The Unruly Dead

Critical Human Rights

Scott Straus and Tyrell Haberkorn, Series Editors; Steve J. Stern, Editor Emeritus

Books in the series Critical Human Rights emphasize research that opens new ways to think about and understand human rights. The series values, in particular, empirically grounded and intellectually open research that eschews simplified accounts of human rights events and processes.

The Unruly Dead

Spirits, Memory, and State Formation in Timor-Leste

Lia Kent

The University of Wisconsin Press

This book will be made open access within three years of publication thanks to Path to Open, a program developed in partnership between JSTOR, the American Council of Learned Societies (ACLS), University of Michigan Press, and The University of North Carolina Press to bring about equitable access and impact for the entire scholarly community, including authors, researchers, libraries, and university presses around the world. Learn more at https://about.jstor.org/path-to-open/

The University of Wisconsin Press
728 State Street, Suite 443
Madison, Wisconsin 53706
uwpress.wisc.edu

Copyright © 2024
The Board of Regents of the University of Wisconsin System
All rights reserved. Except in the case of brief quotations embedded in critical articles and reviews, no part of this publication may be reproduced, stored in a retrieval system, transmitted in any format or by any means—digital, electronic, mechanical, photocopying, recording, or otherwise—or conveyed via the Internet or a website without written permission of the University of Wisconsin Press. Rights inquiries should be directed to rights@uwpress.wisc.edu.

Printed in the United States of America
This book may be available in a digital edition.

Library of Congress Cataloging-in-Publication Data

Names: Kent, Lia, author.
Title: The unruly dead : spirits, memory, and state formation in Timor-Leste / Lia Kent.
Other titles: Critical human rights.
Description: Madison, Wisconsin : The University of Wisconsin Press, 2024. | Series: Critical human rights | Includes bibliographical references and index.
Identifiers: LCCN 2023051521 | ISBN 9780299349301 (hardcover)
Subjects: LCSH: Dead—Social aspects. | Victims of political violence—Timor-Leste. | Collective memory—Timor-Leste. | Transitional justice—Timor-Leste. | Timor-Leste—Social conditions—21st century. | Timor-Leste—Social life and customs—21st century. | Timor-Leste—Politics and government—2002-
Classification: LCC HN710.3 .K467 2024 | DDC 959.8704—dc23/eng/20240510
LC record available at https://lccn.loc.gov/2023051521

Contents

List of Illustrations — vii
Acknowledgments — ix

Introduction — 3

1 From Necropower to Necro-governmentality: State Responses to Massive Bad Death — 21

2 The Martyred Youth of the Metropole: Re-membering the Santa Cruz Dead — 46

3 Civilian Sacrifices in the Town: Re-membering the Liquiçá Church Dead — 73

4 The "Participating Population" of the Hinterlands: Gathering the Dispersed Dead — 97

5 The Treacherous Dead of the Badlands: Re-membering Those Killed by the Resistance — 123

Conclusion — 148

Glossary — 163
Notes — 165
Works Cited — 173
Index — 191

Illustrations

Map

Timor-Leste, including study locations — 2

Figures

All Souls' Day in the Natarbora cemetery — 4

The Nicolau Lobato statue, Dili — 34

The Garden of Heroes, Metinaro — 39

Families of the missing at the Santa Cruz commemoration, Dili — 47

Santa Cruz T-shirt "I sold my body to buy liberty" — 48

Poster showing photos of martyred youth outside the 12 November committee office — 69

Young girl with candles, Santa Cruz commemoration, Dili — 70

Families of the Liquiçá church massacre victims outside the São João de Brito church — 75

Woman prays at the Garden of Heroes, Liquiçá — 88

Families gather at the Liquiçá church angel memorial — 94

Uma Mahon (shade house) for the dead — 106

The *deskoñesidu* (unknown), Ermera ossuary — 115

Eating with the dead — 120

Angelo's recently completed cemetery	125
Statue of Francisco Xavier do Amaral, Dili	135
Makeshift cross at the former RENAL prison, Remexio	137
Neglected grave of UDT and Apodeti victims in Aileu	138
Nicolau Lobato's empty tomb in the Garden of Heroes, Metinaro	152

Acknowledgments

This book has been written, with respect, on the lands of the Ngunnawal peoples. It has had a long gestation, and there are many people who have helped to bring it to fruition. My deepest thanks go to my East Timorese interlocuters who have generously shared their insights, in some cases over many years. I have been privileged to be welcomed into their lives and invited to many family and public events and commemorative rituals. I have benefited enormously from their experiences and insights into the urgency and challenges of caring for the dead. Special thanks to Angelo, Pedro, José Ramos, Eliza, Fernanda, Ana Maria, and Gregorio Saldanha. Thanks also to Mau Kuri and Maun Gray for introducing me to several commissions for the recovery of human remains and Kiko Moniz for intrepid driving skills and good company.

I am privileged to be part of an inspirational network of Timor-Leste studies colleagues scattered around the world. The many and varied conversations I have had with these people have profoundly shaped and helped to sharpen my ideas. I would like to thank Lisa Palmer, Meabh Cryan, Sara Niner, Kelly Silva, Vannessa Hearman, Hannah Loney, Soren Blau, Michael Leach, Nuno Rodrigues Tchailoro, Joaquim Fonseca, Josh Trindade, Hugo Fernandes, Manuela Leong Pereira, Susanna Barnes, David Webster, Andrew McWilliam, Gordon Peake, Kelly Silva, Pat Walsh, Ines Almeida, Fidelis Magalhães, Pat Walsh, and Faviola Monteiro. A collaboration with Rui Feijó provided a wonderful, collegial opportunity to begin thinking seriously about the themes of this book. I am especially grateful to Damian Grenfell and an anonymous reviewer for providing invaluable feedback on the draft manuscript.

Some recent collaborations have also been important for the evolution of my ideas. I thank Simon Robins for an energizing collaboration on a series of workshops that have introduced me to an inspiring academic community working on the "dead" and the "missing" in diverse contexts of conflict and migration. I also thank Cressida Fforde, Steve Hemming, Geoff Langford, and other colleagues involved in the ARC Discovery Project, Heritage and Reconciliation, for fascinating conversations through which I have learned a great deal about memory work and the dead in settler colonial Australia.

Much of this book has been written at the School of Regulation and Global Governance at the Australian National University, which has provided a collegial academic environment to share early ideas. I am grateful to all my RegNet and ANU colleagues for their support and encouragement, in particular, Hilary Charlesworth, John Braithwaite, Kate Henne, Rosanne Kennedy, Shameem Black, David Oakeshott, Sinclair Dinnen, Bina d'Costa, Sarah Milne, Miranda Forsyth, and Christoph Sperfeldt. I also thank colleagues in Sri Lanka (where some of this book was written) for stimulating conversations, in particular, Chulani Kodikara, Radihika Hettiarachchi, and Malathi de Alwis, who sadly passed away before this book was finished. Nuno Rodrigues Tchailoro, Viyanga Gunasekera, and Achalie Kumarage provided valuable research assistance during the book's final stages of preparation. ANU CartoGIS generously produced the map.

I acknowledge the Australian Research Council for a Discovery Early Career Research Award, which enabled me to conduct several periods of fieldwork. I also thank Amber Rose Cederstrom and the editorial board at the University of Wisconsin Critical Human Rights series, who have been enthusiastic and supportive of this project from the beginning.

The book could not have been written without my writing group, the Bunsen Burners. Nick Cheesman, Carly Schuster, Rachel Hughes, and Tom Cliff are the most inspiring, supportive, and smart colleagues I could wish for. Their intelligence and insights have improved this book immensely, while their encouragement has helped get me through to the finish line. May the flame live on.

Parts of this book have previously been aired in earlier forms. Parts of chapter 4 appeared as "Gathering the Dead: Imagining the State?" in *The Dead as Ancestors, Heroes, and Martyrs in Timor-Leste*, edited by Lia Kent and Rui Graça Feijó (Amsterdam: Amsterdam University Press, 2020). Parts of chapter 2 appeared as "Travelling and Multiscaler Memory: Remembering East Timor's Santa Cruz Massacre from the Transnational to the Intimate," *Memory Studies* (online first, 2023).

I am profoundly grateful to family for supporting me throughout this project. My parents, Randall and Desleigh, have offered love and encouragement. My son, Ezra, has tolerated my absences and occasional grumpiness, made me laugh, and provided much-needed diversions. My husband, Tom, has been with me every step of the way. Tom, although editing draft chapters goes well beyond wedding vows, you did so anyway. I am immeasurably grateful for your love, patience, and sense of humor.

The Unruly Dead

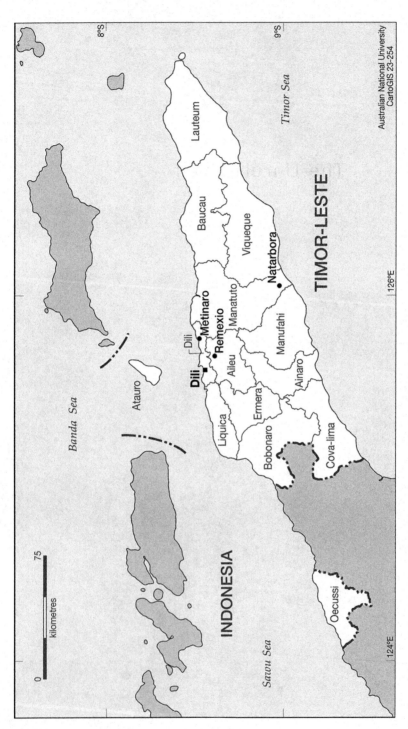

Timor-Leste, including study locations. Map courtesy of Australian National University CartoGIS.

Introduction

It is 4 p.m. on All Souls' Day, the 2nd of November 2019, a time when it is customary for East Timorese to return to their home villages to remember and care for their dead. In the public cemetery in Natarbora, a *posto* (subdistrict) in the hinterlands in central Timor-Leste, a Catholic mass for the dead is about to begin. Although it is late in the afternoon, the sun is fierce and I try to find some shade under a spindly acacia tree. Hundreds of people have gathered in large family groups around the graves, which, for the most part, are simple cement constructions scattered in an eclectic fashion. Having been cleared of weeds the day before, the graves are neat and tidy; many are adorned with flowers and the remnants of candle wax. Pickup trucks and minibuses continue to arrive from other parts of the municipality and from as far away as Dili, with loud music blaring from their speakers. People spill out holding brightly colored baskets containing bunches of (mostly plastic) flowers, *bua malus* (betel nut) flower petals, and candles. The atmosphere is lively, joyful.

The service begins and a man standing in a small chapel at the center of the cemetery—a local teacher dressed in long pants and a neat white shirt—begins to read the names of the dead from the surrounding area, one by one, in alphabetical order, along with their date of death. After each name or set of names, relatives of the dead come forward and place their baskets in front of the chapel to be blessed with holy water by the local Catholic priest. The list is seemingly endless, and I begin to hear the teacher's voice as a mesmerizing drone. Entire families seem to have perished during the early years of the Indonesian occupation. It takes around thirty minutes before the name reading finally draws to a close. I feel a sudden sense of heaviness, of profound sadness, as the magnitude of these losses seeps in.

It is estimated that up to two hundred thousand people—or up to one-third of the East Timorese population—lost their lives during the twenty-four-year

All Souls' Day in the Natarbora cemetery. Photo by author (2019).

Indonesian occupation of the territory (1975–99), although the number could be much higher (CAVR 2005; see also Cribb 2001; Roosa 2007).[1] Some, including guerrillas active in the armed resistance known as the Forças Armadas da Libertação Nacional de Timor-Leste (FALINTIL, Armed Forces for the National Liberation of East Timor), died while fighting the Indonesian security forces. Many more, including civilians like those in Natarbora, perished in remote locations in the mountains from hunger and disease as they sheltered with the FALINTIL guerrillas in the early years of the Indonesian occupation. Those who were part of the extensive, unarmed, clandestine resistance network, including urban youth activists, were killed during political protests against the Indonesian regime or executed as political prisoners. Still others died at the hands of the East Timorese resistance, accused of being traitors or collaborators. Many bodies have not been recovered.

In a new era of national independence, East Timorese are responding to these profound experiences of violence, loss, and missing bodies through what I call "memory work": practices of commemoration, memorialization, and monument building and of exhumation, reburial, and care for the dead. What might it mean to take the dead seriously as participants in this memory work? Through my conversations with relatives and close friends of the dead, resistance veterans, activists, and members of NGOs, it became impossible to ignore the ways in which the legacies of the Indonesian regime were being experienced as the demands of the dead upon the living. And just as Heonik Kwon (2008) found for the Vietnamese dead of the "American war," it seemed that Timor-Leste's dead were principally concerned with their suffering than with the political causes of their deaths and the punishment of those responsible, demanding proper burial and care (see also Langford 2013, 211). The dead appeared to be both animating—and animated by—the memory work I was observing across Timor-Leste. I came to realize that just as people were *working with* their memories of the dead as they sought to rebuild their lives and imagine a future, the dead were *working on* the living as the living encountered human remains, restless spirits, and charged landscapes.

This book is a response to the concerns of my East Timorese interlocutors, which have motivated me to reexamine the ways in which questions of agency, power, and the material and spectral legacies of mass violence are treated in studies of postconflict repair and rebuilding. In concert with other critical peace and conflict scholars, I have pushed for and welcomed the critique of liberal peacebuilding, which has decentered the state, allowing for more attention to the political agency of a diverse array of actors in postconflict rebuilding (e.g., see MacGinty 2013; Brigg 2018). The burgeoning ethnographic work on locally grounded practices of social memory and repair has also been important, disrupting assumptions about trauma, social repair, remembering, and agency derived from Western experiences and epistemologies (e.g., see Kidron 2012, 2020; Kirmayer, Lemelson, and Barad 2007; Lincoln and Lincoln 2015; MacDonald 2013; Shaw 2007; Stoller 1994; Willerslev 2007; Zucker 2013). In another significant development, as the currents of "new materialism" or posthumanism (Barad 1996, 2013; Haraway 2015) have rippled through the social sciences and humanities, there has been a reorientation to the "mutual constitution of the human and nonhuman" in studies of peacebuilding, disrupting narratives of human exceptionalism that treat humans alone as having agency (Squire 2014, 18; see also MacGinty 2017). Despite this, the agential dimensions and political implications of the dead remain underexplored.

The book examines how, more than two decades since the end of the occupation, Timor-Leste remains acutely troubled by the legacies of the large scale "bad" (violent or untimely) death of the Indonesian occupation. I explore how these legacies are felt as the demands of the restless and unhappy spirits of the dead. These spirits are lively, if sometimes tragic, beings. They press their demands for proper burial and care upon the living, activating practices of exhumation, reburial, and commemoration in what is a politically charged period of postconflict state formation. Furthermore, the dead, as they "resurface," transform from a spectral presence into a visible material presence, making further demands of the living.

In Natarbora, as in many other rural areas devastated by massive bad death, local residents have begun to comb the landscape in search of the remains of their loved ones so that they may be given a proper burial. They gather eyewitness accounts from survivors, enlist the advice and support of ritual experts, interpret the dreams of relatives (in which the spirits of the dead may provide clues about the location of their material remains), and travel to remote areas to camp for weeks at a time to conduct searches and carry out exhumations with rudimentary tools. Local Natarbora residents describe the motivating impact of a locust plague, which destroyed crops and caused widespread hunger and economic misfortune. One local man's dream had revealed these locusts to be the unsettled spirits of dead whose remains lay in the surrounding landscape, abject and neglected, devoid of care and attention. Experiences such as these provide a preliminary sense of what is at stake for the well-being of the living in memory work.

Yet this book is not simply about cultural responses to death. My interest is in how "massive bad death" (Sakti 2020) opens up a complex terrain shaped by the interplay of multiple actors (families, NGOs, veterans' groups, state agents, activists, the dead themselves); diverse personal, familial, and political imperatives and struggles; and the materialities and spectral legacies of mass violence. Just as massive bad death animates a local ethics of care for the dead, so too does it give rise to other discourses, logics, and political struggles. These include the globally circulating discourses of human rights, transitional justice and forensic humanitarianism, the logics of state building and "necro-governmentality" (Rojas-Perez 2017, 19), and struggles for recognition and resources.

What emerges from the encounter and interplay between these diverse logics, discourses and ethics? How do they gain currency as they speak to shared experiences of loss and violence as well as urgent needs and preoccupations in the present? To answer these questions, I pay close ethnographic attention to the new spaces of memory, new communities and new forms of political action that are being generated by practices of commemoration, exhumation, memorialization, and care. I explore how the dead, as they prompt the living to act, are active participants in these practices, which are part of the ongoing remaking of social and political worlds after massive bad death.

This is the first book-length study to bring the dead to the center of the analytical frame in examining the afterlife of the violent Indonesian occupation in Timor-Leste. It builds on a rich and burgeoning literature that spans memory and commemoration (Arthur 2019; Feijó 2020; Grenfell 2012; Leach 2008; Rothschild 2015, 2017; Viegas and Feijó 2017); reconciliation (Grenfell

2008; Kent 2011); social repair (Bovensiepen 2014; Grenfell 2012, 2015; Kent 2015; McWilliam 2008, 2011; Palmer and McWilliam 2019; Sakti 2013); state building, nation building, and governmentality (Brown 2009; Kammen 2009; Leach 2017; Roll 2014, 2018a, 2018b; Silva 2017); and a growing number of book chapters and articles on the dead (Bovensiepen 2009, 2018; Grenfell 2012, 2015; Kent and Feijó 2020). The book demonstrates that much can be learned about the interplay between social repair and state formation by attending to the agential dimensions and political implications of the dead. It uncovers the ways in which the dead activate practices within and across multiple geographic and political scales, reconstituting diverse allegiances, responsibilities, and social networks and contributing to debates about suffering, sacrifice, reward, and national belonging. These insights are relevant well beyond this specific case study. The book tells a complex story of how large-scale bad death creates enduring and disruptive material and spectral legacies that must be negotiated by the living. In doing so, it foregrounds imperatives and forms of power, communication, and meaning-making that are often neglected and yet are vital to the remaking of social and political order after mass violence.

The Affective Force of Timor-Leste's Dead

What is at stake in practices of searching, reburial, care, consolation, and remembrance of the dead in Timor-Leste? How can the dead be understood as participants in these practices? And what does "remembering" the dead entail? To begin to answer these questions, it is necessary to recognize that in Timor-Leste, as in many other parts of the world, death is not a final event or simply a physiological phenomenon but a social process that requires the dead to be eased from the world of the living and safely settled into another realm, in this case the realm of the ancestors (Laqueur 2015, 10; see also Hertz 1960 [1907]). Mortuary rituals are fundamental to facilitating the dead's transition to the ancestral domain, enabling the containment of the "negative aspects of death"—that is, "the decay, putrescence and pollution that underscores the finality of life"—making way for death to contribute to the regeneration of the social order (Stepputat 2014, 22).

Mortuary rituals in Timor-Leste involve a blend of customary and Catholic practices, which have themselves been shaped by legacies of colonization (Bovensiepen 2018, 59; Grenfell 2012). Taking varying forms across the half island, their aim is to facilitate the transference of the dead into the ancestral realm, which is necessary for the well-being of the living. Until that takes place, the dead remain suspended in a dangerous "liminal" realm between life and death (Huttunen 2016); they are, in Mary Douglas's (1966) words, "matter out of place," "excluded from the order of the living but not yet included in the order of the dead" (Stepputat 2014, 21; see also Turner 1967).

Following mortuary rituals, the dead do not become mute or passive or retreat to a remote afterlife. They maintain an ongoing relationship with the living, who regularly visit and tend their graves and converse with them. And once they are cared for, the dead can care for the living, providing them ancestral protection and assistance and advice in everyday matters. The dead often impart messages and forms of care to the living through dreams and other embodied experiences. For instance, one young woman told me how she had recently been visited by her father's spirit in a dream just prior to her midwifery exams, giving her the courage and the strength to pass the exams.

In cases where deaths were "bad" (violent or untimely) and where bodies cannot be found, the spirit's journey into the ancestral domain becomes difficult and complicated, and the cycle of regeneration is broken (Bovensiepen 2015; McWilliam 2019; Sakti 2020). As for many people around the world, it is almost unbearable for East Timorese to contemplate deceased loved ones lying abandoned and neglected in the bush, devoid of familial care and attention. This challenges the moral order and blocks the social process of death in the most fundamental of ways. The unburied dead produce senses and atmospheres of disorder, which are magnified in a context where the dead are experienced as agential beings who hold the capacity to inflict illness, famine, and other misfortune on the living, especially their kin. In Timor-Leste as in many other societies, the spirits of the dead are experienced as haunting the living, making onerous demands on them (see Bennett 2018 on Cambodia; Fontein 2022 on Zimbabwe; Kwon 2008 and 2006 on Vietnam; Perera 2001 on Sri Lanka; Rojas-Perez 2017 on Peru). Dreams, visitations, and bodily afflictions such as pain and illness are among the channels through which the dead communicate their demands (McWilliam 2019; Bovensiepen 2009). The inability of families to carry out the required obligations to the dead thus causes acute distress. While these spirits have the most impact on their close relatives and friends, who have responsibility for but have not yet seen to their proper burial, they can also trouble the wider landscape that they inhabit.

The landscape is not a passive backdrop in Timor-Leste. Visceral memories of the Indonesian occupation may be prompted by encounters with different places and landmarks. During my research, people stopped to point out places where they hid from the enemy or where they prepared plants to ward off starvation, sometimes describing the bitterness of these plants and the severe hunger they felt. Some parts of the landscape were described as *lulik*. Often glossed as sacred, forbidden, taboo, or spiritually charged, *lulik* is "at once an idea, an object, a being, a place, a phenomenon, a word or a practice" (Palmer 2021, 15; see also Trindade 2011). It is a "vital energy or force that resides in ancestral houses and objects, as well as animating the environment" (Bovensiepen 2014, 122). *Lulik* places are often talked about in hushed tones, and approached with caution, fear, and reverence. They are part of what anthropologist Judith Bovensiepen (2009, 327), drawing on Allerton (2009) refers to as the "spiritual landscape": a landscape animated by ancestral spirits, nature spirits that "inhabit trees, springs and the sea," and spirit owners of place. The spiritual landscape has a "life-giving and spiritual potency" and is an "active and at times creative and productive resource." It has "desires and preferences and it needs to be looked after and cared for" (Bovensiepen 2009, 327–28). Passing through *lulik* areas may require people to perform small rituals such as throwing coins into rivers, offering prayers to the ancestors for protection, or carrying material objects such as protective amulets or charms (*biru*) (Winch 2020). When walking through areas that one has not previously visited, it is also necessary to be "introduced" to the spirits that inhabit that area as a form of protection against potentially dangerous *lulik* land (Bovensiepen 2009, 333). One woman explained that for her, this introduction was established by kissing the ground in the unfamiliar region so that the land would "know" her.[2]

Thousands of "corpses out of place" (Warren 1993, 31) add to the potency of this already potent landscape. Studies of the material residues of war and violence in diverse contexts have shown how landscapes, places, and sites—especially those containing human remains—can become imbued with atmospheres of disorder for those who have knowledge of the events that took place there (Colombo and Schindel 2014; Maddrell and Sidaway 2010; Till 2012). The powerful, embodied emotions provoked by such atmospheres can impact how such spaces are used, experienced, and imagined, even in cases where no visible traces of violence appear to have been left or when such spaces are relegated to the margins of the national imaginary (Colombo and Schindel 2014, 3; see, generally, Navaro-Yashin 2009). This sense of disorder takes on an added dimension in Timor-Leste, where the restless spirits of the not properly buried dead are believed to inhabit the sites of their death, exacerbating the dangers of the land for the living (Bovensiepen 2015, 148–49). For instance, the blood of those who died bad or "red" (bloody) deaths during the Indonesian occupation is sometimes said to make the land hot (*manas*), making it difficult to grow crops and causing dangerous traffic accidents. For agriculture to flourish, and for dangerous land to be made safe for travel, rituals are required to "cool" the land. In some areas these incorporate the sprinkling of young coconut water mixed with pigs' blood on the land. Another common story tells of how *rai nain* (spirit owners of the land), working with the ancestors, ritually "closed off" parts of the landscape during the Indonesian occupation. These acts of "closing the door" produced a protective force field that prevented the Indonesian military forces from entering certain areas and killing the resistance forces and the population sheltering them. Until rituals are undertaken to request the spirits to "reopen" these areas, exhumations of the dead cannot take place, and cultivation and state-sponsored development (including road building) will not be able to proceed. People are also liable to experience motorbike and other accidents as they travel through them.

These experiences help make sense of the urgency that imbues practices of searching for, exhuming, reburying, and caring for the dead. This work can be understood, at least in part, as a means of facilitating the transference of the dead who died bad deaths from their liminal, abject state into the world of the ancestors (Bovensiepen 2018, 67; Sakti 2013, 443). Through these practices, the living are not simply remembering and making sense of the violence and massive bad death of the past by producing and sharing narratives about it. They are also *re*-membering the dead, reembodying them in material practice (Langford 2009, 701; see also Myerhoff 1982) and re-enfolding them within what Damian Grenfell (2020, 144) refers to as a "cognate community" of the living and the dead. These are practices that restore the dignity of the dead and their place within the genealogy of the family. They renew kinship obligations and connections to the ancestors and to place and help to recalibrate relationships and reassert social networks. By restoring the dead to their "proper place," both physically and spiritually, harmony can be restored in the spirit world and the world of the living (Robins 2013, 195). In these ways, control is asserted over a precarious present and future as the living and the dead create "new social and political roles" that are aimed toward stability and security (Bennett 2018, 203).

At the same time, rituals to placate restless spirits are fragile and contingent. The dead may elide attempts to console, control, or contain them. The spirits of the dead can be unruly, unpredictable, their demands never fully comprehended (Bovensiepen 2018, 67). The spirit world generally can only be partially grasped; people can only speculate about it by, for example, "interpreting signs in the landscape and by examining the consequences of spirit agency in the form of human illness or misfortune" (Bovensiepen 2021, 47; see also Fontein 2010, 2022 on Zimbabwe; Langford 2013 on Cambodia). This leaves residue of doubt or uncertainty as to the completeness and success of mortuary rituals, including whether they have been able to facilitate the spirit's safe transference to the realm of the ancestors.

Adding to these complications is the massive scale of bad death during the Indonesian occupation. This poses a profound challenge for the usual ritual processes that make the deceased safely dead and also makes caring for the dead much more than a family affair. Just as Guillou (2020, 327) found for the violence of the Khmer Rouge period in Cambodia, in Timor-Leste, the main issue is not—or not only—that people must take care of their own dead but that they must "'reorganize' the chaos created by too many deaths in dreadful circumstances." That there are many missing bodies that perhaps may never be recovered causes additional anxiety and uncertainty; unfulfilled mortuary obligations augment the dead's suffering and their grievances.

These uncertainties not only highlight the centrality of the category of "bad death" in Timor-Leste and the implications of disrupted mortuary rituals but also resonate with broader scholarly insights into the unsettling and "excessive indeterminacies" of dead and missing bodies (Fontein 2022, 2014; see also Krmpotich, Fontein, and Harries 2010, 372; Fontein and Harries 2013). Scholars have begun to probe the "disturbing, animating, constraining and enabling power" that imbues the human corpse (Stepputat 2014, 25–26). Joost Fontein, for example, argues that the dead body possesses an "emotive materiality" that derives from the fact that it is a material substance that was once a living human; unlike many other material substances it seems to demand respectful treatment and proper care (Fontein 2022, 84; 2014). Yet caring for the dead is complicated by the unstable nature of the corpse's materiality. Dead bodies are "flowing, transforming materials": "leaky, fleshy, messy material stuff" (Fontein and Harries 2013, 118). This instability imbues the human corpse with "excessive indeterminacies," which both drive urgent attempts by the living to "stabilize" its meanings and identity while also working against the "containment" or "fixing" of those meanings and that identity (Fontein 2022, 31–32; Fontein and Harries 2013, 118; see also Stepputat 2014, 27). Human corpses are continually "negotiated as persons or things, subjects or things, meaning or matter" (Stepputat 2014, 26; Krmpotich, Fontein, and Harries 2010, 372), remaining "implicated in problematic, open-ended processes of 'becoming'" (Major 2015, 176). These indeterminacies are compounded by those that imbue the dead in their immaterial "affective presence," which in Timor-Leste is experienced as the demands of restless spirit agents (see also Fontein 2022, 31; Ngo 2021).

New Uncertainties in a New Era of National Independence

The uncertainties surrounding Timor-Leste's dead and their demands are exacerbated in an era of rapid and intense political and social change, which has followed on from a tumultuous history of colonialism and occupation. A Portuguese colony from the sixteenth century, East Timor experienced a brief opportunity for self-determination following a rapid process of decolonization in 1974. However, nine days after the radical pro-independence party FRETILIN (Frente Revolucionária de Timor-Leste Independente, Revolutionary Front for an Independent East Timor) declared independence on 28 November 1975, Indonesia invaded and then brutally occupied East Timor for two and a half decades (1975–99). A tenacious resistance struggle against the Indonesian occupation and for national independence continued throughout this twenty-four-year period, involving a vast network of armed guerrillas, unarmed clandestine actors based in the villages and towns, students in Indonesia and East Timor, and an active diaspora in Australia, Portugal, and Canada, among others. This tenacity paid off, and in 1999 a referendum was held under United Nations (UN) supervision, in which an overwhelming majority of East Timorese voted in favor of separating from Indonesia. The Indonesian government reluctantly accepted the result but not before unleashing a scorched earth policy that, with the involvement of East Timorese militia, led to the killing of over two thousand five hundred people, the destruction of all significant government and commercial infrastructure, and the displacement of around four hundred thousand people (Kent and Feijó 2020, 21; CAVR 2005, part 7.5, 48). National independence was finally achieved in 2002 after a two-and-a-half-year period of UN transitional administration.

While national independence has been overwhelmingly welcomed, struggles over citizenship, political power, resources, rights, reward for sacrifices, and compensation for suffering remain far from settled, subject to ongoing negotiation. The transformative promises of independence are also far from a reality for many East Timorese, with poverty remaining entrenched and new forms of precarity emerging. The stakes of official recognition of the dead as "martyrs" have become high, connected to both financial reward and elevated political status for the dead and their families. As I discuss more fully in chapter 1, in the wake of the profoundly disruptive experiences of massive bad death, the state has deployed technologies of "necro-governmentality" (Rojas-Perez 2017, 19) to control and contain its destabilizing legacies. State-sponsored practices such as large-scale commemorations of violent events, the reburial of martyrs in Heroes cemeteries, and a veterans' valorization program that provides medals and pensions to former resistance actors are crafting new (militarized, masculine) martyr subjectivities, spatiotemporally containing (some of) the dead, and providing a new language to talk about grief and loss. The symbolic—and at times material—presence of some dead bodies in these practices generates powerful emotional responses (including solidarity and patriotism) that work to bind a national community and legitimate a new political regime (Drozdzewski, Waterton, and Sumartojo 2016; Verdery 1999). Yet the dead are an unruly source of power and may disrupt these technologies and performances.

Just as the excessive indeterminacies that surround the dead and their demands can confound attempts by their living relatives to placate them, so too do they trouble and disrupt attempts to harness the dead in the service of state building (see, generally, Stepputat 2014, 26; see also Fontein 2022, 30–31). This is a key theme of the book. The profound uncertainties that have been precipitated by bad death on a massive scale defy the ultimate stabilization or "fixing" of definitive narratives and any final "remaking" of the dead into martyrs (Fontein 2022, 32). This book shows how the dead are transforming necro-governmental logics in unexpected ways. They demand individualized care, not only collective and symbolic recognition, and refuse to be rendered docile, silent corpses that can be treated as objects and therefore controlled. The state's creation of hierarchies of the dead is also activating demands among those who are excluded and giving rise to new uncertainties about the dead's spiritual power. The dead whose bodies have not been recovered are especially problematic, remaining troubled and troubling spirits that remind the living and the state that the violence of the Indonesian occupation is not yet over but inhabits the present.

This book examines how memory work is part of the ongoing remaking of social and political order in the aftermath of the occupation. This remaking is taking place through the entangled agency of the living and the dead and through an uneven interaction between diverse logics, ethics, and practices. The spheres of the intimate and the political emerge as mutually constitutive; just as necro-governmental logics are permeating local political and social imaginaries, introducing new subjectivities and new modes of political action, they are being transformed in unexpected ways as they encounter a local ethics of care, local power struggles, and the dead as unruly political actors.

Researching Memory Work in Timor-Leste

The book draws on insights gleaned through twenty years of engagement with Timor-Leste in both research and policy roles. My early research on local responses to transitional justice mechanisms led me to the realization that recovery and rebuilding after the violent Indonesian occupation was a far more protracted, dynamic, and multilayered process than the literature on peacebuilding would suggest (Kent 2012). I grew intrigued by the intensive local activity focused on the construction of monuments and cemeteries;

the search for, and exhumation and identification of, human remains; and the performance of commemorative rituals and reburials. This activity appeared to be catalyzed by a multiplicity of actors: members of veterans' groups, former clandestine resistance actors, survivors' groups, and extended family networks. I was driven to learn more about what motivated these actors in a context where material resources are often limited and there are many competing priorities. I was also interested in what close attention to memory work might illuminate about wider political processes in Timor-Leste during the formation of a new state.

I examined these themes through ethnographic research between 2015 and 2019 and analysis of primary and secondary literature (legislation, government and NGO reports, media releases, and scholarly literature). As part of my fieldwork, I had open-ended conversations with around one hundred memory workers, including relatives of the dead, resistance veterans, human rights activists and NGO workers, local clergy, and state officials.[3] I participated in *kore metan* (taking off the black) rituals, church services, a family gravesite picnic, and commemorations, and I also visited ossuaries and *uma mahon* (shade houses, protective houses) for the dead, cemeteries, and memorials. This fieldwork was conducted over multiple visits and involved several open-ended conversations with key interlocutors, allowing time to build trust. This trust was further facilitated by my preexisting relationships with families, local NGOs, and policymakers and my ability to communicate in Tetum (the lingua franca of Timor-Leste). My fieldwork was multisited, spanning Dili as well as several district capitals, subdistricts, and rural areas. This was necessary because in many cases a specific example of memory work (for instance, the recovery of human remains and the remembrance of the Santa Cruz massacre) turned out not to be as site-specific as initially supposed but, rather, geographically extensive.

While my early conversations focused on the goals of my interlocutors and what motivated and constrained them, their concerns quickly pushed me to pay attention to the more-than-human realm and to the "more-than-representational" domain of affect, smell, touch, interaction, and embodiment (Lorimer 2005). I began to realize that memory work not only involved the conscious or deliberate "working through" of traumatic memories but also encompassed experiences and emotions that may not be the subject of conscious reflection (MacDonald 2013, 52; Muzaini 2015, 111). Just as the living were remembering the dead, the dead seemed to be working on the living as the living encountered their remains and spirits through dreams, visions, feelings, and other bodily sensations or when they traveled through dangerous, enspirited landscapes. I increasingly asked my interlocuters questions about their dreams, their experience of places and landscapes, and the ways in which they felt the dead—and the domain of the spirit world generally—to be present in their lives. I also began to pay more attention to people's body language and embodied reactions during ritual performances and at specific sites, including my own.

The book invites the reader to be open to diverse ways of knowing and being, unsettling assumptions about personhood, agency, trauma, social repair, and remembering that are derived from Western experiences and epistemologies. East Timorese foreground relational ways of being and doing: relations to other living humans, the dead and the not-yet-born, and the natural world, including places in the landscape and animals (Palmer and McWilliam 2019, 476; see also Bovensiepen 2015; Palmer 2015; Sakti 2013, 449; Trindade 2015). The spirits of the dead and other nonhuman entities (including land spirits and water spirits) are part of the social and political world. Rather than bracketing experiences of spirits as "cultural beliefs" or viewing stories about them as metaphors that reflect traces of a violent past and fears and insecurities in the present, I suggest, following Jean Langford (2013, 215), that it is more productive to allow spirit agents to direct us toward "another possibility for apprehending the world." For my interlocuters, spirits are "salient, social beings" (Bennett 2018, 185; see also Lincoln and Lincoln 2015) who inhabit multiple temporalities and have the power to influence the living (in both positive and negative ways), prompting action and shaping the world around them. For these reasons I treat them as political actors. As Sophie Chao argues, taking alternative ontological frameworks seriously does not mean treating them as "unequivocally real, but as if they *could* be" (Chao 2022, 212).

In the chapters that follow, I examine the myriad ways in which the dead, as human remains and restless, unburied spirits, are prompting responses from the living. Conceptually I draw insight from the burgeoning anthropological scholarship on the politics of the dead. While the power of dead bodies to enliven politics and "give new meaning to political communities," particularly following times of crisis, is now well established (Verdery 1999, 28; Stepputat 2014), there is a growing insistence that dead bodies are not simply passive objects that "symbolize" aspects of social and political life; rather, they are imbued with "something that comes close to agency" in the way that they act on the living and "animate social and political processes" (Stepputat 2014, 26; see also Auchter 2014; Fontein 2022; Fontein and Harries 2009). The new materialisms movement, which recognizes that material things, landscapes, and bodies can be *actants*—"source[s] of action that 'make a difference, produce effects, alter the course of events'"—has been an important influence on this burgeoning scholarship (Freeman, Nienass, Daniell 2016, 5; see also Barad 2007; Braidotti 2013; Crossland and Bauer 2017; Everth and Gurney 2022, 51;

Fox and Alldred 2019; Haraway 2015; Winchell 2023). However, the materialist "turn" has also led to a tendency to focus primarily on the *material* properties of dead bodies, downplaying the power of the dead in their immaterial presence (see Johnson 2020, 167). In this book I explore how the agency of Timor-Leste's dead emerges from their entangled material and spectral presence (see also Fontein 2022; Ngo 2021).

However, let me make two important caveats. First, heeding the insights of Indigenous scholars, I strive to avoid generalizing statements about the agency of matter, things, and spirits, attempting to engage respectfully with *particular* relational entanglements between the human and the more-than-human world, the living and the dead (Rosiek, Snider, and Pratt 2019, 9). In Timor-Leste as elsewhere, dead bodies and spirits are "incorporated into socially and culturally particular life-worlds" where they have a specific resonance (MacDonald 2013, 85). These life-worlds are not static or stable but are continually brought into being and remade through practice. The Indigenous studies scholarship also provides an important counter to the claimed "newness" of the new materialisms movement, reminding us that Indigenous philosophies have long foregrounded the social self as constituted relationally with other people and with the natural world, anticipating the limits of Cartesian binaries between mind and body, subject and object, that would—much later—be destabilized by "new materialists" (Bignall et al. 2016, 457; see also Allerton 2009; Brown 2020; Byrne and Ween 2015; Graham 1999; Willerslev 2007). Furthermore, it reminds scholars of the inequalities that surround knowledge production and citation in the academy, challenging us to decolonize our own practices. Taking these calls seriously pushes me to collapse the "hierarchical distinction between Western theory and non-Western cosmology" (Jackson 2013, 682, in Chao 2022, 7), a distinction which, as Sophie Chao (2022, 7) identifies, reinforces and exacerbates the logics of colonialism that have historically oppressed Indigenous and other marginalized peoples.

Second, I do not view Timor-Leste's dead as outside modern politics but as deeply entangled with it (see Winchell 2023). The practices of care for the dead I describe in this book do not inhabit a separate realm of "culture" but are deeply intertwined with contemporary discourses and practices of state building, nation building, development, human rights, and Catholicism. They address the lingering impacts of colonial and occupation violence that have profoundly disrupted relational attachments between the living and the dead (see Winchell 2023) *while also* responding to the silences and exclusions of the state's necro-governmental projects, which have focused overwhelmingly on "the category of heroic sacrifice," ignoring the civilian dead (Kwon 2012, 230). They need also to be contextualized within the uncertainties wrought by the rapid political, social, and economic changes ushered in by a new era of national independence, which have fostered a resurgence of ritual practices and the reinvigoration of relations with the spirit realm (Barnes 2011; Bovensiepen 2021; McWilliam and Traube 2011; Shepherd 2019). Throughout the book I remain attentive to how the dead become enmeshed in political struggles around identity, power, and resources and can both assimilate and transform modern configurations of power (see MacDonald 2013, 85; Winchell 2023, 5).

Memory work is therefore best understood as an *assemblage* that draws together diverse discourses, practices, emotions, spaces, landscapes, resources, political struggles, and actors (both the living and the dead) (see MacDonald 2013; Sather-Wagstaff 2017, 18). An assemblage is not a static arrangement but, rather, "open-ended and productive": an ongoing process through which heterogeneous bodies, things, or concepts come "'in connection with' one another" and may, in turn, dissemble (Kennedy et al. 2013, 45, 47). As Jane Bennett insists, the effects generated by assemblages are "emergent properties, emergent in that their ability to make something happen is distinct from the sum of the vital force" of each part considered alone (Bennett 2010, 23–24). These insights enable an appreciation that Timor-Leste's dead do not act alone but collaborate, cooperate, and interact with other "bodies and forces" (Bennett 2010, 21). The dead's affective force interacts with other forces that derive, for instance, from ethical imperatives, economic needs, political agendas, and other human and more-than-human beings to "make something happen." As the elements involved create "patterns of unintentional coordination" (Tsing 2015, 23), we can never fully know what the outcome will be.

The book's concern is precisely to make sense of the new forms of memory work that are emerging from the productive intersection of diverse logics, understandings, and practices that, I argue, are an integral part of the ongoing and uneven formation of a new nation-state. I am especially interested in what emerges from the spaces of encounter and engagement between necrogovernmental logics and technologies on the one hand and local responsibilities and practices of care for the dead on the other. Ultimately, I hope to reveal something of the urgency, creativity, and imagination that imbues the remaking of the social and political order in the face of profound structural inequalities and in the wake of the enduring effects of state violence.

Overview of the Book

Chapter 1 sets the scene for the chapters that follow by providing a brief history of the evolving modalities of "necropower" (Mbembe 2003) that operated during the Indonesian occupation of East Timor (1974–99). It examines how the radical devaluation of the dead has created a "disordered landscape" of "corpses out of place" (Warren 1993) and unleashed dangerous and unruly spirits. Managing the legacy of "massive bad death" (Sakti 2020) is now central to postconflict projects of state and nation building. I mobilize Rojas-Perez's (2017, 19) concept of "necro-governmentality" to examine how the state is attempting to structure social responses to the dead, control and contain the legacies of the violent Indonesian occupation, and legitimize a new political order. This involves the ascription of fixed martyr subjectivities to some dead bodies and the creation of hierarchies of the dead. The state's necro-governmental projects have evolved in critical dialogue with another, very different, form of the same power, one that was at work in the UN's state-building program, including its transitional justice mechanisms.

The dead emerge as key protagonists across chapters 2, 3, 4, and 5. Through a granular focus on location- or issue-specific memory work, the complex struggles of different categories of the dead are illuminated: the martyred youth of a civilian massacre in the metropole; older, town-based civilian massacre victims; the dispersed dead of the hinterlands who died of famine and illness; and the treacherous dead who died at the hand of the resistance movement in the Badlands. As we move figuratively and geographically away from the metropole, state power becomes more diffuse, and the negotiations and transformations of the state's necro-governmental logics become increasingly apparent. Far from containing and controlling the dead, these logics are enlivening them, providing opportunities for them to make their power felt in new ways. Those who are not officially recognized as martyrs push for the acknowledgment of their sacrifices while also demanding ongoing care and consolation from their families. Those who have not yet been given a proper burial and continue to inhabit disordered landscapes closely proximate to the living are prompting practices of reburial and care that are allowing some to "resurface" and make their presence felt in new ways. Those whose bodies cannot be found continue to be dangerous and unruly actors.

Chapter 2 examines how the unruly spirits of young clandestine activists who died during the 12 November 1999 Santa Cruz massacre prevent the memory of the massacre from being fully co-opted by the state's necro-governmental logics. I show how, at first glance, the memory of Santa Cruz appears to have increasingly solidified as a hegemonic narrative of the emergence of the Timor-Leste state: the remembrance of martyred youth has become a powerful mechanism through which to impart a pedagogical lesson that crafts ideal, patriotic youth citizens in the present. However, by looking beyond the state-sanctioned performance of the annual public commemorations to other, highly localized and informal spaces of memory, it is possible to see how the dead whose bodies have not yet been recovered continue to exert their demands for a proper burial, activating practices of searching for and caring for them. The continual questioning of losses and absences by their families imbues the memory of Santa Cruz with an unsettled, dynamic quality, reminding the state of unfulfilled responsibilities.

Chapter 3 focuses on the spirits of civilians who died in the church massacre in the small town of Liquiçá on 6 April 1999. I show how the meanings of the Liquiçá church massacre, like Santa Cruz, are continually evolving. As this church massacre is increasingly recognized by the state, new pathways for families to respond to the demands of the restless dead are emerging as well as new dangers that must be negotiated. The tensions generated by a new Garden of Heroes cemetery is a particular focus of the chapter. I examine how the logics associated with this key technology of necro-governmentality are troubled as they encounter a local ethics of care for the dead that responds to the demands of the dead for care and consolation from their families. These logics are further unraveled by the restless spirits of those whose bodies have not been recovered. Inhabiting the sites where violence was done to their bodies, these spirits create dangerous and unruly spaces that sit just beyond, and yet trouble, town limits.

Moving beyond cities and towns, chapter 4 examines those who died in the mountains and hinterlands during the first five years of the occupation as a result of hunger, inadequate nutrition, or lack of medicine, and who now prompt the living to act. Addressing the problem of solitary, dispersed, and unhappy restless spirits is urgent given the proximity of these dangerous enspirited landscapes to rural communities. The living live here among the dead. Through a case study of a veteran-led "commission for the recovery of human remains" in Natarbora, Manatutu, I open a window on the widespread efforts to recover, identify, and categorize human remains that are taking place in similar locales across Timor-Leste. This unique form of memory work intersects with the state's necrogovernmental project in complex ways that go beyond resistance or acquiescence. We see how the gathering of human remains is generating new forms of political and social action in which the dead are active participants.

Chapter 5 considers the memory work that responds to the dead who are deemed publicly "ungrievable" (Butler 2009)—those deemed to be "traitors." Two key groups of dead are examined. The first are members of the UDT (União Democrática Timorense, Timorese Democratic Union) political party who were killed during the brief internal conflict between UDT and the radical pro-independence party, FRETILIN, just prior to the 1975 Indonesian invasion. The second are those who died or were killed in FRETILIN-run "rehabilitation" prisons for traitors and reactionaries in the early years of the Indonesian occupation. I show how the memory work that responds to the demands of these dead is allowing the "public secret" (Taussig 1999, 5) of resistance violence to leak into the public sphere in ways that might do justice to the dead's suffering and sacrifices and allow their incorporation into the local and national community. Through this leakage, the dead reveal the conditions by which lives are deemed visible, grievable, and count as political lives, questioning the preconditions for entrance to the political community and pushing for a more inclusive and democratizing narrative of what constitutes sacrifices for the nation.

The conclusion revisits the new social and political practices, spaces of memory, and communities that are being activated by Timor-Leste's unruly dead, which are unsettling—and at times transforming—the state's necro-governmental logics. These dynamics suggest different ways of thinking about postconflict rebuilding and repair. I invite the reader to consider the value of bringing the dead, who have traditionally been marginalized, silenced, or overlooked in analyses of postconflict state building and memory politics, into the center of the frame. By treating the dead as political subjects rather than objects, it becomes possible to foreground imperatives and forms of power, agency, subjectivity, and meaning-making that are often overlooked and yet are central to the remaking of social and political worlds after mass violence.

1

 From Necropower to Necro-governmentality

State Responses to Massive Bad Death

In 2015 the Timor-Leste government announced an ambitious initiative, the Kore Metan Nasional, to mark "the end of mourning of the whole nation in relation to those who fell for national liberation."[1] The name of the initiative referenced the widely practiced ritual known as *kore metan* ("taking off the black"), signifying the end of the mourning period. This takes place a year after death, when family members remove the small pieces of black cloth they had pinned to their clothing in remembrance of the dead. The Kore Metan Nasional would be bookended by two significant dates: 4 September—the anniversary of the date when the results of the UN-sponsored 1999 referendum on self-determination were announced—and 31 December, "National Heroes Day," which marks the date in 1978 of the killing of key resistance leader Nicolau Lobato by the Indonesian military in the mountains outside Dili.

To launch the Kore Metan Nasional, the government invited customary leaders, senior political figures, and representatives of the Catholic Church to participate in a series of ceremonies in Dili. Animist and Catholic rituals were performed. A mass was held in the Dili Cathedral; pigs and chickens were sacrificed, and white candles were lit around a *biti* (mat) in front of the government's administrative offices. Major leaders from the resistance era were present, as was the then prime minister Rui Maria de Araújo. Similar events were held in each district. Black ribbons were widely distributed throughout the country to offer every family the opportunity to publicly display a symbol

21

of mourning while the national process lasted. The idea was that the ribbons would be collected at the end of the period and placed in a central location to provide personal recognition to the sacrifices of every "martyr" (Kent and Feijó 2020, 31).

The underlying goal of the Kore Metan Nasional was to provide a contained and time-bound mechanism to acknowledge the dead with a view to moving forward as a nation. This was an opportunity, the government's press release explained, "to look back on the past, recognizing the struggle, and then to look forward, to embrace the future with unity, committed to the journey of nation building and development.... By remembering and then pressing on together to build Timor-Leste we know that those who went before us would be proud and those who come after us can enjoy a promising future."[2]

The program also had other less explicit aims. The Kore Metan Nasional is widely understood to be a response to government concerns about the growing number of elaborate, locally organized practices centered on the recovery and reburial of the dead. These practices involved expeditions, often by large family groups, to remote bush locations to search for and recover the remains of those who died during the twenty-four-year Indonesian occupation. They often involved months of planning and considerable expense (sometimes hundreds of thousands of dollars) and were regarded by the government as an irrational use of resources that should be channeled to other, more economically productive ends.[3] In a context where it would not be practicable to locate, exhume, identify, and rebury each and every body, the Kore Metan Nasional would serve as a collective, national ritual of symbolic recognition that would assign the dead to a past temporality and persuade the living to focus on the future (Kent and Feijó 2020, 32).

The Kore Metan Nasional is among many state-led initiatives in independent Timor-Leste that respond to diverse experiences of grief, loss, disrupted burial rituals, and missing bodies by attempting to enfold them within a collective and forward-looking national narrative. This chapter conceptualizes these initiatives as technologies of "necro-governmentality" that aim to "structure social responses" to the large-scale bad death of the occupation and remake the political order (Rojas-Perez 2017, 19). In Timor-Leste this social structuring takes place through the crafting of a new heroic narrative of the Indonesian occupation, the ascription of new fixed martyr subjectivities to (some of) the dead, and the containment of martyrs bodies in Garden of Heroes cemeteries. The example of the Kore Metan Nasional exemplifies how the symbolic state recognition of the dead is often offered as a substitute for the recovery of missing bodies and their proper burial. The chapter traces how the state's attempts to structure social responses to bad death have evolved in critical dialogue with other forms of necro-governmentality, in particular those that were at work in the discourses and practices of transitional justice that were prominent during the period of the United Nations Transitional Administration in East Timor (UNTAET) (2000–2002).

The varied uses of necro-governmentality in Timor-Leste cannot be understood, however, without first appreciating the extent and brutality of the necropower (Mbembe 2003) exercised by the Indonesian regime. It is only by grappling with the destabilizing and enduring legacies of this necropower that we can begin to grasp the urgency that imbues necro-governmentality in independent Timor-Leste. Both necropower ("the power that kills") and necro-governmentality ("the power that cares") (Rojas-Perez 2017, 14) are part of a broad field of "necropolitics" that encompasses the "multiple modalities of power entailed in the production and management of dead bodies" (Ferrandiz and Robben 2015, 3; see also Stepputat 2014, 5; Huttunen forthcoming, 33).[4] The emergence of necro-governmentality indexes the urgency of reversing the Indonesian regime's "power over life and death" (see Robben 2015, 56) by imbuing death and suffering with new meaning. Put differently, the imperative of structuring social responses to the dead in Timor-Leste can be understood as a direct response to the necropower of the Indonesian regime: as an attempt to reorder chaos and disorder—to manage the emotions of grief and loss, the disruptions to communal self-understandings, the mass graves, and the unburied bodies.

Necropower and Massive Bad Death during the Indonesian Occupation

"Necropower" formed a key dimension of the Indonesian regime's exercise of authoritarian sovereignty over the territory of East Timor. Mbembe (2003, 11) claims that "the ultimate expression of sovereignty resides, to a large degree, in the capacity to dictate who may live and who must die." For Mbembe, necropower entails both the "exposure to death" of an entire population and the killing of "those subjects who are categorized as 'wrong,' as ethnically or politically outside the desired nation" (Huttunen forthcoming, 53). It is a strategy naturally aligned with "territoriality": the exercising of sovereignty through the claiming and absolute domination over territory (Mbembe 2003, 11; see also Robben 2015, 55). In East Timor, a less absolute conceptualization of necropower is needed than that offered by Mbembe. Here, as in many other contexts (see Huttunen forthcoming, 43; Robben 2015, 71–72;), necropower gave rise to countervailing forces that disrupted the power of an authoritarian regime. In this case, a tenacious and continually evolving resistance struggle emerged as a powerful counterforce to the Indonesian occupation.

In the invasion and occupation of East Timor, the twin strategies of necropower and territoriality were bound up in the overarching goal of integrating the half island into Indonesia as the nation's twenty-seventh province. The Indonesian regime asserted a violent form sovereignty through the spatial occupation of territory, the attempted elimination of the resistance, and the re-education of East Timorese to be loyal Indonesian citizens through the imposition of "Indonesian state ideology, national language and cultural practices" (Loney 2018, 88; see also CAVR 2005, 7.2, 774). Necropower was enacted through multiple modalities. Mass killings and aerial strafing and bombings were compounded by the "small doses of death" (Mbembe 2003, 36–38) administered by the regime through torture and sexual violence, executions, extreme deprivation and enforced disappearances, and the "exposure to death" of large swathes of the population through disease and starvation. Western states, including the United States, Australia, and the United Kingdom, facilitated these practices by supplying advanced weaponry and aeroplanes to the Indonesian military.[5]

Over the course of the twenty-four-year occupation, these modalities of necropower underwent several shifts as the regime responded to changing geopolitical circumstances and evolving forms of East Timorese resistance. During the first five years of the occupation, up to one hundred thousand people are thought to have perished from the "slow violence" (Nixon 2011) of disease, malnourishment, and starvation, many in remote locations of the landscape (Taylor 1999, 71). This was a time of massive displacement, when thousands of civilians sought shelter in the mountains with the resistance support bases (*bases de apoio*) established by the radical pro-independence political party FRETILIN (Frente Revolucionária de Timor-Leste Independente, Revolutionary Front for an Independent East Timor) under the control of its armed wing FALINTIL. The protection initially afforded by the bases soon evaporated. People were forced ever further into the mountains as the regime engaged in a violent separation of civilians from FALINTIL guerrillas through aerial bombardments (CAVR 2005, chapter 3, 79; Roll 2014, 66). Livestock, agricultural lands, and wild food sources were destroyed or contaminated, resulting in a rapid diminishment of food sources. Exhaustion also took hold as people were continually forced to move, living their lives on the run and eating wild foods to survive. Young children and the elderly "died in great numbers" (CAVR 2005, chapter 3, 79). Some of the dead were hastily buried by their relatives or resistance comrades in shallow bush graves marked with small rocks or makeshift crosses. Many were left to rot (CAVR 2005, chapter 3; Loney 2018, 50–55). Still others died in unknown locations, separated from their families.[6] The forced abandonment of bodies and the inability to conduct mortuary rituals was experienced as another form of violence.

As FRETILIN's *bases de apoio* were destroyed in the late 1970s and life in the mountains became increasingly untenable, further deaths through starvation and disease ensued. Tens of thousands of civilians "surrendered" to the Indonesian authorities and, already weakened from lack of food and illnesses, were held in transit camps with inadequate supplies and medical relief before being moved into resettlement camps. The Indonesian military exerted tight control on their movement. There was no capacity to farm and grow food, and the regime prevented international relief organizations from entering the territory (CAVR 2005, chapter 3, 83). The result was a devastating famine that between 1978 and 1980 caused the loss of many thousands of lives (CAVR 2005, chapter 7.3, 4).[7] Indonesia's Western allies, while aware of the famine, deliberately concealed its severity and the extent to which it was a "deliberate, calculated policy to starve the enemy" (Hearman 2022b, 5; see also Fernandes 2015).

Further modalities of necropower emerged from the late 1970s as the Indonesian security forces looked for ways to destroy a new incarnation of East Timorese resistance based in the urban areas, towns, and villages. By this point the armed resistance had experienced devastating losses; many of the key resistance leaders were either dead or captured or had surrendered, leading the Indonesian regime to declare the territory of East Timor "pacified" (CAVR 2005, chapter 5, 26). Yet the resistance continued and an emerging "clandestine front"—a network of civilians based in the villages and towns—became increasingly significant, providing critical support to the surviving FALINTIL guerrillas and developing new protest strategies. The regime arrested, tortured, and executed suspected members of the resistance, reducing them to the status of what Agamben refers to as *homo sacer* (sacred man), a form of "bare life" who could be killed with impunity (Agamben 1998; see also Acikcoz 2020, 9). The regime's killings, as the final report of the Commission for Reception, Truth, and Reconciliation (CAVR) notes, had a "particularly horrific character." The methods used "ranged from death by severe deprivation in a prison cell to public executions committed using the most extreme brutality, in which villagers were sometimes forced to participate, at supposedly secret sites, which in fact became widely notorious, to indiscriminate shooting of large numbers of persons in confined spaces" (CAVR 2005, 7.2, 7).

Killings could also be arbitrary. For instance, civilians could be targeted "while looking for food or going about their daily activities, when encountered by Indonesian security forces on operations, in retaliation for Falintil attacks, and on suspicion of having contact with or having knowledge about Fretilin/Falintil" (CAVR 2005, 7.2, 7).

From the late 1980s, necropower increasingly involved the violent suppression of large-scale protests as the streets of Dili became arenas of struggle for a new generation of urban-based youth clandestine activists (Hearman 2022a, 46). Urban protests grew in number and size during a period of "opening up" East Timor to foreign visitors from 1989, a strategy which, while designed to legitimize Indonesian rule and bring in tourism revenue, led to new contact between resistance activists and journalists and allowed for "new witnessing" of their struggle (Hearman, 2022a, 42). The costs of such activism were high; many young people lost their lives, including the hundreds of young activists and high school students who were killed in the 1991 Santa Cruz massacre in Dili (chapter 2).

Enforced disappearances were another modality of necropower used to break down the resistance (CAVR 2005, 7.2, 6). Laura Huttunen (forthcoming, 39) suggests that enforced disappearance is a specific strategy that entails the "practice of taking lives and simultaneously hiding both the act of killing and the fate of the victims" (see also Robben 2015). It is a strategy that is at once "individualizing," in that it targets specific people identified as "suspicious," and "collectivizing," in that "the circle of potentially targeted people" is often large and porous, feeding into a political atmosphere that is already "imbued with fear" (Huttunen forthcoming: 53). Writing of the practices of the Argentinian military junta in the 1970s, Huttunen makes the point that the destruction of corpses (or the prevention of families from recovering them) was aimed at giving the perpetrators a sense of "absolute control" and "creating a culture of fear that repressed opposition" (Huttunen forthcoming, 43). In addition to "re-educating" what it took to be "the mistaken youth," the military used disappearances of their children to punish those parents who had not succeeded in raising "proper citizens" (Huttunen forthcoming, 43).

The Indonesian regime had similar goals. The potential to be accused as a member of the resistance, and hence arrested, disappeared, or executed, was a constant threat hanging over everyday life. The fate of the disappeared often remained hidden as bodies were thrown into the sea, burnt, buried in remote locations, or stuffed down wells. In other cases, sites of execution were notoriously well-known. One such site was "Jakarta 2," which was used because of the difficulty of retrieving bodies. This was a sheer cliff face about three hundred meters high south of the town of Ainaro, off which the Indonesian military would throw their victims (Blau and Kinsella 2013, 2; CAVR 2005, 7.2). These actions of destroying or hiding bodies seem to have been aimed at both giving the military a sense of absolute control and preventing the dead from becoming martyrs by eradicating them physically, socially, politically, legally, and spiritually (see Robben 2015; Huttunen forthcoming, 43).

For families, these disappearances enacted another form of violence, profoundly disturbing the ritual practices that facilitate the dead's transformation from restless spirits to benevolent ancestors and generating a deep sense of anxiety about the fate of their loved ones (see Fontein 2010, 439–40). This anxiety was deliberately cultivated by the regime's use of various euphemisms to refer to these acts. The disappeared were said to have "gone for a bath," "gone to Jakarta/Bali/Quelicai," "gone hunting," or "gone for an operation." The most common euphemism, that a victim had "gone to school" (CAVR 2005, 7.2, 67), is a powerful reminder of the violent pedagogical intent of the regime.

The regime's necropower was further extended through the recruitment of East Timorese spies, informers, and militia (Budiardjo and Liong 1984; Loney 2018; Robinson 2009; Taylor 1991). As thousands of people were coerced into units designed to assist the Indonesian armed forces in detecting and combating the FALINTIL guerrillas, society became increasingly militarized, the demarcation between the public and intimate realms violated. Fear, suspicion, and distrust circulated widely, and it was never possible to know who could be trusted, even among one's own family. This strategy culminated in the army's formation of local armed militia groups in the late 1990s, which perpetrated much of the widespread terror and killings that occurred in the lead-up to, and in the aftermath of, the referendum on self-determination, including the 1999 Liquiçá church massacre (chapter 3).

Resistance to Necropower

Ultimately, the regime's modalities of necropower failed to destroy political opposition and re-educate East Timorese to be loyal Indonesian citizens. Demonstrating a remarkable capacity to withstand and oppose oppressive violence, the resistance continually reorganized itself; guerrilla warfare extended to encompass clandestine resistance in urban areas, student-led activism in Indonesia, and international activism and diplomacy, creating and sustaining networks of support that kept alive the dream of independence. The dead were reclaimed discursively if not materially, their deaths resignified as martyrdom. This inscribed them with a sacred, sacrificial logic (see Acikcoz 2020, 10) that helped delineate the boundaries of the "imagined community" of the East Timorese nation. East Timor's martyrs came to "embody the sense of 'consanguinity' or shared blood, spilled in the struggle for liberation," which became fundamental to the cultivation of nationalist sentiment (Leach 2020, 69; see also Loney 2018, 4; McWilliam and Traube 2011, 18).

Catholic discourses and practices reinforced these understandings of martyrdom, imbuing the resistance struggle with a "political-spiritual dimension" (Viegas 2020, 58). Indeed, insofar as "martyrdom involves actively opting for death rather than abandoning belief" (Van Henten and Saloul 2020, 22), martyrs came to embody the simultaneous embrace of political and moral positions that opposed the powerful Indonesian regime. Numbers of baptized Catholics increased markedly during the occupation, from nearly 30 percent in the 1970s to 90 percent in 1990, as the church transformed from an instrument of colonialism into an ally of the East Timorese struggle (Braithwaite, Charlesworth, and Soares 2012, 55; Durand 2004, 94; Hodge 2013, 164). Over time, the church helped create what Bear (2007, 53) refers to as a "sacred form of continuity in community" and a "transcendent reality" to which East Timorese could be drawn into. The suffering experienced by ordinary people at the hands of the Indonesia state came to be equated with the brutality of Christ's crucifixion. As Catherine Arthur (2019, 84–85) writes, the idea that "Jesus Christ suffered and died, sacrificing Himself for the salvation of mankind from sin, and that freedom and redemption are the positive consequences of suffering and sacrifice," helped the church's teaching "come to the fore of the national imaginary."

The unifying aspects of the church's narratives and its framing of suffering were reinforced by its ceremonies and rituals. Joel Hodge (2013, 158) writes, for example, of the processions of Catholic images such as the national tour of the statue of our Lady (Mary), which, especially during the 1980s, "constituted a source of unity and hope" and even involved local resistance fighters from the forested mountains (see also Viegas 2020, 58). Masses conducted in Tetum further cemented the church as a marker of East Timorese identity. So too did other important everyday rituals such as the priests' reading of the names of the dead during Mass, which both kept their memory and the resistance struggle alive.

At the same time, Arthur (2019, 84) makes the important point that Catholicism was not simply adopted but was reinterpreted "within the cosmological context" of East Timor, where there were preexisting understandings of death and suffering "as an act of sacrifice for the sake of others" (Arthur 2019, 85; see also Traube 2007). Catholicism did not replace animist practices but rather mingled with them such that a "unique East Timorese form of the faith" emerged, one that rested on an alliance between the church and indigenous conceptions of *lulik* (the sacred) (Arthur 2018, 80; Bovensiepen 2009, 331; Viegas and Feijó 2017).[8] Over time, Catholic and animist rituals came to be creatively combined and to some extent mutually reinforcing, as can be seen in the case of funerals, which incorporate both indigenous ritual speech and communication with the spirit realm and Catholic components, such as the placing of flowers on graves, a Catholic mass, and blessings (Grenfell 2012, 2020).

While discourses of martyrdom helped to reframe East Timorese experiences of bad death, imbuing them with new meanings, this has not been sufficient to address the damaging legacies of necropower, which reverberate well beyond the violence of the deaths themselves. The dead have effectively been dis-membered from their communities, divested from their social identities (see Fontein 2022, 112). Communities and families have been fractured and diminished (see Robben 2015, 57). The inability to recover bodies left abandoned in the bush in the early years of the occupation or disappeared by the regime has left a particularly damaging legacy of disrupted mortuary rituals. By preventing relatives from burying and caring for their dead in accordance with the demands of custom, the regime disturbed the usual "material, social and symbolic processes and techniques through which things and substances become human remains, bodies become bones and living people become or are made safely dead" (Fontein 2022, 112). Put simply, the not properly buried dead have been unable to make the transition to the ancestral realm, remaining trapped in an unsettled, liminal realm and leaving a space of deep uncertainty among the living.

These deaths have created a disruptive and unsettling force that, in a new era of national independence, must be negotiated by political leaders and citizens alike. Jean Langford (2009, 704) invites us to consider how "the very actions that radically devalue the dead have the effect of backhandedly acknowledging their uncanny power." "Desacralization," for Langford, "involves active ritual effort (machine-gunning the grave, carving up the liver), which, as Michael Taussig observed 'may stir up a strange surplus of negative energy . . . from within the defaced thing itself'" (Langford 2009, 704; citing Taussig 1999, 1). In Timor-Leste, this surplus takes the form of a "disordered landscape" of thousands of "corpses out of place" (Warren 1993), which remain scattered in unknown shallow graves and sites or submerged in watery graves. These corpses give massive bad death an unsettling material and spectral presence, embedding it in the landscape and prompting urgent responses from families and the state alike.

The State's Necro-governmental Project: Structuring Social Responses to the Dead

Since the end of the Indonesian occupation, necro-governmentality has replaced necropower as the dominant means through which the state attempts to use the dead to exert power over the living. The term necro-governmentality, coined by Isaias Rojas-Perez (2017, 17) captures how the governance and management of dead bodies emerges as a critical priority in the aftermath of mass violence, a time when the (re)establishment of national identity and the transformation of a violent past into a prosperous and peaceful future is perceived as urgent (see Stepputat 2014, 5).

Necro-governmentality, as the name suggests, takes Foucault's concept of governmentality as its point of reference. Governmentality—the "attempt to shape human conduct by calculated means"—is a form of power that operates by "educating desires and configuring habits, aspirations and beliefs" such that the individual subject participates in their own governance, becoming a self-regulating citizen (Li 2007, 5; de Cesari 2010, 626). Its purpose is to secure the "welfare of the population, the improvement of its condition" (Li 2007, 5). By analyzing the state and state building through the framework of governmentality, scholars have honed in on the "microprocesses of governing" (De Cesari 2010, 626), drawing attention to "the diverse political rationalities of government, on its 'technologies,' and on the considerable intellectual labour involved in bringing into being the things, people and processes to be governed" (Jeffrey 2013, 24; see also Painter 2002, 116; Roll 2014, 30). This has allowed the "constructed or imagined" dimensions of the state to come to the fore, including the everyday political, social, and cultural processes through which the state comes to be recognized by citizens as legitimate (Jeffery 2013, 24; Roll 2014, 22). From this perspective, state building emerges as an unstable, ongoing, and never totalizing process.

From these starting points, it is possible to see that necro-governmentality and necropower are distinctly different modalities of power. While necropower "operates within frames of [absolute] sovereignty" (Rojas-Perez 2017, 17), and its purpose is absolute control, necro-governmentality expresses a less violent and more "caring mode of necropolitics" (Huttunen forthcoming, 33), aiming to structure "the field of *possible* action and speech of survivors, relatives and the population [in relation to the dead] so as to conduct their conduct as free subjects" (Rojas-Perez 2017, 17). It does so by bringing together "different legal, political and disciplinary technologies" to produce "particular kinds of objects and subjects, as well as narratives of suffering and recovery" (Rojas-Perez 2017, 17). It promises to settle the dead, to control and contain them, so that a new future, a new political community, can be imagined.

Let me make three additional points about necro-governmentality that clarify how I use this concept in this book. First, the Timor-Leste state's version of necro-governmentality is a form of power firmly addressed to the living. It is grounded in the presumption that only living humans have agency in the world. While the dead are its emotionally charged objects, they are treated as passive and mute, symbols of the suffering of the living rather than subjects in their own right. Second, necro-governmentality is not just exercised by the state but is also a wider, more diffuse form of power. In Timor-Leste, the state's version of necro-governmentality shapes the discourse and practice of veterans' groups, NGOs, and victims' groups as well as popular expectations of reward and recognition. Yet it is also transformed as it intersects with different, sometimes competing, visions of control and containment of the violent past and as it encounters other sources of power and priorities. My understanding of necro-governmentality, therefore, resonates with recent reconceptualizations of governmentality that seek to overcome the state centrism and European bias of Foucauldian approaches (De Cesari 2010; Ong 2006). I am interested in how necro-governmentality operates under conditions of "multisited, graduated authority," where a range of actors, from the local to the transnational, perform governance functions (de Cesari 2010, 626).

This speaks to the third, related point, which is that necro-governmentality takes diverse *forms*. Rojas-Perez (2017, 18), researching Peru's central southern Andes, foregrounds the forensic excavation and exhumation of mass graves scattered in former war-torn areas, the identification of the bodies of the dead, and their return to their families for care and proper burial as key technologies of necro-governmentality; however, this does not reflect Timor-Leste's experience. There has been limited international support for exhumations, even when it comes to prominent massacres such as Santa Cruz (see chapter 2). The Timor-Leste state does not have the resources to undertake a large-scale process of searching for, exhuming, and identifying the dead, and in a constrained and unequal geopolitical environment, there is little political will to press Indonesia to reveal the sites where bodies were hidden, dumped, or buried. The fact that many deaths during the occupation were solitary, isolated deaths is a further challenge to any organized search for the bodies of the dead. Finally, in a society where there are localized ritual practices for identifying the dead (see chapters 2 and 4), there are not (yet) widespread social expectations and demands for state-organized exhumations involving forensic technologies.

Unlike Peru and other examples where exhumation, identification, and the return of bodies is central, the Timor-Leste state is attempting to structure social responses to the dead through three key technologies: the enrollment of grief and loss in a new heroic narrative; the fashioning of new martyr subjectivities who are rewarded, categorized, and set apart from other bodies; and the containment of martyrs' bodies in designated Garden of Heroes cemeteries.

Ascribing a New Heroic Meaning to Death and Suffering

In the aftermath of the occupation, political leaders have attempted to create a new language to talk about grief, loss, suffering, and bad death. Painful memories and experiences are being enfolded into the stable, linear time of the nation-state (Legg 2005b: 496–97; Edkins 2003), imbued with new, less painful meanings and creating what Charles Maier (1988) refers to as a "useable past." The dominant narrative is a story of heroic resistance, invoking the strength and resilience of the East Timorese people and their capacity for suffering and forbearance (Leach 2008, 145; Kent 2012, 108). It is commonly plotted as a story in which the East Timorese resistance won its struggle for liberation after centuries of consecutive colonial rule via tenacious acts of determination, self-sacrifice, and heroism (Kent 2012, 108). It is a story that makes some stories present while rendering others absent; it emphasizes wholeness and continuity, reinforcing the presumed collective future of the polity and a bright and prosperous future.

Within this story, martyrdom has been reimagined. Once central to the fashioning of a national identity that contested Indonesian state power, martyrdom has been resignified as sacrifice for the nation that was necessary for the emergence of the new Timor-Leste *state*. This reimagining indexes the critical shift that, as Laleh Khalili (2007a, 21–22) has pinpointed, takes place in the aftermath of successful liberation struggles, from the nation as the powerful mobilizing force to the nation-*state*. In this shift, histories of struggle and suffering are "domesticated and institutionalised in the apparatus of the state," reconfigured into a linear progress narrative in which the nation-state represents the "preordained telos of the struggle" (Khalili 2007a, 21–22). In Timor-Leste, stories of martyrdom now not only regenerate and re-member a national community violently dismembered and torn apart; they also work to consolidate the state and craft ideal citizens. They offer a pedagogical lesson to today's citizens, especially the youth, reminding them of their fortunate lives, their indebtedness to the sacrifices of past heroes and martyrs, and their responsibilities to work for national development (see chapter 2).[9] They also legitimate the right to rule of the current political leadership, many of whom were resistance leaders themselves.

The heroic narrative performs other important work for the state. It is especially needed at a fragile and formative period of state formation, when ordinary people's high hopes of *ukun rasik an* (self-government) have been frustrated by a lack of structural and material transformation in their lives. In the aftermath of colonialism and occupation, and its legacies of poverty, low levels of literacy, urban-rural inequalities, and malnutrition, this story appeals to popular desires for starting anew and building a modern nation-state. It enrolls citizens in a vision of national unity, progress, and "development," which, at this point in time, takes the form of the pursuit of "cosmopolitan and technocratic futures": large-scale infrastructure projects, road construction, and gas pipeline development (Palmer and McWilliam 2018, 273–74, 265). The heroic narrative is also directed outwardly. It conveys to Western states, ever skeptical of the new nation's viability, an ideal of its coherence, self-reliance, strength, and continuity with the past. And it facilitates the rebuilding of political and economic relations between Timor-Leste and its near neighbor, Indonesia. Specifically, it diverts attention away from the pursuit of prosecutions of members of the Indonesian military for war crimes or the search for "truth" about the location of mass graves, which, political leaders argue, would be destabilizing to the young nation-state. This is because the resignification of those who died during the struggle as martyrs rather than victims of human rights violations means there is no need to pursue justice for their deaths (Rothschild 2020, 236). Their bodies, too, need not be recovered. Those who willingly offered their lives for the cause of national liberation are rewarded with "justice" in the form of national independence and symbolic recognition.

The heroic story is reinforced, reiterated, and solidified through the official commemoration of significant historical days and the placement of monuments in strategic places. National Heroes Day (31 December), for example, has been created to mark the anniversary of the death of key FRETILIN leader Nicolau Lobato. Lobato became East Timor's first prime minister after FRETILIN declared national independence in 1975 and was allegedly shot dead in the mountains outside Dili by Indonesian forces led by then Lieutenant Prabowo Subianto. His body has yet to be recovered. A towering statue of Lobato also stands at the intersection of the international airport (also named in his honor) and the main road into Dili. In his monumental form, he holds an automatic weapon aloft. Dressed in military fatigues, he projects a militarized, masculine vision of strength, fortitude, and self-reliance to recently arrived visitors. Another key site of memory is the National Resistance Museum located in Dili near the parliament building, which contains exhibits depicting the important contributions of the three "fronts" of the resistance—the armed, the clandestine, and the diplomatic fronts—and the key "turning points" in the story of the liberation struggle and the becoming of the nation-state.[10]

Fashioning New Martyr Subjectivities

The fashioning of martyr subjectivities occurs through an elaborate program that "valorizes" martyrs and living veterans through the provision

The Nicolau Lobato statue, Dili. Photo by author (2018).

of medals and pensions. "Valorization" refers to the constitutionally enshrined imperative to "protect all those who participated in the resistance against the foreign occupation" and to develop mechanisms for "rendering tribute" to national heroes.[11] Living veterans (or "national liberation combatants") are defined by legislation as Timorese citizens who "exclusively dedicated" themselves to the independence struggle for more than three years and were "part of the structures and organizations of the resistance."[12] "Exclusive dedication" is defined as "full-time service within a resistance organization and/or incarceration" (Roll 2014, 100). Martyrs are defined as "all militants of the struggle for national independence who have perished or disappeared between 15 August 1975 and 25 October 1999 as a result of their participation in that struggle."[13] While there is no exclusive dedication or minimum number of years required for martyrs, like veterans, martyrs must have been a member of resistance structures or organizations.

These criteria privilege a militarized, masculine subjectivity, constructing a narrow understanding of the resistance struggle that overlooks its messy lived realities. For instance, the requirement for exclusive dedication to the resistance, while not a requirement for martyrs, favors armed guerrillas over the thousands of East Timorese who were members of the unarmed "clandestine" front who generally juggled their resistance activities with study, work, or farming (Kent and Kinsella 2015, 217). That the legislation only recognizes those who had been members of *formal* resistance organizations also overlooks the degree to which the resistance was supported by the everyday resistance tactics of many ordinary Timorese through the ties of kinship, extended family networks, and systems of house affiliation (Loney 2018, 146).[14] By elevating weapons, rank, length of service, and uniforms, women, who often sustained the resistance through everyday practices of cooking, caring for children, and coordinating safe havens, are rendered invisible (Vásquez 2022, 212; Kent and Kinsella 2015). Generational exclusion is also at play, as student activists who only joined the resistance in its later years find themselves cut out by the exclusive dedication requirement (Roll 2014, 101). As the hypermasculine subject is elevated, complex gendered subjectivities are devalued, rendered invisible.

When it comes to the dead, the valorization program identifies, categorizes, recognizes, and rewards some bodies. It engages in "ordering and bordering," (Auchter 2013, 293; 310) distinguishing the publicly grievable from the ungrievable and constructing hierarchies of the dead . Those whose deaths are deemed to fall into the category of the martyr are made "sacred through the logic of sacrifice" (Acikcoz 2020, 10), imbued with national fantasies of masculine heroism and ideals of collective action, national service, and patriotism. Martyrs' bodies are lifted—both symbolically and, where possible, physically—

from the realm of the family into the realm of the state. Altruistic martyrs who sacrificed their lives for the resistance struggle are distinguished from categories of the "inconvenient dead": civilians, women, children, those who supported the "wrong" side (i.e., the Indonesians), and those killed by the resistance movement itself. These categories do not fit with the state's useable past, it's narrative of heroic and unified struggle and of willing sacrifices for the nation.

The sizeable material benefits that are offered to veterans and martyrs speaks to how another governmental aim of the valorization program is, as Kate Roll (2014, 116; Roll 2018b) has argued, to placate unruly veterans' groups by registering, ordering, managing, and pacifying them, a theme to which I return in chapter 4 (see also Metsola 2006, 1126). Living veterans are entitled to receive: a special retirement pension if they have at least fifteen years of full-time service to the resistance; a special subsistence pension if they have between eight and fourteen years of full-time service (or if they are disabled) or; a single lump sum payment if they have between four to seven years of full-time service. The monthly pensions range between USD 276 per month and USD 750 per month, depending on rank and the length of time in the resistance. Family members of martyrs are entitled to receive substantial "survival" pensions of between USD 230 and USD 287 per month depending on the rank of the martyr. These pensions are paid (in order of priority) to widows/widowers, children, parents, or siblings.[15] In a country where the current minimum wage is USD 150 per month and where, according to the United Nations Development Program, 48.3 percent of the population experiences multidimensional poverty, these amounts are not trivial.[16] The pensions are also complemented by other material benefits, ranging from preferential access to healthcare, scholarships for veterans' children, and entitlement to be buried in an official Garden of Heroes cemetery. The program is also known to be associated with several *ad hoc* benefits, for instance "preferential access to lucrative government contracts" for powerful veterans (Roll 2020, 307).

These generous benefits have created a problem for the state: the valorization program has grown exponentially as tens of thousands of East Timorese have registered themselves or their family members as claimants. More than two hundred thousand individuals have registered over two nationwide registration processes, a figure that is close to 60 percent of the population over thirty years old (Roll 2020, 308).[17] While around 25 percent of claims are still awaiting verification by commissions operating under the auspices of the Ministry for Veteran's Affairs, payments to veterans now account for over 5 percent of the total Timorese national budget—"an expenditure almost double that of the Ministry of Health" (Roll 2020, 308). Given that pension recipients (including children of veterans and martyrs) will receive the pension until they die, these payments are expected to continue for another ninety to one hundred years, representing a significant burden on the national budget.[18] These high numbers also suggest that, as Roll (2018a) argues, many do not meet the narrow legal criteria of a veteran or martyr and that these categories are not as fixed as they may seem, a theme that I return to in later chapters.

Garden of Heroes Cemeteries

The Timor-Leste state's third necro-governmental technology involves the construction and reburial of martyrs (whose bodies have been able to be recovered) in centralized spaces, the Garden of Heroes (Jardin do Herois) cemeteries. These bodies have been recovered through a range of means, including searches and exhumations by the Timor-Leste armed forces (F-FDTL, Falintil-Forcas de Defesa de Timor-Leste) and, more commonly, the localized efforts of families and "commissions" for the recovery of human remains (see chapter 4). The largest Heroes cemetery is in Metinaro, in the municipality of Dili (and is designated for the most senior martyrs). Strategically located next to the main army base of the new armed forces, it establishes a connection between the heroes of the past and the military of today (Myrttinen 2014, 100). The cemetery is described as a "national memorial and place of reflection." (Democratic Republic of Timor-Leste 2010), containing, at its center, a platform for hosting official ceremonies, three flagpoles, a national memorial garden, a chapel, a large cross, and two ossuary houses for the temporary storage of human remain (Arthur 2019: 78).

Heroes cemeteries are now also being constructed beyond Dili. The state's initial plan was to build a cemetery in each municipality. At the time of writing, there are cemeteries at various stages of planning or completion in all of Timor-Leste's municipalities, with the exception of the Oekussi special economic zone, with the Liquiçá cemetery the first to be completed, in 2017 (see chapter 3).[19] Some cemeteries remain unfinished due to construction delays (which are often said to be caused by the misuse of funds by local construction companies). Not all have been fully embraced by local residents. For instance, the Los Palos cemetery contains only a handful of graves, and it is often said that local *adat* (custom) will not permit the reburial of the dead far from their ancestral land (see Viegas and Feijó 2017, 101). This is part of the reason for the more recent emergence of Heroes cemeteries at the scale of the *posto* (subdistrict). There are no official criteria for the establishment of such cemeteries, which have largely come about as a result of the human-remains-gathering efforts and the advocacy of local veterans' groups, who argue that these cemeteries are needed because of the large number of deaths in their region. At this point in time, heroes cemeteries are being planned or built in Natarbora, Kelikai,

Iliomar, Uato Lari, and Laga, some of which will become official municipality cemeteries.[20]

The Heroes cemeteries draw martyrs into the heroic resistance narrative, rewarding and categorizing. Like other modern war cemeteries around the globe, the graves are constructed within a grid-like pattern that expresses a "commonality of destiny" among the dead, bringing them into connection with one another owing to their deaths for the nation (Viegas and Feijó 2017, 101; Grenfell 2012, 99). Reburial ceremonies are presided over by members of the armed forces, who, dressed in military uniform, carry coffins draped in *tais* (woven cloth) in the colors of the Timor-Leste national flag from the ossuary to the graves, emplacing them in the ground to the accompaniment of a gun salute. The designation of different spaces for the burial of the clandestine and FALINTIL dead and those of different rank establishes "clear hierarchies of state recognition," demarcating the ways in which some bodies matter more than others (Grenfell 2020, 152).

The Heroes cemeteries perform other work for the state. They can be understood as a key mechanism for "spatializing" the state, "projecting a taken for granted spatial image of a state that sits above and contains its localities, regions and communities" (Ferguson and Gupta 2002, 982). Perhaps more so than other spatializing strategies such as the policing of borders, the strategic placing of national flags and monuments, the renaming of streets, and the creation of grand boulevards (e.g., see Till and Kuusisto-Arponen 2015, 294), the emplacement of dead bodies in the material landscape through reburials is a powerful technique of statecraft. The material presence of dead bodies—their "thereness"—and their association with ideas of the "sacred" imbue graves with a symbolic effectiveness in projects of state and nation building (Verdery 1999). Furthermore, through the enclosure of identified bodies in distinct spaces, and their labeling and categorization (Johnson 2008), the state's "ownership" over those bodies is asserted and the boundary between the state and family is delineated.

Reburials in these cemeteries also serve as a mechanism through which the land is cleared of painful memories and "corpses out of place." They promise to settle the dead, offering closure to their living relatives and rendering the land safe for development. This settling seeks to cultivate a "reformed sensibility" toward the dead, to curtail fluid, unruly, and spatially dispersed familial practices of remembrance, reburial, and care (Johnson 2008, 781). A recent decree law, for instance, governs arrangements such as which bodies are entitled to be buried in the cemeteries, the correct spacing of graves, their shape and depth, the material out of which the coffins are to be constructed, and their thickness. It also sets out the minimum time required after death before

The Garden of Heroes, Metinaro. Photo by author (2018).

burial can take place, the ornamentation permitted on graves, and the behaviors that are prohibited in the cemetery grounds.[21]

Finally, the cemeteries provide "proof" of the extent of sacrifices for the resistance. The vast numbers of bodies that now lie in the Heroes cemeteries around the country provide evidence of the scale of the resistance movement against the Indonesian occupation and the large number of people who were involved. This, in turn, validates the current political order led by many former resistance leaders.

Necro-governmentality through Transitional Justice

The technologies of necro-governmentality deployed by the Timor-Leste state have evolved in critical dialogue with others, including those that operated during the period of the United Nations Transitional Administration in East Timor (UNTAET), 2000–2002. It could in fact be argued that the state's necro-governmental project has evolved in part as a reaction to the power asymmetries reproduced by UNTAET, one of the most substantial UN state-building missions to have ever been undertaken. The mission has been widely critiqued for replicating colonial logics by ignoring preexisting social and political structures and reinforcing imaginings of the East Timorese population as passive and vulnerable, in need of external assistance (Arthur 2018, 177; Brown and Gusmao 2009, 64; Rothschild 2020, 237).

The UNTAET mission was established at a time when "liberal peacebuilding efforts were in ascendancy around the world" (Grenfell 2020, 137). There were widely held assumptions that East Timor's successful transition to a peaceful, prosperous nation-state would require a liberal democracy, functioning public institutions, and an open market economy (Kent 2016b, 225). The idea that an internationally supported transitional justice process would be necessary to "deal with" a violent past and respond to victims' suffering was also in wide circulation among UN actors, donor agencies, and NGOs (both local and international). Transitional justice had by this point become a "global project" (Nagy 2008), reflecting an apparent global consensus that justice is essential to sustainable peace (Kent 2016b). Criminal prosecutions, truth-telling mechanisms, and reconciliation and reparations programs had become "key tools" in the international peacebuilding infrastructures (Jones 2021, 165). The UN established two transitional justice mechanisms in East Timor: a truth commission known as the Commission for Reception, Truth, and Reconciliation (referred to by its Portuguese acronym CAVR) and a serious crimes investigations process that consisted of a specialized investigations unit (SCIU—Serious Crimes Investigations Unit) and a hybrid tribunal comprised of international and domestic judges.

Transitional justice projects are not power free but provide "frameworks that 'structure' the possible field of action of others" (Obradovic-Wochnik 2020, 121; see also Jones 2021). They produce "power hierarchies, regulatory practices, disciplinary rules and subjectification" that make some forms of action possible, and some forms of violence visible, while concealing others (Obradovic-Wochnik 2020, 119; see also Jones 2021, 165). As these frameworks become naturalized and taken for granted, these hierarchies and silences become difficult to "see." In Timor-Leste, transitional justice mechanisms assigned new "victim" subjectivities to those who had experienced harm. They also assigned new meanings to the violence of the past, framing massive bad death as human rights violations, crimes against humanity, and genocide: crimes that demanded a prosecutorial response and "traumatic" experiences that needed to be exposed and worked through publicly. Furthermore, they introduced new practices of public truth telling and criminal prosecutions. The assumption was that transitional justice would not only contribute to personal healing but provide a pedagogical lesson that would instill the historical consciousness required to deter future violent conflicts and secure a democratic and accountable state (Kent 2019, 190; see also David 2017; Kidron 2020, 308).

These technologies of necro-governmentality, just like those at work in the Timor-Leste state's projects, treated the dead instrumentally, as the means to a broader end. As Damian Grenfell (2020, 141) observes, the discourse of liberal peacebuilding (of which transitional justice discourse is a part) is concerned with restoring relations between the living, not between the living and the dead. The dead are important insofar as they help to achieve broader institutional goals: to establish a conclusive "truth" about past violence, to serve as "evidence" in prosecutions, and to provide a pedagogical lesson to the citizens of the present and future that will contribute to peacebuilding. The individual demands of the dead, as they are expressed through their families—for exhumation, identification, and reburial—cannot be heard.

For the CAVR, the dead were necessary to achieve a number of goals that are intrinsic to the work of truth commissions. Key among these was truth seeking. The CAVR was tasked by the government with "establishing the truth regarding past human rights violations" committed during the Indonesian occupation and presenting "factual and objective information" (CAVR 2005, chapter 2, 1). Counting the dead was presumed to be a critical part of this process, facilitating the construction of what John Roosa (2007, 574) has termed a "truth by numbers" (see also Auchter 2016, 40; Rothschild 2020). The CAVR went about this counting by combining a qualitative research approach focused on gathering witness testimony with investigative techniques that were claimed to be based on "verifiable scientific best practices" (Chapman and Ball 2001, 42). The assumption behind these latter techniques was that an authoritative, objective, undeniable truth could be achieved through the use of "quantitative statistical data" (Rothschild 2020, 225). A key technique involved a retrospective mortality survey, which consisted of a random survey of East Timorese households to investigate the numbers of individuals who died during the commission's mandate period, as well as a graveyard census database, in which data was collected from public cemeteries (Chapman and Ball 2001; see also Roosa 2007, 58; Rothschild 2020). The goal was to produce "macro-level" conclusions on the "broader patterns underlying gross violations of human rights" and come up with an accurate number of those who died during the Indonesian occupation (Chapman and Ball 2001, 10). Yet many have questioned the CAVR's "truth by numbers," suggesting that it is likely to be well below the number of actual deaths. Roosa (2007, 576), for instance, has argued that the CAVR's focus on counting bodies that lay in known locations produced an inaccurate figure of conflict deaths that failed to account for all those who were not buried in cemeteries. Bodies that could not be found could not be counted.

The CAVR's concern with counting the dead was also a reflection of its reparative, reconciliatory, and justice-seeking goals, goals that underpin the work of all truth commissions. Jessica Auchter notes that the counting of the dead of conflict is seen as important to "rehumanize" the dead, to "redeem their humanity" (Auchter 2016, 42). The drive to rehumanize, she suggests, is underpinned by the "moral notion that each death matters, and that each production of a dead body should not only be measured but also *accounted for*" (Auchter 2016: 40). Conversely, it is assumed that not to account for deaths is dehumanizing (Auchter 2016, 42). Determining an accurate number of conflict dead is also assumed to promote an awareness of loss that will promote reconciliation among a divided population (Auchter 2016, 42). Finally, it is seen as a necessary measure to "do justice to the memory of those killed" that might allow communities to acknowledge suffering and sacrifices and for victims to be recognized (Auchter 2016, 41). In the case of the CAVR, the counting of the dead fed into the commission's recommendations for: the memorialization of significant sites of killings of deaths; assistance for families to locate and rebury the remains of deceased loved ones; the establishment of a public register of the disappeared; a National Day of Remembrance of the famine of 1978–79; and investigation of significant massacre cases with a view to prosecutions (CAVR 2005, chapter 11, 6–7, 25).

The SCIU's mandate was narrower than that of the CAVR. The dead were valuable insofar as they helped to meet the broader goal of prosecutions. Selected exhumations were conducted in cases where dead bodies were needed as "criminal evidence"—as a "preamble to the desired prosecution and conviction of war criminals" (Ferrandiz and Robben 2015, 11; see also Grenfell 2020, 143). The dead were evidence of an event, necessary to establish that event as one of international gravity, as a war crime or crime against humanity (see Auchter 2016, 42). For these reasons, little attention was given to the role exhumations might play in meeting families' needs, and few resources were devoted to this task. In fact, there were times when the work of the SCIU caused distress to families and disturbed spirits of the dead. These included cases where families were requested to exhume the remains of loved ones already buried to provide evidence for trials. The SCIU did not provide families with sufficient resources to conduct rituals to request the permission of the spirits to disturb their bodies (Kent 2012: 167). Another issue was that human remains exhumed for the purposes of criminal investigations were not always returned to their families for reburial. In one case of institutional incompetence described in detail by Douglas Kammen (2015, 150–52), the SCIU effectively "lost" a body it had exhumed from a family grave in Maubara for the purposes of a murder investigation and was unable to return it to the family, creating deep spiritual disturbances (see also Blau 2020). In these cases, far from delivering justice, the SCIU inflicted a form of "epistemic violence" as it was unable to engage with East Timorese ways of knowing and being in the world (see Jamar 2022).

Not only were the dead treated as a means to an end in the UN's transitional justice process; the CAVR and Serious Crimes Process were also ultimately unable to meet many of their own liberal, justice- and truth-seeking goals. Both mechanisms became entangled in what Alex Jeffrey (2011, 2019) and Rachel Hughes (2015) refer to as a "geopolitics of justice," framed by the possibilities of the initial international response to the conflict. As Hughes astutely observes, international justice responses (and in this case transitional justice mechanisms) do not simply "arrive" after war but are "already constrained and continually challenged in highly consequential ways" (Hughes 2023, 160). These constraints tend to be obscured by the framing of transitional justice as a set of technical, apolitical "tools" that can be applied in diverse contexts. In Timor-Leste, the "hybrid" or "internationalized" tribunal established by the UN was from the outset a compromised response to widespread demands for members of the Indonesian military to be brought to justice. A United Nations Commission of Inquiry in 1999 had released a report recommending the establishment of an international criminal tribunal, along the lines of those established for the former Yugoslavia and Rwanda. Despite this, the UN secretary general, responding to assurances from the Indonesian government, declared that the Indonesian courts must first be given an opportunity to investigate and prosecute, noting that he would also strengthen UNTAET's capacity to conduct investigations and collaborate with the Indonesian process. Yet the tribunal's jurisdictional restrictions and the absence of Indonesian government cooperation with investigations ultimately meant that no member of the Indonesian military was prosecuted. The absence of Indonesian involvement also constrained the "truth" that could be revealed about the location of mass graves and the fate of the disappeared. The truth that was pieced together by both the SCIU and the CAVR was heavily reliant on accounts gathered from East Timorese witnesses.

Since the departure of the UN transitional administration, the transitional justice version of necro-governmentality has been superseded by the Timor-Leste state's heroic version, which, endowed with significant resources, is increasingly gaining traction in the public imaginary. However, the subjectivities, discourses, and practices of transitional justice remain powerful, kept alive by a small yet active group of Dili-based domestic human rights NGOs and activists and the Centro Nasional Chega! (CNC, National Chega! Center), established by the state in 2016 as the successor institution to the CAVR. These actors maintain an ongoing campaign for the establishment of an international criminal tribunal and support the local memorialization and commemoration of civilian massacres (a theme to which I shall return in chapter 3).

Transforming Necro-governmentality

The Kore Metan Nasional, discussed at the beginning of this chapter, was a key state technology to bring about closure and containment of the massive bad death of the Indonesian occupation. It was a failure. It quickly became clear that families were not prepared to trade the search and individualized, ritual treatment of their deceased loved ones for the symbolic, collective recognition of all the nation's dead. Picking up on this rejection, the government did not bother to collect the black ribbons that it had distributed to families and place them in a central location, recognizing that an end to mourning could not be so easily declared (Kent and Feijó 2020, 32–33). Many of those I have spoken to about the Kore Metan over the past five years have dismissed it as an ineffective exercise that imposed a premature form of closure. As one interlocutor laughingly stated, it is "not time for kore metan—there are too many missing bodies!"[22] The Kore Metan Nasional brings to the fore a fundamental limit of the state's necro-governmental logics: the treatment of the dead as passive and inert is unable to engage with widespread, embodied experiences of the dead as agential beings.

Even as the state's necro-governmental logics are permeating local lifeworlds, they are far from all encompassing. This is a key theme of this book. These logics are transformed as they intersect unevenly with alternative logics of necro-governmentality and other forms of power and as they open up spaces for maneuver and resistance. These dynamics become especially evident as the book moves geographically and figuratively beyond the national capital, Dili. While the state's necro-governmental logics and technologies are not necessarily resisted locally (as they were in the case of the Kore Metan Nasional) the capacity of political leaders and bureaucrats to control them is limited in rural communities where the state, such as through welfare programs, institutions, and development projects, is often experienced as a remote presence. Not only that: "the edges of the state," as Timothy Mitchell (1991, 88) puts it, emerge as hazy and uncertain, complicated by other forms of power, legitimacy, and authority. These technologies and logics enter a complex necropolitical terrain where diverse actors (for instance, veterans' groups) seek to harness the power of the dead for their own necro-governmental goals and where other forms of power (including the power of the dead to act on the living) are also at work.

The chapters that follow explore how the dead and the living participate in the ongoing transformations of necro-governmentality, transformations that come further into view as the state is decentered as the site of analysis. I pay attention to the new communities, spaces of memory, and sociopolitical practices that are emerging from the productive frictions between diverse necro-governmental logics and other forms of power. I show how the dead, in their emotive materiality as human remains and their affective presence as spirit subjects, are a potent and at times unruly source of power in these transformations.

The next chapter turns to the Santa Cruz massacre that occurred in the urban space of Dili. This case is interesting because it seems, at first glance, that the memory of Santa Cruz has been fully enrolled within the state's necro-governmental logics. This massacre occurred in the national capital, the center of the national imaginary, and the thousands of young people who lost their lives have been recognized as martyrs and their families provided with material compensation. They are now symbolically remembered through annual, state-funded commemorations that involve thousands of people. The remembrance of martyred youth has become increasingly useful to the state as a pedagogical lesson that crafts ideal, patriotic youth citizens in the present and reinforces hierarchies of the dead. However, a closer look reveals that the Santa Cruz dead have not been fully captured by the state. A key issue is that many bodies have not been recovered; their restless spirits continue to press their demands for proper burial and care on their families and close friends, calling attention to unfulfilled responsibilities.

2

The Martyred Youth of the Metropole

Re-membering the Santa Cruz Dead

Each year, on the morning of 12 November, outside the pretty, whitewashed, Portuguese-era Church of Santo António de Motael (Motael church) in Dili next to the sea, thousands gather to commemorate the Santa Cruz massacre. They mark the anniversary of the day in 1991 when hundreds of young, unarmed East Timorese protestors were killed by Indonesian troops at Dili's Santa Cruz cemetery. In 2017 I joined the commemoration, which began with a festive, early-morning atmosphere. Many people were dressed in their Sunday best, having just emerged from the mass in the church grounds led by Dili's bishop, Father da Silva. Student groups, youth groups, church groups, and families greeted each other with enthusiastic cries of "Viva Timor-Leste!" The symbolic presence of the dead was everywhere. The faces of martyred youth gazed out from the frames of photographs carried by family members and were emblazoned on T-shirts and banners alongside slogans such as "They died so we could live" and "They woke us up to continue sacrificing in a new struggle for a better Timor-Leste." Some messages were addressed to the audience in the first person, such as "I sold my body to buy liberty" (see also Rothschild 2020, 234). Mostly depicting happy moments of young people, posing in their favorite clothes, wearing sunglasses, astride motorbikes, these photos were also an unsettling reminder of the unnaturalness of victims' deaths and the loss of their youthful potential. We then began a slow walk to the Santa Cruz cemetery, following the path that the young protesters took on the day of the massacre, stopping at different points along the way to listen to one of the survivors describe the events that took place there. This part of the ritual evoked the Catholic stations of the cross. By walking the original route, it felt as if these events were being powerfully inscribed into the spaces and into our bodies, the bodies of the walkers.

By the time we reached the cemetery the mid-morning sun was high above us, the heat intense. The crowd congregated near a large stage, adorned with Timor-Leste national flags, that had been set up outside the cemetery walls. Everyone did their best to find pockets of shade, some perching on shaded gravestones just inside the cemetery walls. Relatives holding framed photos of their missing and deceased loved ones sat in plastic chairs in rows along one side of the stage under a covered tarpaulin. Beside them, various dignitaries reclined in more comfortable couches. The main ceremony then began. Political leaders and members of the 12 November Committee—the nongovernment organization representing the interests of over two thousand survivors of the massacre and the families of the dead—addressed the crowd, making impassioned statements about the sacrifices made by resistance youth and the significance of this day as a turning point in the independence struggle.

Halfway through the ceremony, a group of young people representing each of Timor-Leste's districts arrived on foot. Dressed in colorful *tais* (woven

Families of martyred youth at the Santa Cruz commemoration, Dili. Photo by author (2017).

Santa Cruz T-shirt: "I sold my body to buy liberty." Photo by author (2017).

cloth) and carrying national and district flags, they had been bussed into Dili and had walked from various sites just outside of town. Shouts of *Viva mate restu!* (Viva Survivors!), *Viva Timor-Leste!*, and *Viva Unidade Nasional!* punctuated the air. The bishop delivered an oration, and we all stood for the singing of the national anthem and for one minute's silence to remember the dead, led by then president Francisco Guterres, aka Lú-Olo. Iconic nationalist music was then blasted through speakers and people began dancing the *tebe-tebe*—a collective dance of "social and community cohesion"—holding hands in large circles (Siapno 2012, 436). White doves were released into the air by the political leaders on stage. The final ritual act involved a slow winding of people through the crowded, higgledy-piggledy cemetery to the grave of Sebastião Gomes, whose death sparked the initial massacre, to perform the Catholic ritual of laying flowers and lighting votive candles. The intense heat emanating from the blazing fire created by thousands of small candles melding and merging created another powerful sensory experience of Santa Cruz.

The Santa Cruz massacre has become a foundational narrative of the Timor-Leste state, a "chosen trauma" (Volkan 2001) that signifies a turning point in the liberation struggle. This chapter examines how the young people who lost their lives during the massacre now hold a critical place in the public discourses and performances of Santa Cruz memory, imbued with the sacred, sacrificial aura of martyrdom. State-sponsored annual commemorations and associated events such as media interviews, seminars, and film screenings not only harness the symbolic power of martyred youth to remember a national community violently dismembered by Indonesian necropower; they also work as necro-governmental technologies that fashion ideal youth citizens in the present and reinforce hierarchies of remembrance of different dead bodies. The spirits of those martyred youth are not permitted to disrupt these performances. Yet those whose bodies have not yet been given a proper burial remain restless, unhappy, not easily dispensed with. While there is little space for them to make their demands known during the large, annual commemorations, there are moments and spaces outside this event when they succeed in pressing themselves into, and making themselves felt within, the assemblage of Santa Cruz memory work. The dead's insistence that the symbolic, collective recognition of their suffering is not sufficient pushes back against attempts to render the memory of Santa Cruz "safe" for the state to claim for its own.

The first part of the chapter tracks the trajectory of Santa Cruz remembrance over space and time, showing how this massacre became a powerful "traveling" memory that galvanized Western audiences and transnational resistance activists before coming "home" after national independence to take on new and powerful meanings for the state. This tracking is important for several reasons. First, it provides a compelling illustration of how the necropower of the Indonesian occupation unleashed countervailing forces as the resistance claimed the Santa Cruz dead as martyrs. Second, it sets the scene for the more recent incarnation of Santa Cruz as a central narrative within the state's necro-governmental project, a narrative that, in elevating the sacrifices of martyred youth, molds a forward-looking youth citizenry, creates hierarchies of the dead, and delineates publicly grievable lives from those that are ungrievable. Third, it shows how these shifts have been less due to the "top down" engineering of the state than from the long-term efforts of prominent Santa Cruz survivors to keep the memory of the massacre alive. However, these survivors are also propelled by responsibilities and imperatives that complicate and at times subvert the state's necro-governmental logics.

These complications become especially visible in the chapter's second part, when I turn away from the official annual commemorations to the less publicly visible work of searching for the bodies of Santa Cruz victims and to memory work in the intimate space of the home and neighborhood. I first explore the exhumation work of the International Forensic Team (IFT), which, while imbued with its own necro-governmental logics, was gradually transformed as it intersected with socioculturally situated understandings of evidence, identification, and agency. I then turn to the home and neighborhood, where practices of care and remembrance respond to the demands of the restless spirits of the martyred for the recovery of their bodies and proper burial and care. These practices reveal the powerful, embodied ways in which the dead remind their living relatives and close friends of their unfulfilled obligations. It is precisely because Santa Cruz has a unique, personal, and embodied significance to close friends and families of the dead that its memory is unable to be "fixed," fully contained, and owned by the state.

The Santa Cruz Massacre

While the events of Santa Cruz are well known, let me briefly recount them here, as they provide an important window into the evolving modalities of necropower deployed by the Indonesian regime to deal with an increasingly sophisticated resistance movement based in the urban areas and towns. In addition to violently suppressing a civilian youth protest and disappearing or destroying the bodies of the dead, the regime would desecrate a church, setting in train a pattern that would later be replicated in the killings of 1999 (Leach 2017, 108; Loney 2018, 134), including the Liquiçá church massacre (see chapter 3).[1]

The immediate trigger for the massacre was the Indonesian military's killing of young resistance activist Sebastião Gomes Rangel on 28 October 1991 in the Motael church. Sebastião had been a member of one of East Timor's youth resistance groups that were part of the "clandestine front" of the resistance. This was the loose network of civilians organized into small cells based in the villages and towns that became increasingly important as an emphasis on armed resistance began to give way to international diplomacy and urban-based protests (Nicholson 2001, 19; Wigglesworth 2013).[2] Clandestine youth groups helped to pass messages, food, and medical supplies to the FALINTIL, organized demonstrations, and educated young people and civilians about the struggle for independence. They also engaged in public actions such as asylum seeking in foreign embassies in Jakarta. In this instance, clandestine youth activists had been preparing for a demonstration that was to coincide with a visit by a Portuguese parliamentary delegation. Under intense political surveillance, they were creating flags, posters, and banners declaring East Timorese resistance to the Indonesian occupation (Crockford 2007). When the delegation was suspended by the Portuguese parliament on 25 October, the Indonesian military escalated its harassment of activists, which culminated in a raid on Motael church in which Sebastião was killed (CAVR 2005, chapter 7.2, 199). At the time, Indonesian military officials in East Timor denied claims that they had killed Sebastião, insisting that his death was a consequence of a clash between pro- and anti-integrationist youths at Motael church.

In its violent transgression of "sanctified religious space" (Crockford 2007), the raid was especially provocative. The Catholic Church had by this point come to occupy a central place in East Timor. Critically, it was present in people's lives in an everyday sense, providing education and spaces of sanctuary and refuge for those targeted by security forces and offering spiritual solace to those who were mourning the loss of their loved ones. In an environment where "there was death all around, everywhere and constantly in people's minds, the Catholic Church was a place to find hope—otherwise there was just death" (Hodge 2013, 153). At a time when churches remained one of few spaces respected by the Indonesian authorities (see Loney 2018, 133), the raid was a potent signal that nowhere was safe from necropower. It disrupted peoples' sense of "being at home in the world" (Ingold 2005, 503), rendering a familiar, safe, and sacred space strange, violent, and dangerous. This point is powerfully made by former resistance activist Naldo Rei (2007, 49), who writes in his autobiography that the attack was experienced as a profound "assault on our values, spirituality, identity, and culture. . . . we felt our last refuge, our peaceful churches, had been sucked into the horror."

This provocation motivated clandestine youth groups to transform their initial plans for a demonstration into a decision to hold a memorial service for Sebastião on 12 November. This would also be an occasion to demonstrate for a referendum on East Timor's future, as the UN Special Rapporteur on Torture would be visiting Dili (Pinto and Jardine 1997, 199). The 1991 Santa Cruz memorial service for Sebastião was, then, a powerful expression of "memory activism" (Gutman and Wustenberg 2023). Resistance activists consciously used Sebastião's death as an occasion to express their anger and frustration at the oppressive conditions in which they lived. They were under no illusions about the dangers they faced. One of the key organizers, Liurai Tasi, described how his sense of foreboding increased when, the night before the service he had a dream in which all the flags of the world suddenly hovered close to the demonstrators, but the Portuguese flag, which was the closest, was black.[3] Liurai Tasi interpreted this dream to mean that many of the demonstrators would be killed. Despite expressing his misgivings to other activists the next day, collectively they decided to proceed—"because we had to move the process, we decided to die."[4]

Eyewitness accounts and footage of the events of 12 November 1991 indicate that a crowd of over three thousand mourners attended the early-morning memorial service at Motael that day. This was a powerful, embodied expression of public contestation of the military's power to circumscribe and control space in the capital city (Crockford 2007, 89). Following the service, a procession of mostly young people began to walk from the church toward the Santa Cruz Cemetery, metamorphosing into activists as they unfurled banners, waved FRETILIN flags, punched the air, and shouted "Viva" (Crockford 2007; CAVR 2005, chapter 7.2). As the procession wove its way to the cemetery, the crowd grew to four or five thousand. While some remained in front of the cemetery entrance, standing on the walls and on the gate with their banners unfurled, others continued through the cemetery gates to pray and lay flowers at Sebastião's grave. Those in front of the cemetery were soon confronted with a line of Indonesian military troops bearing automatic weapons who began shooting into the crowd, driving them into the cemetery (Braithwaite, Charlesworth, and Soares 2012, 80).[5] The military then began moving through the cemetery shooting and bayoneting those inside, including protesters who tried to scramble for cover behind cemetery tombstones or flee into the streets nearby. Bodies began piling up at the gate to the cemetery. The killing continued for about fifteen minutes before orders were issued to cease and pile the wounded and dead into trucks (Braithwaite, Charlesworth, and Soares 2012, 80).

The number of those killed during the Santa Cruz massacre remains unknown. While some suggest the figure could be as high as 271 dead, with 250 missing (see CAVR 2005, part 3, 117; Braithwaite, Charlesworth, and Soares 2012, 80), determining a precise number is complicated by the Indonesian military's success in covering its evidentiary traces; many bodies have not been recovered, thought to have been burned or dumped in the sea. A further complication is that some killings took place after the massacre itself (Blau and Fondebrider 2011, 1251). Interviews conducted by the Commission for Reception, Truth, and Reconciliation (CAVR) with witnesses suggest that some of the wounded were taken to the Wira Husada Hospital, and then to the morgue. Soldiers crushed the heads of some of the seriously wounded with a large stone and ran over bodies in the morgue area with a truck.[6] Tablets of formaldehyde were given to others to hasten their death. Witnesses also observed the bodies brought into the hospital later being placed on trucks and driven to unknown locations (CAVR 2005, chapter 7.2, 203). In the days and weeks after the massacre hundreds of young people were rounded up and interrogated, not only in Dili but throughout East Timor. Executions of massacre witnesses took place on 15, 17, and 18 November, and again later in November. In this sense, Santa Cruz was not a single massacre but a continuum of events (Blau and Fondebrider 2011, 1251) in which different technologies of necropower were deployed to cultivate fear and uncertainty and demonstrate the regime's absolute control. This was a strategy that unraveled.

Santa Cruz as a Traveling Memory: International Outrage and Condemnation

The Santa Cruz massacre propelled East Timor's struggle into the imaginations of Western audiences. Several, intersecting factors help to account for this impact. First, while similar atrocities had taken place during the occupation, this was the first time that the brutality of the Indonesian military had been captured on film. The British photojournalist Max Stahl, who filmed the massacre, managed to smuggle the footage out of the country.[7] The events were then shown worldwide, reaching international audiences at a time when information on what was happening inside the territory was scarce. Santa Cruz took place at the end of an almost two-decade period during which the Indonesian government had virtually banned international media and aid agencies from the territory and had permitted official delegations only in tightly controlled circumstances (CAVR 2005, chapter 3, 85).

Contributing to its powerful impact was the nature of the massacre itself. Ann Rigney (2020, 717–18) makes the point that civic massacres, which involve the transformation of a "peaceful demonstration into a bloodbath" are "highly memorable." They present a powerful opposition between good and evil, "capturing in a condensed form the opposition between right and might, between the rights of citizens to make their voices heard and the repression of that right on the part of the state" (Rigney 2020, 718). In the case of Santa Cruz, the contrast between "might and right" is augmented by the poignant distinction between the young age of the victims and the ruthless foreshortening of their lives (see Rigney 2020, 718). Martyred youth have a special power due to their associations with vulnerability, innocence, disrupted lineages and promising lives cut short in their prime. In the case of Santa Cruz, where demonstrators used "banners not bullets," their actions, and subsequent suffering and death, came to be associated with an innocence, vulnerability, and purity (Rothschild, 2016, 99).

A third factor that contributed to the impact of Santa Cruz was the power of the images themselves. Filmic images possess what Roland Barthes (1980, 81, 82) has described in the case of photographs as an "evidential force": a form of "tangible evidence of otherwise invisible processes and events" that invokes a sense of the "immediate and real" (Crossland 2009, 71; 73). In the case of the Santa Cruz footage this force is magnified owing to a sense that the images before our eyes are constantly moving and unfolding in real time (McCosker 2004, 74). Filmed on a shaky handheld camera, Max Stahl's footage has a fast-paced quality, creating the effect of a "collective flow of terror" (McCosker 2004, 74). Amid this collective flow, there is one point when the camera zooms in on two individuals, an injured and bleeding young man being cradled in the arms of a friend, apparently dying before our eyes. This moment of zooming in gives a face to the memory of protest, making it "concrete, condensed, portable" (Rigney 2020). In its portrayal of immediacy, urgency, collective terror, and individual suffering, the footage of Santa Cruz produces a powerful affect that, at the time of its reception by international audiences, was experienced as the "shock of catastrophe" (McCosker 2004, 74).

Enabled by global media infrastructures, footage of the massacre circulated widely. While Tomsky argues that, as memories of violence travel, media outlets tend to frame them in ways that resonate with preexisting political or economic agendas (Tomsky 2011, 58), in the case of the Santa Cruz footage, the opposite was true. This large-scale spectacle of violence achieved a political force that disrupted dominant political agendas (McCosker 2004, 74). Santa Cruz inspired demonstrations around the world, galvanizing a new era of international solidarity for East Timor's independence. This began to wear away at the realpolitik positions promoted by Western states and to undermine the reputation of Suharto and the Indonesian military (Braithwaite, Charlesworth, and Soares 2012, 73). From this point on, it became increasingly difficult for Western states to simply ignore the violence taking place in the territory.[8]

Just as the memory of Santa Cruz was generating support and solidarity for East Timor's independence cause among Western audiences, so too did it become incorporated into evolving understandings of struggle and national identity among geographically dispersed East Timorese resistance activists. This was a time when, along with the increased focus on international diplomacy and urban-based clandestine resistance, the language of anticolonial liberation was gradually being displaced by a "church inspired message of human rights and deliverance from suffering" (Webster 2013, 12). This discursive shift was not only a pragmatic strategy designed to appeal to an international audience; it was also critical to evolving imaginings of national identity grounded in ideas of shared suffering and self-determination (Webster 2013, 6). Santa Cruz gave shape to these imaginings, providing evidence of the brutality of the occupation that countered Indonesia's claims to "territorial integrity" with claims to the "collective right to self-determination as a people" (Webster 2013, 18).[9] Claiming those young people who died as "martyrs" inscribed those deaths with a sacred, sacrificial logic. Martyred youth came to embody both the "bravery and courage" associated with East Timor's armed guerrilla movement and the "innocence and moral high ground" associated with their status as young people engaged in a peaceful, unarmed protest (Rothschild 2016, 99).

The relative freedom enjoyed by solidarity and diasporic activists contrasted with the hostile and suffocating environment within East Timor, where activists deemed it too dangerous to publicly remember the dead for much of the 1990s. Yet Santa Cruz remained a powerful embodied memory, carried and transmitted through interpersonal encounters, stories, and private acts of remembrance. The lengths to which the Indonesian regime went to suppress this memory suggests that they recognized its danger, that it could become a mobilizing force for the resistance. On the first anniversary of the massacre, Indonesian authorities required permits to visit the Santa Cruz cemetery, banned remembrance masses, and ensured that armed soldiers and police tightly guarded the cemetery and patrolled the streets and university.[10] The small number of mourners who visited the Santa Cruz cemetery to place flowers at a site marked by a large black cross were closely watched.[11] In 1995 Dili residents were still reporting widespread harassment around the time of the Santa Cruz anniversary.[12]

It was not until 1998, when activists, emboldened by the recent political opening in Indonesia that followed President Suharto's fall from power, attempted a large public commemoration in Dili. Accounts of those who participated suggest this was a moving and powerful event that brought together people from Dili and beyond at the Santa Cruz cemetery. Liurai Tasi, key organizer, recalls how the priest at the Balide church (the closest church to the Santa Cruz cemetery), still scarred by the events that occurred during the original commemorative mass in 1991, refused activists' requests to conduct a special mass. The mourners/protesters had brought flowers to the Balide church and, finding that the priest had barred the doors, went directly to the Santa Cruz cemetery to place flowers on Sebastião's grave. He jokingly describes how, because no priest was present, he took on the role of sprinkling the flowers with holy water and blessing the mourners.[13]

According to Liurai Tasi, the crowd that gathered at the Santa Cruz cemetery on 12 November 1998 numbered around twenty thousand people.[14] Around three hundred trucks had driven from Baucau (some three hours from Dili toward the east) carrying protesters. In the cemetery, students displayed banners depicting acts of torture perpetrated by the Indonesian military and performed a reenactment of the 1991 massacre. They held banners aloft with Tetum and Indonesian slogans such as "Gather, those who live to light a candle for those who are no longer here"[15] and "East Timorese pro-independence activists remain pro-independence."[16] In a sign that this performance was directed as much to an international as a local audience, the few foreigners present were urged to take photographs to "show to the world" (Crockford 2007, 159).[17] Heavy rain fell that evening. For those present at the commemoration, this was a sign that the *matebian* (ancestors) were pleased.[18]

Through the sustained efforts of international and diaspora activists and clandestine youth activists in East Timor, then, the memory of Santa Cruz was transformed by the end of the 1990s into a powerful story of youth resistance, heroism, and martyrdom that undermined the Indonesian regime's necro-power. While the story of Santa Cruz fostered empathy and outrage among Western activists, for East Timorese resistance activists it became central to evolving understandings of national identity, struggle, and self-determination. As geopolitical circumstances altered once more, the memory of Santa Cruz would transform into a powerful tool of necro-governmentality.

Post-independence Remembering: Santa Cruz as a Narrative of State Becoming

Since national independence, a key geographic shift has occurred in the remembrance of the Santa Cruz massacre. While once commemorated by international human rights activists and members of East Timor's diaspora, it is now those within Timor-Leste's borders who do the work of public remembering. Annual commemorations take place in Dili and around the country, signaling the affective power and continued relevance of Santa Cruz to contemporary concerns. The significance of Santa Cruz is also reflected in the growth of the number of participants. While once involving a handful of families and survivors, the Santa Cruz commemoration in Dili is now a large event involving thousands of people. Many are young people who also organize their own parallel events, including seminars, concerts, film screenings, sports competitions, and tree plantings. These transformations have been possible because of funding and endorsement by the state. The 12th of November is now designated "national youth day" and celebrated as a national holiday (Arthur 2019, 95–96). Government funding for the commemorations, now organized by the secretary of state for youth and sport, has grown to over USD 120,000 annually. A state-funded monument to Santa Cruz has been built across the road from the Motael church, which reconstructs the famous Max Stahl image of a young man cradling his injured and bleeding friend. A new USD 1.3 million memorial is now being built at the Santa Cruz cemetery.

These transformations have been accompanied by a shift in the meanings attached to Santa Cruz. The story of the massacre has increasingly solidified as a foundational narrative of the new nation state, coming to symbolize the key "turning point" in the struggle—the moment when the mass slaughter of youth finally "woke up" the outside world to the suffering of the East Timorese people—leading, seemingly inexorably, to national independence. This narrative is reinforced by the embodied experience of those participating in the annual commemorations. As thousands walk the original route of the 1991 demonstrators, physical space is linked with understandings of what is known to have happened there. As shared memories of suffering merge with feelings of solidarity, togetherness, and connectedness, the idea of the nation is experienced in an immediate and visceral way (see Drozdzewski, Waterton, and Sumartojo 2019, 255, 257, 265). Reclaiming and recognizing the young lives that were blatantly disregarded and their families and communities violently dismembered might be understood as an embodied and collective ritual of re-membering a fractured national community, making it whole through ritual practice (see Myerhoff, 1982, 111). It is a ritual that works as a powerful counterforce to the necropower of the Indonesian regime, reversing its "power over life and death" (Robben 2015, 56) and imbuing death with new meaning.

Importantly, the regeneration of a national community is now connected to the legitimation of the nation-*state*. Indeed, Santa Cruz now works in the service *of* the state. It has become a powerful vehicle for structuring social responses to the massive bad death of the Indonesian occupation and imagining a collective future, cultivating a patriotic, forward-looking citizenry that is firmly focused on the "development" and future prosperity of the state. Today's youth are its main audience.

The symbolic presence of martyred youth and those who narrowly escaped death is central to the performance of Santa Cruz. They have become the vehicles through which a current generation of East Timorese are instructed on the values of patriotism and self-sacrifice, held up as a lesson to mold ideal youth subjectivities. In the speeches of political elites, priests' sermons, and television and radio talk shows, where survivors of the massacre tell their personal stories, the sacrifices of those who died on 12 November 1991 are repeatedly acknowledged and celebrated. Today's youth, who have no lived experience of the Indonesian occupation, are reminded of their "easy" lives, their freedom, and their opportunities, which contrasts with the hardship and suffering experienced by the youth of the past. Told that they are too easily led astray by drugs, martial arts gangs, and the internet, they are implored to learn from and uphold the values of their predecessors by studying hard, displaying leadership, discipline, and unity, and contributing to national development. These lessons remind the youth of today that, unlike the incorruptible youth of the past, they lack the validity and prerogative to engage in political action and protest and cannot match their purity and blood sacrifices for the nation. On the rare occasions when student and youth activists attempt to mark Santa Cruz by protesting about contemporary issues of injustice (for instance government corruption), this is deemed disrespectful to the martyrs of the past, inappropriate and illegitimate. In these ways the pedagogical lesson of Santa Cruz stifles the energies and activism of the present and future.

The necro-governmental logics that permeate Santa Cruz remembrance were acutely apparent during several commemorative events in which I participated in 2017 and 2018 in Dili and beyond. These events were organized by local youth groups. In Liquiçá, young people from several districts sat patiently, in the afternoon heat, through a seminar several hours long in which they were instructed on leadership and patriotic values by local political leaders. In Natarbora, young people climbed slippery poles and engaged in other group sports competitions aimed at fostering teamwork and national unity. Among the most memorable event was a film screening in the Dili neighborhood of Motael (where the Motael church is located) on the eve of the Santa Cruz massacre anniversary, organized by a group of young university students. I had bumped into one of the organizers, Mario, earlier that day at the office of the human rights NGO Asosiasaun Hak (Rights Association), and he had invited me along. When I arrived around 7 p.m., the group was arranging plastic chairs in front of a small stage on a plot of empty land. A small table had been set up with snacks for audience members, most of whom were young residents from the *suco* (village). Organizers were dressed in specially designed T-shirts that read "Suco Motael Komemorasaun Massacre 26 years" (the village of Motael commemorates twenty-six years of the massacre). The key part of the event involved the screening of Max Stahl's footage of the massacre while a survivor from the neighborhood provided commentary over a microphone. At various points, the master of ceremonies paused the film and quizzed the children in the audience about facts. "Whose death are we commemorating?" "Sebastião Gomez!" "Who is the priest who gave the mass?" "Bishop Ricardo!"

After the film, we lit candles to honor the martyrs, and the master of ceremonies led the audience in one minute's silence. A young man then got up on stage and passionately performed a piece of poetry titled "One Minute's Silence" (written by famous resistance-era poet Francisco Borja da Costa). During this part of the event, graphic images of mass graves, of young, blindfolded bodies, and tortured and scarred young bodies, were displayed one after another as part of a slide presentation. I found myself averting my eyes from these individualized and yet highly decontextualized and mute images of vulnerability, suffering, and death. The presentation was undoubtedly directed at the youth in the audience, conveying, in an emotional and visceral way, the sacrifices of the youth of the past and the stark difference between the violent past and the peaceful present.[19] The evening ended with a lengthy speech from a 12 November survivor that reminded the young people in the audience of the sacrifices of their *maun sira, biin sira* (older brothers and sisters) who had brought an end to conflict and ushered in this new period of peace.

The Memory Work of the 12 November Committee

The symbolic efficacy of the martyred youth of Santa Cruz to the imagining and building of the new Timor-Leste state is easily appreciated. Yet the growing significance of the memory of the massacre within the state's necro-governmental project is less due to the deliberate engineering of political elites than it is to the efforts of prominent survivors. Sharing embodied histories, experiences, and knowledge, these survivors, once clandestine youth activists, have been powerful carriers of the memory of Santa Cruz, keeping it alive in the public imaginary. Many are now members of the 12 November committee, the nongovernment organization that represents families of victims and survivors of the massacre. They occupy a unique position as those who narrowly escaped death. Referring to themselves as *mate restu* (the Tetum term for survivor, which literally means "leftovers from the dead"), they are imbued with a special form of moral power and legitimacy—a power to retell the story of Santa Cruz, impart its lessons, and act in the name of the dead. All of this makes their voice difficult to ignore by the political elite.

The 12 November committee is neither wholly resistant to, nor completely supportive of, the state's policies and projects. Its work has been at different times (and sometimes simultaneously) an anticolonial assertion of the self-determination and collective identity of an oppressed people, a critique of the state's militarized, masculine narrative of national sacrifice, *and* a mobilization of its own necro-governmental logics that seek to harness the power of the dead to govern the living. During the early years of national independence, the committee's efforts to publicly remember Santa Cruz formed part of a critique of the state's veterans' valorization program that had placed armed resistance fighters at the top of the hierarchy of heroism and martyrdom, downplaying the suffering and sacrifices of the clandestine resistance, including youth activists. This had both symbolic as well as material effects, overlooking clandestine activists for medals, pensions, funeral honors, and other benefits.[20] Over time, as the committee's advocacy has successfully transformed the state's narrow conception of national service and sacrifice into one that recognizes the actions of Santa Cruz protestors, its interests and those of the state have become more closely aligned. The committee actively works to mold ideal youth citizens and reinforce (new) hierarchies of the dead.

Among those who have advocated the most vigorously for greater state attention to youth sacrifices is Gregorio Saldanha. Gregorio is the chairperson of the 12 November committee and a former clandestine youth activist. A *mate restu* par excellence, his advocacy efforts are imbued with a powerful moral legitimacy. Born into a family who supported the resistance, and with an older brother involved in FALINTIL, he became involved in clandestine youth groups in 1985 when he was 15 years old.[21] Gregorio was a key organizer of the original 1991 Santa Cruz demonstration. Shot in the back at the Santa Cruz cemetery, he was taken to the military hospital, where he watched as corpses were kicked out of the military vehicle and witnessed the death of a friend before his eyes. After Gregorio's wounds were treated, he was interrogated by Kopassus (Special Forces) colonels before being transferred to a police station, where he was imprisoned for eight months. He was then moved to the Balide Comarca (Balide prison) in Dili, a notorious Indonesian interrogation center, where he was detained for nine months and regularly tortured. He was later moved to Cipinang prison in Indonesia, eventually being released on 10 December 1999 after the UN-sponsored referendum.

The efforts of Gregorio and other members of the 12 November committee have not only ensured the growth and continuity of the Santa Cruz commemorations and the state recognition of youth sacrifices but also influenced the state's determination of entitlement to veterans and martyrs pensions. Those who took part in the Santa Cruz demonstration—both the living and the dead—are now entitled to receive pensions on the grounds of "special service" (Roll 2014, 201–2), allowing the living to bypass the legislative requirement that they must prove more than three years of "exclusive dedication" to the resistance (see chapter 1). The bodies of those martyred at Santa Cruz (and survivors who have died since national independence) are also now permitted to be buried in the state's Garden of Heroes Cemetery in Metinaro.

These transformations reveal that the categories of veteran and martyr, far from being fixed, are *negotiated* categories that are "largely determined in the field, independent of the legal framework and the world of policymakers" (Roll 2018a, 263). As Kate Roll's work has compellingly demonstrated, politically powerful groups such as the 12 November committee have a significant influence on members of the commissions tasked by the state with registering and verifying potential veterans' claims (Roll 2018a). As these commissions—composed of high-ranking former resistance members—travel around the country to record and check biodata, they "modify" or "rework" the veterans' legislation by applying alternative eligibility criteria ("correctives") (Roll 2018a, 263–64; see also Vásquez 2022). This is not simply a case of corruption or nepotism (although it does display those patterns) (Roll 2014, 194). It also responds to popular understandings of sacrifice, service, and contribution, which are more expansive than the state's narrow, militarized framing (Roll 2018a, 263).

Through its advocacy efforts, the 12 November committee has become increasingly formalized. While it currently has a modest, temporary office at the site of the former Balide prison (which was renovated by the Commission for Reception, Truth, and Reconciliation [CAVR]), the government has promised it a permanent office with space to display memorabilia and photos from the original demonstration and host school visits. Gregorio Saldanha expresses pride in the 12 November committee's achievements, suggesting that the growing state attention to Santa Cruz and the enthusiastic participation of today's young people in the commemorations is testament to the committee's success in "transmitting the spirit of nationalism."[22] At the same time, he also acknowledges that something has been lost. As more and more people participate in the annual commemoration, it has become increasingly less intimate, and he says he must concentrate extremely hard to "feel" the presence of the dead.[23]

Gregorio's comment about the difficulty of "feeling" the presence of the dead is important. It gestures toward how, as the dead have been enrolled in the state's necro-governmental logics, collectively valorized as martyrs, the presence of the dead as *actors* is no longer immediate. In the noise, the crowd, and the nationalistic fervor, the spirits of the dead have become distant—in fact, they are no longer welcome. While they are assembled, symbolically displayed on photos and banners, and referenced in instructive speeches to the youth of today, there is little space for them to be heard or "felt," to express their demands for reburial or care. The dead are deemed passive and mute, assigned to the temporality of the past. The state's necro-governmental imaginings, directed as they are toward a community of the living and promising the containment of the violent past with a view to development, prosperity, and new beginnings, make little space for the agency of the dead. No unruly spirits are therefore permitted to disrupt the regeneration of the nation, the legitimation of the state, and the formation of youth citizens that takes place through the Santa Cruz commemorations and the state's claiming of its collective, martyred youth. A more complex picture emerges, however, if we move beyond the formal, state-sponsored commemorations to the less publicly visible work of searching for the bodies of the dead.

Searching for the Dead

The limited official attention that has been directed into the search for the bodies of missing Santa Cruz victims compared to the energy and resources that goes into the commemorations is striking. While the search for and exhumation of the dead is in some contexts a key means of legitimizing the state, as already noted (chapter 1), there are a range of reasons why this has not been the case in Timor-Leste. Foremost is the reluctance of Timor-Leste's political leaders to disrupt the rebuilding of diplomatic relations with Indonesia, deemed necessary to ensure the future economic and political stability of Timor-Leste. The prohibitive cost of any such search is another factor. These factors need to be placed within a broader geopolitical context marked by global inequalities. Indonesia has systematically refused to cooperate with requests for information, and following the closure of UNTAETs serious crimes investigations process, Western states have displayed little interest in pressing the Indonesian state to reveal the locations of mass graves, support exhumations, or pursue prosecutions. While the Santa Cruz massacre may have prompted a more activist and human-rights-oriented stance among some Western governments when it came to their dealings with Indonesia during the 1990s, this stance has been reversed now that it no longer serves their interests.

More than thirty years after the massacre, only a handful of bodies have been located and recovered. According to the 12 November committee, the bodies of only seventeen victims have been recovered and identified, while sixty-eight are listed as still missing.[24] Because of the iconic status and transnational impact of Santa Cruz, there has been at least some international support for the search for victims' bodies, which is not the case for other massacres that occurred during the occupation. For instance, the UNTAET Serious Crimes Investigations Unit (SCIU) organized a limited investigation into Santa Cruz in 2001. Yet only two staff were assigned to an exploratory dig, and after it failed to locate any human remains, no attempt was made to take the investigations further (Blau and Fondebrider 2011, 1272–73). A far more significant search began in 2008, when the Victorian Institute of Forensic Medicine (VIFM) in Australia and the Argentine Forensic Anthropology Team (EAAF) joined forces to establish the International Forensic Team (IFT). With funding from the Australian government, they conducted a dedicated search for Santa Cruz victims, which resulted in the recovery and identification of a small number of bodies from a cemetery in Hera, near Dili.

In contrast to the exhumations conducted by the UN-sponsored Serious Crimes Investigations process, in which corpses were treated instrumentally, as "evidence" for trials (chapter 1), those conducted by the IFT can be understood as part of a rapidly evolving field of "forensic humanitarianism" marked by a reorientation of forensic efforts from a legal paradigm (focused on the use of scientific evidence in a court of law) to a predominantly humanitarian paradigm that puts families' needs at the forefront (Rosenblatt 2015: 12). Put differently, forensic humanitarian expresses a different face of necro-governmentality, promising to alleviate the suffering of the living through the exhumation of human remains, their identification, and their return to their families for care and proper burial (Rojas-Perez 2017, 18; see also Moon 2014, 2020). It is field that draws on both "the epistemologies and practices of scientific enquiry" and "the frameworks of humanitarianism and human rights," allowing them to speak to one another in new ways (Moon 2014, 49). On the one hand, its practitioners adhere to strict scientific protocol; they claim to secure, "scientifically and unequivocally," a factual, objective truth about the identity of the dead and how they were killed. On the other hand, because exhumations are often delinked from legal processes, possibilities open up for forensic practitioners to build relationships with families and respond to their needs. Practitioners claim that "forensic service to families" trumps the legal aims of forensic humanitarianism, describing their activities in terms of a "core duty" to the living, which centers on identifying the dead and returning their remains to their families (Moon 2020, 39).

The VIFM's Soren Blau, a forensic anthropologist, had first met the EAAF's Luis Fondebrider in 2003 and had discussed collaborating on investigations into massacres in Timor-Leste. Blau, who had previous experience in Timor-Leste, was attracted to working with the EAAF because of its significant experience in exhumations in Latin America and its reputation for working respectfully with local communities.[25] Much of the EAAF's work had involved exhumations of the graves of the disappeared in Argentina, a context where immunity laws for human rights violators had made it impossible, for decades, for forensic evidence to be used in legal cases. These experiences had led the EAAF to become leaders in the field of forensic humanitarianism, ushering in what Rosenblatt (2015, 4) refers to as a "small scientific revolution" through pioneering DNA testing methods that would later be used to identify missing people in other postconflict contexts.

Between 2003 and 2006, VIFM and EAAF consulted with the Timor-Leste government regarding the potential for investigations into mass graves. This eventually led to the signing of a memorandum of understanding (MoU) and the submission of a funding proposal to the Australian government's aid program (AusAid). Acutely aware that neither the Timor-Leste nor the Australian governments would welcome investigations that confronted the Indonesian government and pushed for prosecutions, the team was careful to highlight the "humanitarian" contributions of the proposed investigation. As Blau puts it, "We never spoke about prosecutions with the East Timorese government, only about emotional healing."[26] The AusAid funding proposal was similarly carefully framed, highlighting the "training" and "capacity building" potential of the IFT initiative.[27]

In its early stages, the IFT was open to investigating any cases of mass killings in Timor-Leste; however, it soon decided to narrow its investigations to the victims of Santa Cruz. This was due to the availability of at least some detailed open-source information on this massacre (in contrast to many other massacres) and Santa Cruz's iconic status. The knowledge and advice of foreigners with long connections to the Timor-Leste struggle for independence, including Max Stahl (who at that point was living in Timor-Leste) and prominent Australian parliamentarian Janelle Saffin, helped the team to make links to potential eyewitnesses and open communication channels with the Timor-Leste government.[28]

Led by available documentation and knowledge gathered from family members of the missing and eyewitnesses, the IFT began by investigating reports of bodies buried in large, unmarked graves in Tibar, close to Dili. This was the site of a former military army base. Several families of Santa Cruz victims had had dreams in which the dead had revealed to them that their remains were in this area, and local residents had created a small cross at one site there. Although initially promising, the investigations found no evidence of graves or human remains at Tibar after several weeks of digging (Blau and Fondebrider 2011, 1256). The investigations then moved on to Hera, to a small cemetery containing a row of unmarked graves where stones had been placed. These investigations achieved a more positive outcome. Twenty graves were found, and of these, sixteen individuals were identified as Santa Cruz victims (Blau and Fondebrider 2011). The identity of some of these bodies was established through families' identification of clothing and personal effects including wallets containing identification documents. In some cases, DNA tests were conducted in Australia (Blau and Kinsella 2013).

There were times when the IFT's scientific epistemologies and methods came into tension with families' truths, which were informed by the felt and sensed presence of the dead. After the first week of unsuccessful digging at Tibar, families confronted the IFT, explaining that the reason for their failure was that the correct rituals had not been conducted to request permission from the ancestors (Sully and Stahl 2010). As frustration at the lack of results at Tibar grew, several families hired their own excavator and began to dig several holes in a manner that the IFT regarded as unsystematic (Sully and Stahl 2010). In another example, two families who had received DNA results identifying their loved ones among the dead at Hera were not willing to accept these results (Blau 2020). Having previously consulted with *lia nain* (owners of the word, ritual experts), removed rocks that had been ritually infused with the spirits of the dead from the Tibar site, and then buried them according to the demands of custom, they were convinced that the dead were now at rest.

The IFT could not problematize the paradigm of forensic humanitarianism that underpinned its work. Those involved fiercely protected the ideal of objectivity and scientific protocol (see Reineke 2022, 29; see also Rosenblatt 2015). Bones were regarded as passive substances. The concern was with the living, not the dead. Yet over time, families' requests and demands pushed the IFT to recognize forms of evidence and agency and methods of identification that would not normally be acknowledged within a legal or scientific framework (see Crossland 2013, 127). For instance, following the confrontation by families, the IFT permitted a ritual expert to conduct an evening ritual at the Tibar exhumation site to seek permission from the *rai nain* (land spirits) to disturb the site and to ask for their help in finding the bodies (Blau and Fondebrider 2011, 1255; Sully and Stahl 2010).[29] A special ritual was also undertaken before the digging at Hera began that included customary elements and a Catholic mass at the Balide church. In cases where families had already buried bodies (or substances infused with the spirit of the deceased) and were unwilling to exhume them, the IFT also provided funds to enable them to deliver ritual prayers and make offerings to the spirit realm to allow a second burial.[30] In one case where it was not possible for DNA identification to determine whether a recovered body was a family's older or younger son, the IFT permitted the final determination to be made by the father. In this case the father deemed the body to be his eldest son as his spirit had appeared to him in a dream (Blau 2020). Examples such as these show that the results the IFT were able to provide were "not a matter of 'objective' knowledge or 'accurate scientific procedures' but, rather, emerged from the relationships of trust built with families and slowly negotiated over time" (see Cruz-Santiago 2020, 363).

Despite the modest success of the IFT investigations, they were not continued when the AusAid grant money ran out. Given the strong relationship between the Australian and Indonesian governments, AusAid had raised questions about the use of its funding to support exhumations under the framework of "capacity building." And while the VIFM had hoped that the East Timorese government would take over the exhumations, this did not happen. Members of the IFT also came to believe that any further investigations would be futile unless they had the cooperation of the Indonesian government and military.[31]

The Unruly Santa Cruz dead

Since the winding up of the IFT, it is surviving relatives and the prominent *mate restu* involved in the 12 November committee who keep alive the demand for the recovery of bodies. They also engage in their own ongoing search for the dead, and practices of care and consolation of their spirits. There are many restless and unhappy spirits. While these spirits welcome the annual commemorations, they deem them insufficient. They demand to be treated not only as abstract symbols of youth martyrdom and sacrifice that help to foster the spirit of nationalism, legitimize the state, and educate today's youth; they also want their bodies to be recovered, and to have individualized, ritual treatment from their kin. They continue to press their demands on their relatives through embodied experiences and dreams.

The dead are persistent. In some cases, they have led their surviving relatives to the sites where their bodies lie. For instance, the body of one young man from Baucau who participated in the Santa Cruz demonstration was located by his family in 2019. He had been captured by the military on 12 November 1991 and taken to Natarbora, in Manatutu district, where he became a forced laborer and had died some years later in an unknown location. After family members had been repeatedly visited by his spirit in dreams, with the assistance of a *matan do'ok* (one who can see far) the location of his body was identified and his remains recovered. Gregorio Saldanha, who was present at the exhumation, describes how the *matan do'ok* threw a chicken egg into the bush; the site where it landed was the site where the digging took place, resulting in the recovery of a small number of small bones. By using a method known as *koko ran* (testing the blood), the *matan do'ok* determined that the bones were the young man's. This involved taking a small blood sample from one of the young man's relatives, placing it on a fragment of bone, and observing it. Because the blood remained *metin* (fixed, i.e., it seeped into rather than running off the bone), it was deemed to belong to the family. The bones were carefully wrapped in a *tais* (woven cloth) before being transferred to the ossuary in the Garden of Heroes cemetery to await reburial.

Cases such as these reveal how the intersection between the demands of the dead and the practices of the IFT is activating new, creative practices of identifying the dead. While the method of *koko ran* is, according to many East Timorese, an age-old practice, there are two aspects that are new. First, it is increasingly referred to as "traditional DNA," and second, it is now being used to address the uncertainties arising from instances of massive bad death where bodies are missing such as the Santa Cruz massacre. It is certainly not novel to observe that the field of forensic humanitarianism is contributing new ideas about what constitutes the identification of the dead. However, there is an assumption that the field is reshaping these ideas around a "science-based and individualistic model associated with the industrialized West" (Rosenblatt 2015, 30). What is taking place in Timor-Leste is suggestive of a different dynamic. On the one hand, the IFT appears to have fostered a faith among ordinary East Timorese in the ability of forensic science to provide invaluable information about the identity of the dead. On the other hand, in light of the virtual absence of the state or international donors in the provision of forensic investigation and analysis, families and others socially proximate to the dead with no formal forensic training are producing their own forensic knowledges and practices (see Cruz-Santiago 2020, 351). Ideas drawn from forensic science are being mobilized in accordance with experiences of the agential dead and pre-existing practices in ways that allow people to meet their obligations to those who died during the Indonesian occupation. These practices are heralding the emergence of a new form of what Cruz-Santiago (2020) calls "citizen-led forensics," which is challenging common forensic science assumptions about the elements necessary to the "proper" identification of a body (Crossland 2015, 243; see also Blau 2020) and transforming "the regular centres of expertise and control" of forensic expertise (Moon 2014, 60). Citizen-led forensics takes many and varied forms, as we shall see in later chapters of this book (especially chapter 4).

The disruptive intrusions of the spirits of the dead also ensure that responding to their demands remains a central component of the work of the 12 November committee. The articulated desire of members of the 12 November committee to pay tribute to those who died and help families locate bodies can be traced to their personal experiences of military violence, the deaths of many of their friends, and the unique moral responsibility that inheres in the category of *mate restu*—the leftovers of the dead. Gregorio's connection to the dead is especially powerful. His memories of Santa Cruz are activated daily, in an embodied and visceral way, through his work at the 12 November committee office—located in the former prison where he was previously incarcerated. Families of the dead are a regular, embodied presence in the nondescript and cramped space of the office, which has only a few small windows and is dark and airless. They stand or sit inside or outside, smoking cigarettes or quietly chatting, waiting to seek practical assistance from Gregorio, inquiring as to whether any new information has become available or providing their own new leads to follow up. The small, enclosed space of the office contrasts to the large, open space of the commemorations and has a vastly different atmosphere—the nationalist slogans and celebrations are gone, replaced with quiet discussions.

Gregorio also describes the motivating impact of a powerful dream he had while in prison in 1993. In this dream, he was given a key covered with red cloth. He is still not sure what it means. "Is this the key to finding the bodies?"[32] While the dream's precise meaning may be elusive, Gregorio has interpreted its broad parameters as a message from the spirit realm that he has been entrusted with the weighty responsibility of continuing the work of the 12 November committee until the bodies of all the victims of the Santa Cruz massacre are found.

The 12 November committee's concern with recovering the dead reveals that while it has its own necro-governmental goals that are increasingly aligned with the state's, it is also motivated by other responsibilities that can challenge the state. For instance, while the committee maintains courteous and diplomatic relations with the government, remains heavily invested in imparting to today's youth the nationalistic messages and lessons of Santa Cruz, and reinforces hierarchies of the dead, it also acts as the custodian of a list of the numbers of dead and missing. This list, created at the time of the massacre, is regularly updated by the committee as it seeks out eyewitnesses, follows up leads, and gathers new information about the whereabouts of the dead. This information is kept safe until such time as future exhumations may be possible (Blau and Fondebrider, 2011, 127). The list provides a form of accounting for and naming of the dead that speaks against the "systematic non-production of knowledge" (Cruz-Santiago 2020, 355) by both the East Timorese and Indonesian governments. From time to time the committee also speaks out publicly, producing statements and media releases calling on the government to demand that the Indonesian military explain and identify the places where the bodies of victims were dumped, thrown into the sea, or buried. As Gregorio explains, unlike many East Timorese martyrs who died in disparate locations in the bush and whose deaths were a product of happenstance, those who died at Santa Cruz were killed *en masse* as part of an orchestrated plan carried out by the Indonesian military. The military must therefore know where their remains lie. Gregorio is acutely conscious that the military actors responsible for transporting, disposing, and dumping bodies will not live much longer and that this information will soon be lost.

The dead are also remembered and cared for in intimate spaces. Liuirai Tasi, for instance, describes how the spirits of his deceased friends regularly visit him in a dream the night before the anniversary of the Santa Cruz massacre. They gather in his house, as a lively and jovial presence, reminding him

Photos of martyred youth outside the 12 November committee office. Photo by author (2017).

not to forget their sacrifices.³³ The neighborhood is another important space of memory. On the evening of 12 November, residents in Dili and other parts of Timor-Leste transform their streets into long, winding rows of twinkling candles. Small groups of families and young people sit nearby the candles in their local areas, reflecting, singing, chatting quietly, or praying. Like the main commemorative event, this ritual cultivates, immediately and viscerally, the idea of the imagined nation; everyone gathered in those small groups would be aware that others around the country were involved in the same collective ritual. The rows of candles form a pathway that materially connects those small communities into a national whole. At the same time, these gatherings conjure a different atmosphere from the official commemorative event. They are smaller, more intimate, less noisy, and less structured. They seem to create a space where local and familial relations are reconstituted and where the dead, in their unique specificity and genealogical connections, can make their presence felt. This space might be thought of as akin to the "dark, enclosed, inner realm" where customary rituals take place, a space which, in vernacular accounts, is contrasted with the "outside" and "light" spaces of politics and administration (Traube 2020, 12; see also Bovensiepen 2015, 37). That this ritual is performed at night, unlike the bright morning light during which the official commemoration takes place, contributes to this different atmosphere and to the sense that it might be possible, in these spaces, for the dead to be re-membered as part of the community.

Young girl with candles, Santa Cruz commemoration, Dili. Photo by author (2017).

In these ways, the dead continue to prompt their families and the *mate restu* to act, creating new practices and spaces of memory. In these spaces, far more so than the crowded, nationalist celebrations of the formal commemorations, families and the *mate restu* can allow themselves to feel and respond to disjuncture, losses, and absent bodies. These are spaces where new relational networks of support and solidarity are created from shared experiences of (disrupted) grief, and where the dead can be re-membered as part of kin and community.[34] These spaces reveal that memory work is simultaneously imbued with different meanings and serves various political and intimate purposes. While it is a form of care for the dead, it also honors the dead's national sacrifices and keeps alive the need to address *continuing* losses and absences, maintaining a demand for absent bodies to be made present (see Walker, 2015, 111).

This vernacular memory work does not resist the enrollment of the Santa Cruz massacre and the dead in the state's necro-governmental project; however, it displays two key points of friction with this project. First, while the state seeks to relegate the Santa Cruz massacre to a past temporality, vernacular memory work refuses to countenance the "pastness" of this past (see Carsten, 2007, 13). The dead whose bodies remain unrecovered press their disruptive intrusiveness into the present, reminding the living that they are not yet at peace. Their continuing suffering, as it makes demands on the living and invokes responsibilities of care, disrupts the linear, forward narrative that underpins the state's necro-governmental project.

Second, and relatedly, vernacular memory work recognizes that the state's *symbolic* remembrance and celebration of martyred youth is not sufficient to respond to the dead's demands; the dead, as children, brothers, sisters, and friends, must be individually cared for, their relational connections with their living kin and others socially proximate to them reconstituted. Vernacular memory work therefore responds to the violent and dismembering effects of Indonesian necropower *and* the violence of both the state's and the "international community's" necro-governmental logics, which have failed to address the demands of restless and unhappy spirits. These complexities imbue the memory of Santa Cruz with an unsettled, dynamic quality, reminding the living and the state of unfinished business and unfulfilled obligations.

Conclusion

This chapter has charted the rise of Santa Cruz as a central narrative within the state's project of necro-governmentality. It has shown that this transformation was less a product of the state's deliberate orchestration than of the sustained efforts of prominent survivors of the massacre, who, over many years, have kept the memory of Santa Cruz alive and pushed for the official recognition of youth sacrifices. The 12 November committee, as it has harnessed the symbolic power of martyred youth to bolster the status of former clandestine youth leaders in the present, has succeeded in drawing the dead into the heart of the state's necro-governmental project. Yet committee members are also motivated by their powerful embodied connections to deceased friends and comrades and their responsibilities to care for them, which complicate and at times subvert that project.

These responsibilities reveal that the dead are another source of power in Santa Cruz memory work, which complicates diverse necro-governmental logics. The spirits of the dead, while not resisting their status as symbolic vehicles for instructing the youth of today, deem this insufficient. Despite the limited opportunities for them to make their felt presence known within the formal commemorations, there are moments and spaces—often outside this event—when they succeed in pushing their disruptive intrusiveness into the Santa Cruz assemblage. By reminding their living relatives and the *mate restu* that they have not been safely consigned to the past, the spirits of the restless dead prevent the memory of Santa Cruz from becoming fully contained and "domesticated" by the state. The painstaking work of searching for and caring for the dead by the 12 November committee and the families entails an embodied questioning of continuous losses and absences that imbues the memory of Santa Cruz with an unsettled, dynamic quality, reminding the state of unfulfilled responsibilities.

The next chapter moves beyond the national capital to the small town of Liquiçá to consider the remembrance of the dead of the 1999 Liquiçá church massacre. Compared with the Santa Cruz dead, the bodies of those who died during the Liquiçá church massacre are less symbolically useful to the state in crafting a heroic, forward-looking narrative of statehood. Their families also have less political capital than the clandestine leaders who are the Santa Cruz *mate restu*. The Liquiçá church massacre is not officially commemorated across Timor-Leste and the dead are excluded (at least in theory) from the category of martyrdom. Yet the restless spirits of the Liquiçá church dead, like those of Santa Cruz, are difficult to ignore. In this case they push not only for consolation and care from their families but also for the official recognition of their sacrifices. They are prompting new practices that disrupt the state's hierarchies of the dead and meet the needs of the living and the dead.

3

Civilian Sacrifices in the Town

Re-membering the Liquiçá Church Dead

Since the end of the Indonesian occupation, a group has gathered annually on 6 April in Liquiçá, a small, sleepy seaside town in Timor-Leste close to the capital, Dili. They mark the anniversary of the 1999 Liquiçá church massacre, when up to one hundred people were shot or cut down with knives and machetes in the compound of the São João de Brito church where they had been sheltering from local militia. Compared with the large, festive, and well-funded Santa Cruz commemorations, those that take place in Liquiçá are relatively modest in size and have a more somber tone. Annual gatherings have only been possible because of the combined efforts of Dili-based human rights activists and members of the Liquiçá victims' and widows' groups. They often involve little more than a simple Catholic mass followed by a ritual at a small angel memorial in the church compound (the site where many of the killings took place) and a visit to a nearby salt lake (where the bodies of victims are thought to have been dumped) to light candles and sprinkle flower petals. When resources are available, a small press conference might be organized, during which survivors of the massacre and families of the dead read out a list of demands to the government; this invariably includes a demand for an international criminal tribunal to prosecute those responsible for the massacre and for reparations.[1]

During the commemorations I attended in 2018 and 2019 it was clear that a shift had taken place. In 2018, hundreds gathered for an early morning mass in the church, among them scores of school children dressed in neat school uniforms. As in previous years, families had placed colorful plastic baskets containing photos of the dead, flowers, and candles beneath the pulpit to be sprinkled by holy water. Following the mass, we congregated by the small angel memorial for more prayers, and the local priest sprinkled holy water on the photos of the dead held by their living relatives. There were so many of us that the crowd spilled out into the road. Following this ritual, rather than visiting the Maubara salt lake some fifteen kilometers from Liquiçá town, a new site of memory, the Liquiçá Garden of Heroes cemetery, was incorporated into the commemoration for the first time. We all walked quietly through the dry and baking-hot midday streets of Liquiçá to the cemetery, relatives of the dead still carrying photos of their deceased loved ones. There, the priest delivered further prayers and sprinkled holy water on the recently completed, neatly laid out, ordered, and identical graves.

In 2019, the twenty-year anniversary of the massacre, thousands were present for the Catholic mass. A two-day seminar was also held on the 4th and 5th of April in the hall of a large municipal government building behind the newly constructed Garden of Heroes Cemetery, involving an audience of over one hundred. A large banner reading "20 Years since the Massacre of Liquiçá, April 1999–2019: A Long Road to Justice and to Preserve the Historical Values of the Resistance" hung behind the stage. The dead were present in their symbolic form, gazing out from photographs displayed on photo boards outside the hall. Invited speakers included representatives of government, key political figures such as José Ramos-Horta, members of Dili-based human rights NGOs, and survivors of the Liquiçá massacre and other massacres that took place in 1999, including in Maliana and Suai.

When I arrived at the hall, two of my long-term interlocuters, Ana Maria and Fernanda—both widowed during the 1999 violence and members of the Liquiçá widows' group—greeted me with their eyes shining. "Finally," said Ana Maria, "we have been able to do things really well. People from other districts have come—this is what we have been waiting for." Her enthusiasm contrasted to her despondency during our conversations over the previous several years, when she had expressed frequent doubts about whether Liquiçá residents had the capacity and funds to keep the commemorations going.

While the Santa Cruz massacre occurred in Dili, the metropole, the Liquiçá church massacre occurred in a small town forty-five minutes' drive west of Dili. It provides an interesting contrast: the Liquiçá church massacre is far less well-known internationally, the date of the massacre is not a

Families of the Liquiçá church massacre victims outside the São João de Brito church. Photo by author (2018).

public holiday, and it is not commemorated around the country. The locally organized commemorations do not have guaranteed, ongoing funding from the state. However, just as the meanings of Santa Cruz continue to evolve, so, too, do those attached to Liquiçá. This chapter traces these changing meanings, which, as in the case of Santa Cruz, are emerging as the state's necro-governmental logics intersect with diverse local priorities, practices, and sources of power.

A key focus of the chapter is the recently constructed Liquiçá Garden of Heroes cemetery, a powerful new site of memory in the center of town. As the first Heroes cemetery to be completed outside of Dili, it offers significant insight into both the power and limits of this key technology for structuring social responses to the dead. I explore how the cemetery has emerged as a site where frictions between the state's necro-governmental logics and diverse local priorities are negotiated. Just as these logics are permeating the narrative frames through which the Liquiçá church massacre is understood, shaping the subjectivities of the dead and influencing the spaces where they are remembered, they are being transformed through the entangled agency of the living and the dead. New practices of caring for the dead and new claims for the official recognition of civilian sacrifices are emerging.

In this chapter's first part, I track the key spatial and temporal shifts in Liquiçá church massacre remembrance over the past twenty years. This story reveals how the massacre is increasingly referred to as an instance of heroic resistance: those who died are assigned martyr subjectivities and their bodies buried in a new Garden of Heroes cemetery. I tell this story through the lens of three sets of actors—Dili-based human rights activists, local veterans, and members of the Liquiçá victims' and widows' groups—allowing their diverse experiences and political struggles to come to the fore. In the chapter's second part, I complicate this story by examining how, as we move beyond the formal, centralized spaces and sites of Liquiçá church memory to other, less formal spaces, including the home and dangerous "deathscapes" (Maddrell and Siddaway 2010), the dead emerge as resistant to control and containment. Let me begin, however, by describing the key events of the massacre before drawing out some of the factors that account for its differential public remembrance vis-à-vis Santa Cruz.

The Liquiçá Church Massacre: Evolving Repertoires of Necropower

The Liquiçá church massacre of 6 April 1999, like the Santa Cruz massacre that took place eight years earlier, involved the killing of unarmed civilians. It also involved the violent desecration of a church. A key difference is that while the Santa Cruz massacre took place while the territory was still under the grip of Indonesian rule, the Liquiçá church massacre occurred during the months leading up to the UN-sponsored referendum, when hopes and tensions around the future status of the territory were high. This was also a time when the training of, and support for, East Timorese militia had become critical to the Indonesian regime's repertoire of necropower. In Liquiçá, as in other parts of the territory, militia—mostly young men whose loyalty to the regime was maintained through drugs, alcohol, and money—had become increasingly visible and active in their attempts to terrorize and intimidate voters (Kammen 2015, 146). In a pattern that would be repeated across East Timor in the months to follow, the Liquiçá church massacre is widely understood to be a deliberate attempt by the Indonesian military to foster an illusion of conflict between East Timorese and derail plans for the referendum.[2]

The Liquiçá church massacre represented the culmination of a lengthy period of intimidation by the local militia group Besi Merah Putih (BMP, Red and White Iron) (CAVR 2005, 7.2; Kammen 2015, 146). After attacking, in January and February, a number of hamlets and villages suspected of supporting the independence movement and having links with FALINTIL (Kammen 2015,

146), members of the BMP burned dozens of houses and abducted and killed several civilians, displacing thousands from their homes on the 4th and 5th of April (Robinson 2003, 192). In response, residents of the Liquiçá and Maubara subdistricts fled to the São João de Brito Catholic church in Liquiçá town to seek refuge. By the 6th of April, there were approximately two thousand men, women, and children in the church compound. While some sought refuge inside the church, others sheltered in the residence of local priest Father Rafael dos Santos next to the church (Robinson 2003, 192).

Early on the morning of 6 April, members of the BMP, wielding firearms, machetes, knives, and spears and accompanied by military troops, Mobile Police (Brimob) from Dili, and local police arrived at the church (Robinson 2003, 160). They taunted those inside, calling on them to surrender and threatening to attack the church. As militia hurled rocks and fired homemade guns in the air, causing injury and damaging vehicles in the yard, the military and police stood by. Around midday, militia members violently entered the compound (Robinson 2003, 160). While women and children were permitted to leave, the men inside, as they sought to flee, were hacked with machetes by the militia waiting for them outside. According to Father Rafael, the militia, Brimob, and the military then entered the priest's residence, searching for those still inside and killing them with machetes and guns. Among them were a group of clandestine youth resistance activists who were pulled down from the roof of the house where they were attempting to hide (Robinson 2003, 161). The violence continued for several weeks after the massacre, as local residents suspected of being involved in pro-independence activities were arrested, questioned, and killed. Some fled to Dili, where they sought refuge at the house of prominent pro-independence leader Manuel Carrascalão. At least twelve people were killed during an attack on the Carrascalão house by the BMP and the Dili-based Aitarak (Thorn) militia on 17 April, where approximately 150 displaced persons were sheltering.[3]

Just as they did for the bodies of the Santa Cruz victims, the Indonesian military hid or destroyed the bodies of those killed in the Liquiçá church massacre. This not only enacted another form of violence, preventing the ritual practices that would allow the dead to become safely dead, but also covered any visible traces of the regime's clandestine crimes. Many bodies have not been recovered. Witnesses suggest that they were taken away in trucks by the militia and dumped or buried in various locations, including the Maubara salt lake (Lagoa Masin), a marshy body of water between Liquiçá and Maubara (Robinson 2003, 162). Many of those thought to be responsible for transporting these bodies later fled across the border to neighboring Indonesia after the referendum and have not returned.[4] The exact number of those killed in the church and its compound remains unknown, with estimates varying widely, from thirty to one hundred people (CAVR 2005, part 7.2, 251).[5]

The Differential Remembrance of the Liquiçá Church and Santa Cruz Massacres

While the Santa Cruz and Liquiçá church massacres both involved the killing of unarmed civilians, there are marked inequalities when it comes to state support for public commemorations. Several factors are important in accounting for this. First, while Santa Cruz took place in the national capital of Dili, the Liquiçá church massacre occurred in the (seemingly less nationally significant) small town of Liquiçá. Second, it was not captured on documentary film and subsequently circulated transnationally. It did not then have the same visual presence as a traveling, transnational memory. Third, although the events of Liquiçá took place at a critical historical juncture, they were not experienced as the abrupt shattering of two decades of media silence as was Santa Cruz. For these reasons, the Liquiçá church massacre was not propelled into the global imagination—and subsequently back into the national imagination—in quite the same way as Santa Cruz.

A fourth factor pertains to the actors who have, at least until recently, been the key organizers of the Liquiçá church commemorations: Dili-based human rights activists. These actors lack the moral power, legitimacy, and close links to the political elite enjoyed by the Santa Cruz *mate restu*. They are part of a younger generation than members of the 12 November committee; many had been young university students in Indonesia during the 1990s, where they had joined the resistance organization RENETIL (Resistência Nacional dos Estudantes de Timor-Leste, National Resistance of East Timorese Students). While they had participated in risky, nonviolent actions in Jakarta to attract international attention, such as mass fence jumping into embassies to seek asylum, their contributions to the independence struggle have been marginalized within a heroic resistance narrative focused on armed struggle and struggle *within* East Timor.[6] Many of these activists now work for prominent Dili-based human rights NGOs with close links to Western donors and international advocacy organizations such as Amnesty International and Human Rights Watch.[7] This, however, is not always an advantage in the current political environment; activists are frequently accused by the political elite of promoting a neocolonial, Western human rights agenda that emphasizes vulnerability and suffering over agency and self-reliance.

Perhaps the most important factor that influences the less prominent status accorded to the Liquiçá church massacre vis-à-vis Santa Cruz is that the events that took place fit less neatly within the state's heroic "usable past." The dead had been sheltering in a church compound rather than engaged in a planned demonstration for independence in which the organizers fully expected military retribution; they are less readily transformed into ideal martyr subjects who teach a lesson to the youth of today and rejuvenate the national community. For the state, the Liquiçá dead fall into a category of the "inconvenient civilian dead" who fall short of the subjectivity of the martyr. By drawing attention to the deliberate slaughter of vulnerable civilians by the Indonesian military, the dead also raise the uncomfortable suggestion that not all those who perished during the occupation were voluntary participants in the struggle who willingly sacrificed their lives.

Despite these differences, there is a similar interplay between citizens, the state, and the dead in the evolving memory work taking place around the Liquiçá church massacre as in the Santa Cruz massacre. The following sections discuss the significant shifts that have taken place in Liquiçá church remembrance over the last twenty years from the perspective of three distinct groups of actors: Dili-based human rights activists, Liquiçá resistance veterans, and the Liquiçá widows' and victims' groups.

Dili-Based Human Rights Activists: Commemorations as a Stepping Stone to Prosecutions

During the early years of national independence, Dili-based activists were at the forefront of the Liquiçá church massacre commemorations. This was a time when there were still hopes that the UN Security Council would establish an international criminal tribunal to prosecute those responsible for war crimes and crimes against humanity during the occupation. Activists took advantage of the abundant donor funding available for peacebuilding and transitional-justice-related activities, supporting a number of local memory initiatives around the country, including commemorations of civilian massacres, the construction of memorials, and oral history projects. They also encouraged the formation of local victims' and widows' groups with the aim of fostering a "bottom up" victims' movement that would keep the memory of past violence and the demand for justice alive. In Liquiçá they assisted those groups to request donor funding and collect small, one-dollar donations from community members to construct the small angel memorial at the site of the massacre, which was completed in 2006 (Kent 2011, 434–35).

With the departure of the UNTAET in 2002, the UN reduced its presence in Timor-Leste, and hopes for an international criminal tribunal began to wane. International peacebuilders, deeming the nation-state no longer in transition, began shifting their attention to other "postconflict" societies. Donor priorities and the project funding that had sustained human-rights-activist-led memory projects (and fostered the increasing "NGO-ization" of civil society) also began to move elsewhere. It became common to hear Dili-based activists complain that there was no longer funding for transitional justice activities, only those related to "development." While these activists continued to support the Liquiçá widows' and victims' groups, the goal of building a grassroots movement for justice seemed far from a reality.

Even in these constrained circumstances, Dili-based activists have continued to support commemorations and associated press releases, vigils, demonstrations, seminars, and petitions. They directly confront the Timor-Leste government's forward-looking focus on building relations with Indonesia and maintain a call for an international tribunal. Indeed, Dili-based activists deliberately adopt a frame of memory that opposes the state's necro-governmental narrative of heroic resistance. The massacre, they argue, was a *crime against humanity* that demands a prosecutorial response. Those who died are *victims*, not martyrs.

In these ways, Dili-based activists keep the discourse of transitional justice, and the categories, practices, and subjectivities associated with it, alive. As already discussed (chapter 1), transitional justice is another form of necro-governmentality; it seeks to contain and control the legacies of a violent past by assigning new human rights meanings to massive bad death, crafting victim subjectivities and promising that, through prosecutions and truth telling, such violence might be prevented in the future and a traumatized population might "come to terms" with its past. Importantly, activists reproduce the assumption—now prevalent in the discourse of transitional justice—that *memorialization* has an important role to play in shaping responses to massive bad death. Memorialization, as Lea David (2017) observes, has recently moved from the margins to the center of transitional justice discourse, a shift that is underpinned by the growing assumption that alongside prosecutions and truth commissions, the public remembrance of past atrocities is essential to successful postconflict recovery.

For Dili-based activists, commemorating the Liquiçá church massacre (and other 1999 massacres) is both a means of honoring the dead and a vehicle through which past crimes and victims' suffering will be made visible to a wider public. Commemorations might, by awakening a public consciousness, lead to increased public demand to put perpetrators on trial (Weissart 2015). Citizens—today's youth in particular—will also learn "lessons" from their history that will ensure they uphold human rights values in the future and that violence is not repeated. For these reasons, activists encourage local victims' groups to organize public seminars targeted at young people (such as the one that took place in Liquiçá in 2019) alongside local commemorations. Finally, it is hoped that public remembrance will foster active, democratic citizens who are aware of and have the capacity to claim their rights.

In these ways, the Dili activist-led memory work surrounding Liquiçá church can be understood as a creative performance of imagining both a nation and a state and crafting new citizen subjectivities. The nation activists imagine is one in which understandings of national belonging are not intrinsically linked to ideas of heroic struggle and willing sacrifice. Activists argue, implicitly, that those who were not active participants in the struggle yet who suffered as a result of the conflict deserve to be acknowledged and remembered in the nation's story. National identity needs to be built not only on the remembrance of the nation's heroes and martyrs but also its victims. The state they imagine is an open, liberal, democratic, and accountable state that acknowledges its "duty to remember" the violent past and pursue prosecutions to respond to victims' suffering and foster long-term peace, development, and democracy. Today's youth citizens are imagined as individual rights holders with the responsibility and capacity to engage in collective action and hold their leaders to account.

While the dead are central in this creative performance, they are treated symbolically and *en masse* rather than in their individual personhood. As already noted, the liberal, secular discourse of transitional justice is concerned with the restoration of relations among the living, holding the dead to be passive and mute, their suffering belonging to the past. The community that is affronted by the "crime against humanity" committed in the Liquiçá church massacre and that must now be remembered is assumed to be composed of living individuals rather than a relational web of the living, the dead, the ancestors, and lives to come (see Brown 2015, 108; Grenfell 2020). The dead are important insofar as they provide important symbolic lessons to the living. They are evidence of suffering, the vehicles through which a societal truth might be told about the violence of the Indonesian occupation that will arouse mass consciousness, mobilize outrage, and encourage the society to remember atrocities they would prefer to forget, while preventing their recurrence (see Lincoln and Lincoln 2015, 201, 208). For Dili-based activists, the living will be liberated from the legacies of massive bad death with prosecutions, the public acknowledgement of suffering, and reparations. There is no opening in this narrative to recognize what Kwon (2017, 7) describes as the "right" of individual restless spirits to be "liberated from the violent history of their death" and make the transition from their current liminal state to the world of the ancestors.

Resistance Veterans: Transforming the Liquiçá Dead from Victims to Martyrs

A decade after the departure of UNTAET there was a question mark over the sustainability of the annual Liquiçá church commemorations. It was at this point that former resistance actors—members of the armed and clandestine resistance in Liquiçá—began to take an interest. These actors, mostly men who had once been regional commanders and leaders of smaller guerrilla units and leaders of village-based clandestine resistance networks or youth groups, not only contributed funding for the commemorations but also a new interpretation. They began to refer to the Liquiçá church massacre as an instance of heroic resistance; those who were trapped in the church and its compound embodied the values of strength and fortitude, those who died were martyrs, not victims.

Much like the Santa Cruz *mate restu*, these resistance actors had their own necro-governmental agendas. Their interest in the commemorations and ascribing a new, heroic meaning to massacre was entangled with a complex politics of veterans' relationships with the state, encompassing veterans' struggles for legitimacy, relevance, and power in the present (issues to which I will return in chapter 4). Those who had been members of the clandestine were engaged in an ongoing struggle for the recognition of their contributions to national independence. Yet this was not simply a case of narrow self-interest; these actors were also influenced by popular understandings of sacrifice and suffering that were more expansive than the state's and that resonated with their own lived experiences of the struggle. They had an acute awareness of how civilians had kept the resistance alive through the everyday and feminized labor of cooking, delivering messages, providing medicines and clothing, caring for children, and maintaining safe havens in their homes.

These shifts in the interpretations of the massacre and the subjectivities of the dead have become increasingly evident. During the 2018 and 2019 Liquiçá church commemorations, the dead were incorporated into a story of suffering victimhood *and* a story of heroic resistance. Emblematic of this dual interpretation was the banner that hung above the stage during the 2019 seminar, which highlighted both the need for "justice" and the preservation of "the historical values of the resistance."[8] A narrative of the *national* significance of the Liquiçá church massacre has also emerged. Just as the Santa Cruz massacre is said to have finally "woken up" the international community to the suffering of the East Timorese during the Indonesian occupation, the Liquiçá massacre is now said to be a critical event that "woke up" the international community to the organized nature of violence in the lead-up to the referendum and the extent of coordination between the militia groups and the Indonesian security forces. In this way, Liquiçá is understood as an important stepping stone to independence—it is "part of the national story of the struggle."[9]

These resistance actors were interested not only in the commemorations but also in the bodies of the dead. From 2012 they began to search for the bodies of all those who died in Liquiçá due to the "consequences of the war" (*konsekuensia funu*). These bodies, they argued, should be buried in the Liquiçá Garden of Heroes cemetery and recognized by the state as martyrs. The first body to be exhumed was that of young clandestine youth activist Martinhu (code name "Tasi Diak"), a survivor of the Santa Crus massacre who was later killed in another incident in Liquiçá in 1999. While the location of Martinhu's body was known because there was a witness to his death, he had no surviving family members to rebury and care for him. Those involved in the recovery of Martinhu's body describe being motivated by a powerful sense of feeling for him as a fellow human being and community member; his body could not be left in its abject, unburied state.[10] Martinhu's body was placed in a coffin and taken to the ossuary in the Garden of Heroes, which was at that point empty, the cemetery far from complete.

Following Martinhu's exhumation, Liquiçá resistance actors formed a local "commission" for the recovery of human remains and, through a concerted five-year effort (2012–17), they gathered the human remains of 284 Liquiçá residents who had died bad deaths during the Indonesian occupation. These remains were placed in the ossuary. In cases such as Martinhu's, where the location of human remains was known, searches were initiated to locate and exhume them. In cases where the dead had already been buried in family cemeteries, the commission provided families with state-issued coffins and a small financial contribution to exhume them. Where the location of bodies was unknown, as was the case for many of the Liquiçá church massacre dead, some families conducted rituals at the massacre site or the Maubara salt lake, enlisting the assistance of ritual experts to call the spirits of the dead to these sites to infuse substances such as soil and rocks. These substances, now the bodies of the dead, were then carefully wrapped in *tais*, placed in the coffins, and taken to the ossuary.

By 2017 the ossuary in the Garden of Heroes was stacked floor to ceiling with coffins, each draped with a *tais* in the colors of the Timor-Leste flag. The affective power and material presence of these coffins formed the basis on which Liquiçá resistance actors lobbied national political leaders to rapidly complete the cemetery and organize a state-sponsored reburial ceremony. They argued that these human remains could not be left too long in the ossuary either from a public health or a "cultural" perspective. These efforts were successful, and the official reburial ceremony in the newly constructed cemetery took place in 2017. Led by the government's Ministry of Social Solidarity and attended by the then prime minister, president, and the bishop of Maliana, it involved a Catholic mass at the ossuary, followed by the emplacement of the 284 coffins in freshly dug graves by the Timor-Leste armed forces while family members stood by. Each identical, state-issued coffin was reburied to the accompaniment of a military gun salute. Members of the FALINTIL and the clandestine were reburied in spatially distinct sections, each identical granite headstone labeled not only with the name of the dead but also, where relevant, their resistance code name and rank.

Importantly, these reburials took place even though many of the dead had not been officially acknowledged by the state as martyrs. Their names were on a list of claimants that since 2009 had been awaiting verification by the state. This provides another example of how the state's category of martyr and its hierarchies of the dead are negotiated "in the field" (Roll 2018a, 263) as they intersect with a complex politics of veterans' relations with the state and popular understandings of suffering and sacrifice.

The Liquiçá Widows' and Victims' Groups: Meeting Obligations to the Dead and Seeking Economic Security

Relatives of the dead in Liquiçá have also contributed to shaping the meanings, practices, and spaces of remembering the Liquiçá church massacre. Far from being passive recipients of the diverse logics of necrogovernmentality promoted by the state, Dili-based activists, and resistance actors, they have engaged with these logics to meet their needs for economic security and their obligations to the dead, seeking opportunities and allies where they can.

In the early years of independence, families of the dead saw Dili-based activists as useful allies. This was a time when the district was in what Caroline Hughes (2015, 917) describes as a "catastrophic" economic state, and families were living in precarious material circumstances. The district was heavily reliant on coffee production; however, the price of coffee internationally had plunged. Prior to independence, East Timor had sold its coffee crop to Indonesia, but this option was no longer available (Hughes, C. 2015, 917). Families willingly accepted the support of Dili-based activists to form the Liquiçá victims' group and the widows' group Rate Laek (Without Graves), which in the case of Rate Laek, enabled the women to establish a small catering business.

That the women chose the name Rate Laek is telling, revealing something of the unique moral responsibilities inherent in the category of the widow in Timor-Leste. At the time of its formation, some Dili activists had felt that a more hopeful, forward-looking name might serve the women better and, that by defining their identities so closely with that of their deceased husbands, they would remain "stuck" in their past trauma. What these activists had perhaps not fully appreciated is that far from evincing a stuckness, this name indexed the women's profound feelings of connectedness to, and obligations toward, their deceased husbands that would be critical to their future well-being and that of their children. It would also endow the women with agential capacities within the domain of their husbands' extended families, a theme to which I will return in the next section.

Families of the dead also embraced the victim identities bestowed on them and their deceased loved ones by Dili-based activists in the hope that this might open up further pathways to resources, in particular, reparations. They supported, too, the movement for an international criminal tribunal, which held out the promise of bringing members of the Indonesian military to trial and forcing them to reveal the locations of bodies (Hughes, C. 2015, 923). Put simply, families recognized that "access to international coercive power" would be needed to meet their obligations to the dead, and in the narrow window when there was international support for Timor-Leste's transitional justice processes, they were willing to accept the discourses, practices, and subjectivities promoted by Dili-based activists in the hope they might fulfil them (Hughes, C. 2015, 923).

By the mid-2000s, however, despondency had set in. From the perspective of members of Rate Laek and the victim's group, transitional justice was achieving few practical results. While these groups continued to organize the commemorations as a means of making their demands to the state for justice and reparations, they were by this point fundraising among a local population with little cash to spare, volunteering their time to clean the church, cook, and advertise the event around the town via motorbike and megaphone. They had begun to despair at the effort required to accumulate the requisite funding, social capital, and legitimacy to organize the annual commemorations.

Transporting families from dispersed and often remote villages into Liquiçá town—and providing them with food—was costly. Timor-Leste's political leaders, despite receiving invitations to the commemorations each year, often failed to show up. Exacerbating the groups' despondency were the legacies of unfinished business and the unfulfilled justice promises of the UN's Serious Crimes Process. In the few cases where the bodies of the dead had been located and recovered, the unit's treatment of them for a broader evidentiary purpose had neglected families' needs to give them a proper burial. In one case, for instance, twelve bodies exhumed from the Maubara salt lake in 1999 by Australian navy divers working for UNTAET—acting from a tip-off from a former BMP militia member (see Agliomby 1999; Robinson 2003, 162)—were sent off to the SCIU for forensic testing and were not returned.

Families had also grown disillusioned at the failure of reparations, which might have facilitated the organization of customary rituals for the dead whose bodies could not be recovered. While the CAVR report, tabled in the national parliament in 2005, had recommended a national reparations program to assist the most "vulnerable victims," the government had made it clear that it would not implement the program. The women involved in Rate Laek were also no longer reaping benefits from their catering business. Most of the customers had been foreigners, and by the mid-2000s most foreigners associated with the UN and NGOs had left Liquiçá (Hughes, C. 2015, 917). Put simply, as the UN peace-building economic "bubble" had burst, so too had the catering business (Hughes, C. 2015, 917). The women drifted apart, only coming together when it was time to organize the annual commemorations.

As the discourse of transitional justice began to lose its sheen, former resistance actors emerged as another, possibly more useful, set of allies for families of the dead. These actors had a high status in the community and many families welcomed their attention to the gathering of the remains of the dead, even if some also complained about the financial burden it placed on families (it was widely held that the commission did not provide enough funding for the ritual practices that would be necessary to request permission from the spirits for the exhumation of their bodies). Many families were willing participants in the exhumation of bodies and the 2017 reburial ceremony of the dead in the new Garden of Heroes cemetery, which held out the possibility of the official recognition of their loved ones as martyrs and a survival pension.

What are the implications of these exhumations and reburials? On the one hand, they seem to be pushing toward an enlargement of the state's narrow category of martyrdom. As already noted, among the human remains interred in the state-sponsored ceremony in 2017 are those who have not been recognized by the state as martyrs (or at least, *not yet*). Their graves now stand as powerful emotional and material evidence of the contributions of unarmed Liquiçá civilians to the resistance: evidence that is difficult for the state to ignore. They remind the state of the struggles and suffering of the *povu kiik* (small people, ordinary people) that are yet to be recognized. As these bodies push for the official recognition of the contributions of young people, women, and others who engaged in everyday strategies of resistance, they cut against "the towering moral hierarchy of death in the state politics of memory" (Kwon 2008, 159).

On the other hand, the cemetery has become a powerful, centralized space of memory that appears to draw the dead into the realm of the state. A replica of the Garden of Heroes cemetery in Dili, its vast open space and ordered rows of graves are a material and spatial embodiment of the state's necro-governmental logics. The cemetery promises to settle Liquiçá's dead by enclosing them within its hard borders, ascribing them new militarized, martyr subjectivities and placing them within a past temporality. It also cultivates a "reformed sensibility" (Johnson 2008, 781, 787) toward the dead by prohibiting unruly behaviors (for instance, loud noise, music, and visits to the cemetery at night). The living are encouraged to contain their grief and curtail expensive practices of remembrance and care. The focus is now on the future development of the district and the nation-state.

Does this mean that understandings of "proper" burial are changing in ways that reinforce the state's ownership of a privileged category of dead bodies? As the dead are firmly emplaced in identical gravesites, in orderly rows, named by their roles and ranks in the resistance (where they have them), and enclosed by the cemetery walls, will dispersed, fluid, and embodied practices and rituals of day-to-day re-membering and care be transformed into more formal, constrained practices? Are individuals who had livelihoods, families, and complex histories and subjectivities being transformed into fixed martyr subjects? Will the dead, as they are claimed by the state, become a passive and compliant community, losing their agential capacities? I do not think so.

While it is too early to know the long-term impact of the cemetery, it is apparent that a more complex dynamic is underway. This becomes especially clear as we move beyond the formal spaces of Liquiçá church remembrance to informal and intimate spaces of memory. In these spaces, the living and the dead seem to be negotiating diverse necro-governmental logics in ways that allow them to meet their needs for economic security, recognition of sacrifices, and continuing reciprocal relations of care. The next section explores these themes through the narratives of two Liquiçá widows, Eliza and Fernanda.

Woman prays at the Garden of Heroes, Liquiçá. Photo by author (2018).

The Dead in Intimate Spaces: Activating an Ethics of Care

Both Eliza and Fernanda are founding members of the Liquiçá widows' group, Rate Laek. Like other women in the group, they were both widowed during the massacre and other violent events that took place in Liquiçá in 1999. Yet in contrast to many others in the group who have had limited access to educational and employment opportunities, they are both employed in district government jobs. Nonetheless, they would self-describe as the *povu kiik*, contrasting themselves to the *ema bo'ot* (big people, political leaders), who are perceived to dominate or direct postconflict state-building agendas. As widows, they feel themselves to be especially marginalized. Not only are widows discouraged from public, political life. The lack of a male breadwinner means there are restricted opportunities for their children to gain an education that might enable them to escape lives marked by poverty (Hughes, C. 2015, 920; Kent 2011).

Fernanda's case is unusual in that unlike many other members of Rate Laek, she has been able to recover the remains of her deceased husband (who I shall call Felis). Felis had been a member of the clandestine resistance in Liquiçá and had been killed by militia while on his motorbike on the 5th of April 1999, the day before the church massacre. Fernanda collected his body amid the escalating violence and buried him soon afterward in her husband's family cemetery. In 2017 Fernanda (who by that point had remarried) and Felis's family consented to the request of the local commission for the recovery of human remains to exhume his body and rebury it in the Garden of Heroes. They participated in the state's reburial ceremony later that year. This was not a straightforward exercise, as a lengthy and expensive set of customary rituals was required to request permission from the ancestors and the land spirits for Felis's body to be disturbed. Felis's extended family came together for a collective feast involving the slaughter and consumption of several pigs and buffalo. Felis's remains were then exhumed with the assistance of the family's *lia nain* and placed in a temporary grave near the family's house. Fernanda described these rituals as *todan* (heavy, burdensome) for the family because the commission, while providing a coffin, did not provide the family with enough money to cover the ritual costs. Despite these difficulties, the family felt it necessary to go ahead with the reburial to achieve recognition of Felis as a martyr. They argued that because he participated in the resistance, his body belonged to the state (*estadu nia ema*). Although Fernanda had registered Felis's details as a claimant for martyr status in 2009, this status had not yet been verified. Fernanda hoped the reburial would show that her husband had died for the nation, which might speed up the verification process and provide the family with a survival pension.

Not long after the reburial ceremony, Felis's spirit came to speak to Fernanda through her teenaged daughter. His spirit possessed their daughter's body and spoke through her mouth. Fernanda knew her daughter had been possessed because her hands suddenly became cold and she started crying and speaking in a rough hoarse voice (her husband's throat had been cut with a machete). She asked Fernanda's mother-in-law "How are you?" in the local language of Tokedere (a language in which the daughter is not fluent). In another sign of spirit possession, the daughter asked for cigarettes and beer (she did not usually smoke or drink). Felis then delivered two key messages. The first was to his younger brother, who was instructed to take better care of Fernanda's three children, whom he had previously neglected, and specifically, to pay for their education. The second message was one of reassurance to the family that he was happy with his reburial in the Garden of Heroes, that he had enjoyed the *festa ramai* (lively festival) in 2017. There was no need for the family to construct a new headstone for him in the family cemetery or conduct additional rituals there. After Felis's spirit left his daughter's body, she fainted before waking up, remembering nothing of these events.

Since the reburial of her husband's remains in the Garden of Heroes, Fernanda regularly visits his new grave to tend it, light candles, and place flowers.

Fortunately, as she is based in Liquiçá town, the cemetery is not too far away. Each time she visits, she finds others there also visiting their recently buried loved ones. But she does not always go to the cemetery—she can also call Felis's spirit to her house by mentioning his name (*temi nia naran*). His spirit, she says, is still alive and can hear and see her even if she cannot see and hear him. His spirit is not confined to the cemetery but can travel. And because his spirit is at peace, no longer wandering and unhappy, Fernanda is now able to call on him to help her with everyday problems.

Like Fernanda's husband, Eliza's husband (who I shall call Joao) had been a key figure in the clandestine resistance in Liquiçá. He had regularly organized meetings in the family house and relayed messages to the FALINTIL. Because of this, Eliza had lived in constant fear. She recalls how at night, as she nursed her small baby and listened to military vehicles driving endlessly up and down the road, she worried about what she would do if she suddenly had to leave the house and run. Joao was killed during the Liquiçá church massacre, outside the priest's house, at the site where the angel memorial now stands. Eliza herself had narrowly escaped being killed.

In 2018 Eliza and her husband's family decided, after many years of experiencing Joao's restless spirit in their dreams, to make a grave for him, even though they had not been able to recover his remains. To do this, the family's *lia nain* called Joao's wandering spirit to the site of the massacre. He removed a rock from the site, which had been infused with his spirt. The "body" was then taken to the family's house for one night of prayers, after which it was taken to the family's *uma lulik* (spirit house, sacred house) for further ritual prayers before being buried close to the family house. This "proper" burial required an expensive set of rituals involving the sacrifice of several buffalo and the exchange of Dutch coins between different sides of the family. This ritual had only now become possible as Joao had recently been officially verified as a martyr by the state and Eliza had begun to receive a monthly pension of approximately USD 230 per month. Eliza explained that after these rituals she felt calm, no longer heavy (*todan*), as Joao's spirit was no longer wandering but was peaceful. He had been given a "good place" (*fatin diak*). He now had "shade" (*mahon*). She had felt his presence watching over her during a recent dream. She is now able to pray to him in the church or in her *uma lulik*, where she asks him to watch over her children and prevent her from falling ill. As well as this, she does not need to go to the *uma lulik* or the church—she can mention his name wherever she is, and he will visit her. Only now that the correct rituals have been performed are Eliza and her family able to use the survival pension to pay for basic necessities, such as urgent repairs to the family house.

Unlike Fernanda, Eliza has resisted requests from local resistance actors to rebury her husband's remains in the Garden of Heroes. Although, like Fernanda, she regards her husband as having died for independence, a reburial would require another lengthy and expensive set of rituals in the family's *uma lulik*, which the family is not yet prepared to countenance. A *lia nain* would be required to "explain" to her husband's spirit that because he struggled for independence, his body needs to be buried with his *maluk* (close friends, comrades) in the Garden of Heroes. While this ritual might be possible in the future, Eliza thinks it is more likely that the family will only permit her husband's photo to be taken to the cemetery and his name inscribed on a headstone. His "body" will remain with the family. In this way, his spirit will not be disturbed.

Several observations can be drawn from these narratives. First, they reveal how memory work has become a vehicle through which Eliza and Fernanda are transforming their interpersonal relationships. For Janet Carsten (2007, 16), memory work in the familial realm can enable the past to be creatively rearranged in ways that allow "alternative scenarios of social engagement" to be asserted "against the perceived restrictions of normative familial life" (Carsten 2007, 16; see also Das et al. 2001; Sakti 2020). For Eliza and Fernanda, dreams and spirit possession are experienced (and recognized by others) as direct, embodied messages from the dead that cannot be ignored. By relaying their husbands' concerns with their well-being and that of their children to their husbands' families, a limited form of recalibration of their status is possible against the constraints of both local patriarchal norms and the deeply gendered dynamics of state building. In other words, the performance of close and continuing relationships with their husbands' spirits enables women who may have otherwise had limited power within their husband's families to find space, agency, and a degree of economic security. The recognition of their dead husbands as martyrs will also satisfy the dead, who remind their relatives and the state that national independence was won not only by those who participated in formal resistance organizations but also by the actions, suffering, and sacrifices of the *povu kiik*. According to a "cultural code" of reciprocity, their "unpaid wages" must now be repaid (Traube 2007).

Second, these narratives provide further evidence of how the state's necrogovernmental logics and technologies are providing the ground for their own transformation. Far from extinguishing a familial ethics of care for the dead, these logics and technologies are providing the conditions for new ways of defining and expressing this care. Families are creating new practices that allow them to enfold the dead into their kinship networks while mitigating the potentially problematic consequences of their reburial in the Garden of Heroes. As these deceased loved ones are cared for, they reveal their complex subjectivities, histories, dependences, and vulnerabilities, challenging fixed, martyr subjectivities. While they may have gained new martyr subjectivities, they are still fathers, husbands, brothers, and kin. They aspire to political recognition, financial compensation, *and* familial regeneration (see Sakti 2020).

Finally, and importantly, even as the dead are reburied, their restless spirits placated, they do not become passive and mute. Nor are they spatiotemporally confined. They are leaking out of, and refusing to be bound by, the space of the Garden of Heroes cemetery. They continue to activate the familial and feminine work of caring for them and re-enfolding them into reciprocal relations with their kin. Emerging practices of caring for the dead are distributed across multiple spaces, including the Garden of Heroes, the church, homes, and *uma lulik*. Importantly, once they are cared for, the dead can also care for their living relatives, including their widows. In these ways, the living and the dead are negotiating and transforming necro-governmental logics and technologies to meet their own needs, forging new relationships that are oriented toward healing, stabilization, and intergenerational well-being.

Sacralized Places and Dangerous Spaces

There is, however, another—altogether more troubling—way in which the dead refuse to be controlled and contained, their power harnessed for diverse necro-governmental goals. That is as restless and unruly spirits who render landscapes dangerous. The formal spaces of remembering the Liquiçá church massacre not only coexist with the intimate space of the family but are also proximate to wild and unruly spaces inhabited by the spirits of those who died bad death. These spaces lie within and just beyond the bounds of the town, troubling its borders.

There remain many restless spirits from the Liquiçá church massacre who linger near the sites where violence was done to their bodies. That their needs and demands can never be fully grasped or understood imbues them with an unknowable, threatening quality (see Bovensiepen 2018, 67). These spirits create disordered spaces that exude powerful affects and are a potential danger to those who live nearby or are passing through. These "deathscapes" (Maddrell and Sidaway 2010) are imbued with a dangerous *lulik* (sacred) potency that can give rise to unexpected, unpredictable, and disturbing experiences to those who live close by or are passing through. Unforeseen visitations of the spirits of massacre victims whose bodies have not yet been recovered can occur in these spaces. These spaces are not, as they are regarded within the state's necro-governmental logics, "mere palimpsests" that bear the traces of violence long past (Till 2008, 103). For local residents they are experienced as "hot" and dangerous spaces that are animated by spirits who have not yet left the world of the living nor reached the land of the ancestors (see Bovensiepen 2015, 148–49).

The threatening quality of these dangerous spaces has prompted Liquiçá residents to attempt to transform some of them into "sacralised" places (Schramm 2011). Far from being an "innate or unchanging" quality (Schramm 2011, 6–7), the sacred emerges through the "work of sacralization," the "ritual and interpretative labor involved in setting certain things, places or objects apart" (Chidester 2000, 30). One such place is the Liquiçá church and its compound. As a sanctified Catholic religious site and a site of massacre, this place is especially *lulik*. The small angel memorial built by the community, which stands in a shady, inconspicuous site in the compound, her head bowed in prayer, was inaugurated with Catholic blessings and customary rituals (including the sprinkling of a mixture of young coconut water and pig's blood). These rituals helped to "cool" the land that had become hot (*manas*) and dangerous with the victims' blood. While these rituals have performed the work of transforming a dangerous space into a sacralized place, the memorial must be continually cared for through the annual gathering of families and Liquiçá residents and the rituals performed there, which remind the dead that their kin still care for them and that they have not been forgotten. Through a blending of Catholic and customary rituals, the spirits of the dead are quelled, the land is cooled, and this place is rendered safe for the living.

The rituals that take place at the angel memorial differ from the more formal rituals that take place during the Liquiçá church massacre commemorations in several ways. While all these rituals seek to remake order in the aftermath of massive bad death, unlike the mass, the seminar, press conferences, and the rituals at the cemetery that are addressed to the living, those that take place at the angel memorial bring together a community of the living and the dead. Second, while the formal rituals have an outward, political purpose—addressing the state, the media, and at times an international community—those that take place at the angel memorial seem to create an intimate and relational space in which families and other members of the community perform an ethics of care for the dead. Absent are the formal, choreographed speeches by state leaders, the military salutes, and Catholic sermons in which families play no active role. The rituals at the angel memorial possess a more fluid, flexible, and improvised quality. They seem to create what Kwon (2006, 94) calls an "alternative spatiality of memory" that is not the wild, dangerous, and unruly space of comingled bodies and unhappy spirits, or the disciplined, enclosed, and ordered space of the Garden of Heroes, or yet, the space of

Families gather at the Liquiçá church angel memorial. Photo by author (2018).

kinship relationships defined by ancestral bonds. It is a space in which the bereaved come together as an affective community of mourners united beyond their distinct genealogical identities, their separate, familial ties to the dead, and their roles in the resistance.

However, it does not seem possible to draw all dangerous spaces into the realm of the sacred. The Maubara salt lake, just outside Liquiçá town, is a space that feels resistant to rituals of memory and care. As the site where local residents believe the bodies of the Liquiçá church massacre victims were dumped, it exudes a feeling of eeriness and desolation to those that know something of its history, although few signs of the events that took place here are visible. I felt something of these affects when, following the seminar that took place during the 2019 Liquiçá church commemoration, I visited the site with Joao, a survivor of the Liquiçá church massacre. We walked over soil parched and cracked by the heat and past dead trees bleached by the sun, without seeing a single person, to find a tiny handmade cement monument. Although there were remnants of candle wax and some dead flowers—outward signs of familial visits—the site is much less cared for than the angel memorial, retaining something of the quality of the *abject*—that which "stands against or is kept outside the personal and socio-political order" (Navaro-Yashin 2009,

160). Visits by families of the dead to this site, Joao told me, were becoming less frequent. While the annual Liquiçá church commemoration had once involved the lighting of candles and the scattering of flower petals at this place, this was no longer the case. Spirit leaders have called the spirits of the dead to enter rocks and soil at this place, and these rocks and soil have now been taken the Garden of Heroes and reburied. The dead are now remembered there.

Even as the salt lake is increasingly relegated to the margins of the national and local imaginary, it cannot be fully expelled. The massive bad death of the Liquiçá church massacre, like that of the Santa Cruz massacre, seems to exceed the reordering promised by diverse projects of necro-governmentality *and* intimate rituals of care and consolation. While rituals of re-membering the dead are possible and can be profound, not all attempts to call and quell restless spirits are successful. And not all restless spirits have surviving family members to care for them. These spirits remain fundamentally unknowable, inhabiting the sites of their death and disposal, generating uncertainty and anxiety and reverberating in the everyday lives of families and residents through unexpected, embodied experiences. As they press their demands on the living for the revelation of the sites of their graves, the recovery of their bones, and official state recognition of their sacrifices through dreams and other visitations, they haunt the living and the forward-looking state-building project. They are *evidence* that the Liquiçá church massacre is not an event safely consigned to the past. This evidence speaks of unreconciled and continuing harms. These dead continue to suffer.

Conclusion

By charting the transformations in the memory of the Liquiçá church massacre since independence, this chapter has revealed that this incident is increasingly interpreted as an incident of heroic resistance, the dead attaining new martyr subjectivities. These interpretations and subjectivities are reinforced by the new Garden of Heroes cemetery. Yet even as it appears to draw the dead into the state's necro-governmental logics, centralizing and "fixing" their meanings, the new cemetery has emerged as a key space for the negotiation and transformation of those logics. First, the state's narrow category of martyrdom is being expanded as diverse interests push for the recognition of the suffering and sacrifices of the *povu kiik* and as the bodies of the dead provide powerful material *evidence* of those sacrifices. Second, as the dead and the living enter into new reciprocal relationships of care, they disrupt logics of spatiotemporal containment and control. Finally, the unhappy spirits that inhabit the area of the Maubara salt lake remain a potent reminder of how the problem of massive bad death not only exceeds state attempts to resolve or contain it but also surpasses the efforts of Liquiçá residents to draw the dead into reciprocal relationships of care. The vernacular memory work of caring for the dead remains fragile, contingent.[11]

The next chapter delves more deeply into the dangerous, wild, and unruly spaces inhabited by restless spirits. We move away from the metropole and the town to the hinterlands, where it is acutely apparent that state power coexists with other sources of power and legitimacy, including that of former resistance actors. The state's municipality-based Heroes cemeteries are geographically remote, and Dili-based human rights activists are absent, which imbues vernacular memory work with an improvised and bottom-up flavor. In these areas, restless spirits are an acute problem for the living. The spirits of those whose bodies lie in remote and mountainous areas after dying solitary bad deaths in the early years of the occupation number in their thousands. They complicate the containment of massive bad death perhaps more so than massacre victims, as geographically dispersed, they render large swathes of the landscape dangerous rather than coalescing around a single site. Addressing the problem of these solitary, dispersed, and unhappy spirits is also urgent for rural communities given the proximity of these dangerous spaces and the precarious nature of livelihoods. I show how one local commission for the recovery of human remains in Natarbora in the municipality of Manatutu is responding to this problem through a unique form of expeditionary memory work.

4

The "Participating Population" of the Hinterlands

Gathering the Dispersed Dead

This chapter moves beyond the urban and peri-urban areas of Dili and Liquiçá to the small *posto* (subdistrict) of Natarbora, in the municipality of Manatutu, about a three-hour's drive from the national capital. Its concern is with the dispersed dead who died in the first few years of the occupation, many in remote locations in the *foho* (mountains) and *ai laran* (forests). Unlike the dead discussed in previous chapters, these dead did not die as the consequence of a single event or set of events but, rather, died individual and often isolated deaths due to the slow violence of starvation and disease. Across the district, intensive efforts to gather and rebury the remains of the dead are underway. As it is more than forty years since some of these deaths, peoples' recollections of sites where bodies were hastily buried are hazy, landscapes have changed, and bodies have decomposed. The terrain is often mountainous and inaccessible. Yet the extensive time and resources directed into this work speaks of its profound significance for the living and the dead.

In rural areas, where the mountains and forests are highly proximate, landscapes generate intense affective reminders of the suffering experienced by family members, friends, and neighbors whose bodies were abandoned. These landscapes can also be dangerous and unpredictable, inhabited by the restless and unhappy spirits of those who died bad deaths. Inspirited landscapes are encountered on a day-to-day basis, including during travels to and from rice fields (*natar*), vegetable gardens (*to'os*), and small orchards that lie some distance from peoples' homes. Rural communities reliant on subsistence and smallholder agriculture for their survival are also acutely conscious of the vicissitudes of the natural and spirit worlds and their potential to cause disaster. Seasonal food shortages and an annual "hungry season" are a reality for many (Thu and Judge 2017, 146–47). Livelihoods can be easily destroyed by floods, droughts, insect plagues, and other natural disasters unleashed by imbalances in the spirit realm.

This chapter takes a deeper look at the phenomena of "commissions" for the recovery of human remains (Komisaun Recolhimento Restus Mortais) in Timor-Leste. My focus is the Natarbora commission which, like the Liquiçá commission I introduced in the previous chapter, is one of the many self-described commissions spontaneously formed across Timor-Leste over the past ten years at the scale of the municipality, posto, or village. Improvised and evolving, they draw together a loose collection of individuals, the majority of whom are male former members of the armed and clandestine resistance.

This chapter considers the complex ways in which the Natarbora commission's practices and the resurfacing dead intersect with the state's technologies and logics of governmentality, generating new and shifting configurations of power. On one reading, the commission's activities of gathering, identifying, and categorizing human remains appear to be contributing to and extending the state's necro-governmental project, allowing the abstract category of the martyr, imbued with national fantasies of masculine heroism and sacrifice, to become a "palpable and intimate figure" (Aciksoz 2020, 56). They produce heroic martyr subjectivities that are legible to the state and can be differentiated from other dead bodies, symbolically recognized, and safely consigned to a past temporality. Yet a deeper reading reveals a more complex necropolitical terrain, a terrain in which the state's necro-governmental logics are transforming as they intersect with veterans' struggles for recognition and legitimacy, an ethics of care for the dead, and the power of the dead, in their entangled material and spectral presence.

I begin by situating the emergence of commissions for the recovery of human remains within the proliferation of veterans' groups since the end of the occupation before providing a brief overview of experiences of the Indonesian occupation in Natarbora. I then offer a reflection on my first visit to the Natarbora commission, drawing out the divergent forms of power that animate its members' narratives. The next sections focus on the commission's practices of identification and categorization of the dead and the emergent spaces of memory in Natarbora. What becomes clear is that the gathering of human remains is generating new political and social practices in which the dead are active participants.

The Proliferation of Veterans' Groups

The emergence of self-described commissions for the recovery of human remains in Timor-Leste needs to be understood against the backdrop of the proliferation of local veterans' groups since the end of the Indonesian occupation. These groups promote the interests of former resistance actors, primarily former FALINTIL members. The commissions are closely connected to—and are sometimes sections within—these diverse groups, which have mushroomed with the development and rollout of the state's veterans' valorization program. The position of these groups vis-à-vis the state is ambiguous and shifting. As Myrttinen (2013b, 209) suggests, many veterans' groups share the "visions and myths" that "lie at the heart of the social imaginary" from which Timor-Leste's political leaders draw their legitimacy. This includes a commitment to valorizing the resistance struggle. Yet they simultaneously unsettle the authority of the state. They do so by alleging that the state is not living up to its obligation to care for and reward the people for their sacrifices to the resistance and by revealing the continuing power and legitimacy of former resistance actors by taking over services such as local security provision and veterans' welfare in a context where the state struggles to deliver them (Myrttinen 2013b, 209).

These ambiguities speak to Kate Roll's (2018b, 140) astute observation that a key state-building challenge in independent Timor-Leste revolves around the renegotiation of the "relationship between the new state and the resistance movement" that, during the occupation, "served as the legitimate site of authority, popular sovereignty and coercive force." Resistance leaders continue to hold significant power within their geographically dispersed territorial domains; their tenacity and leadership during the struggle continues to inspire loyalty and respect from the people in the present. For national political leaders, the question of how to consolidate power with the state has become a central concern. State building has entailed a "delicate dance" of attempting to move "from multiple sites of legitimate force and authority toward a Weberian monopoly" while continuing to harness the symbolic power of the resistance (Roll 2018b, 140). Political leaders have engaged in various strategies, including "incorporation and grafting" as well as "exclusion and delegitimization" (Roll 2018b, 140). The veteran's valorization program has been central to these strategies. By drawing sharp lines between the "state and non-state," and defining and regulating veterans, it attempts to consolidate state power with the center (Roll 2018b, 141).

This state building challenge is reflected in the two divergent discourses that underpin the veteran's valorization program. The first is a discourse of heroism and national sacrifice that involves the resignification of bad death as martyrdom and a sacrifice for the nation and foregrounds the state's obligations to valorize and care for those martyrs. This discourse reinforces the mythology of the national liberation struggle (and "veterans" as the embodiment of that struggle). It imagines a united national political community born from struggle and sacrifice, an imagining that bolsters the legitimacy of current political leaders (many of whom were themselves resistance leaders). Yet there is a second, less explicit discourse, which constructs veterans as a "social problem" because of their perceived potential to resort to violence. This discourse is a response to deep uncertainties about whether the state has a monopoly over the usage of violence (see Metsola 2006, 1128). It is also infused by global demobilization, demilitarization, and reintegration (DDR) orthodoxies, which suggest that without assisting ex-combatants to reintegrate into society, this group will remain a "ticking time bomb" and a destabilizing influence (see de Vries and Wiegink 2011, 38).

In this way, "former fighters are limned as both national standard bearers and decrepit; they are the protectors of the nation but also a threat" (Roll 2014, 174). This dual construction provides the justification for a veteran's valorization program that both rewards and reforms (Roll 2014, 174). As I have discussed (chapter 1), former resistance actors are rewarded with a privileged category of (militarized, masculine) citizenship through the provision of substantial pensions, scholarships for children, and lucrative government contracts to veteran-led businesses. At the same time, the program controls potential political spoilers, who are registered, managed, and pacified through pensions and other benefits (Roll 2014, 116; see also Metsola 2006, 1126). When it comes to veterans' groups, valorization enables the state to exert control over "unruly" citizens through techniques that "register, categorize and track them" (Roll 2018b, 142). Through the regulation of identities and bodies, the authority of the state is communicated. Former resistance actors are encouraged to exchange weapons and political power for pensions and recognition (with that political power to be strategically harnessed by state leaders when it suits their interests).

The discourses and practices of valorization attempt to construct "veterans" as an interest group with shared problems, experiences, and interests. Yet the shared nature of this identity only goes so far. Given the dispersed and highly decentralized ways in which the resistance movement operated, local guerrillas had a great deal of autonomy within their territorial domains, and powerful affective bonds and loyalties formed between guerrillas and between guerrillas and civilians. This imbues veterans' groups with a highly localized dimension. The vocal demands of these groups, which utilize public channels such as media and petitions as well as private "backchannels for accessing high-level political leaders", have enabled the progressive expansion of their entitlements and benefits (Roll 2020, 311). Policymakers are also caught in a bind. While on the one hand they seek to delegitimize unruly and dissident veterans' groups, they are also responsive to their claims owing to these groups' effective mobilization of discourses of suffering and sacrifice and the necessity of "having these groups 'on side' for maintaining political legitimacy" and security (Roll 2014, 175).

During the period I conducted my fieldwork, these tensions were acutely evident. This was a time when the state was encouraging local veterans' groups to set up microfinance schemes, small businesses, and banks in order to use their pension money wisely (rather than "wasting" it on televisions, motorcycles, and cultural ceremonies). These groups were also self-organizing in anticipation of a national veterans' council (CNV) that would give veterans a national political voice.[1] They were choosing their own representatives, who would then elect a national president and three vice presidents (one each from the armed, the clandestine, and the diplomatic fronts). The idea of a national political voice for veterans had emerged, in part, in response to veterans' demands and followed on from the recent establishment of a stand-alone Ministry for Veterans' Affairs. Previously, veterans' issues had fallen under the mandate of the Ministry of Social Solidarity, which coordinates welfare programs for "vulnerable" sectors of society, including the elderly and the disabled. This had been perceived by veterans as disrespectful; as one respondent put it, veterans did not want to be treated as welfare subjects or as "beggars."[2] While the stand-alone ministry and the CNV reinforces veterans as a privileged category of citizens set apart from vulnerable welfare recipients, another implicit aim seems to be the tightening of control over unruly veterans' groups and the delegitimization of those perceived as political spoilers (see Roll 2014, 145–46).

Bad Death in the *Foho* (mountains) and *Ai laran* (forests)

Natarbora lies roughly in the center of the half island of East Timor, not far from the wild coast of the Timor Sea, the *tasi mane* (or "male" sea). Its experiences of the Indonesian invasion and early years of the occupation speak to how the regime's necropower involved both the exposure to death of an entire population and the deliberate targeting of the resistance. Natarbora became a place of hoped-for refuge for civilians and FALINTIL guerrillas from the east and the west who were driven there in the mid-1970s, escaping from airplane bombings and in search of safety and food. Natarbora was known as an area with an abundance of wild food (*hahan ai laran*) and wild forests (*rai fuik*) in which to hide. Yet many died on the journey there because they could not find enough food or were poisoned by eating wild foods that had not been properly prepared and cooked. Thousands of those who made it to the area also perished from starvation, as wild food sources were rapidly diminished or became contaminated after bombings, or from illness and exhaustion.

Natarbora's geographical location and natural advantages meant that the surrounding hinterlands and forests became a site for FRETILIN-controlled *bases de apoiou* (resistance support bases), where from the mid-1970s, thousands of civilians lived together with the resistance. Life in the bases was highly organized and controlled by strict discipline (CAVR 2005, part 5). People worked in communal and personal gardens, and youth and women's organizations established by FRETILIN encouraged people to plant rice, corn, tubers, and other crops, which were distributed to those in need and given to the guerrilla fighters. Women wove cloth and produced traditional medicines from plants. FRETILIN also set up rudimentary schools, which taught both literacy and political ideology (CAVR 2005, part 5).

The period of the *bases de apoio* was brutally ended across the half island with the major Indonesian offensive of 1978–79 known as "encirclement and annihilation" (CAVR 2005, part 5, 23). Beginning in the west of East Timor, the Indonesian army moved steadily eastward, assaulting FRETILIN bases around Mount Matebian, the Natarbora area, and later, Manatutu (CAVR 2005, part 5, 23). This pushed FALINTIL and the civilian population sheltering with them deeper into the mountains, forcing the resistance to abandon the centralized management of its activities and disperse. The loss of life was immense. People were forced to live months of their lives constantly on the move and in extreme secrecy as they sought to evade Indonesian attacks and find food (see Loney 2018, 53). The bodies of the dead frequently had to be abandoned: there was no time for proper burial.

In the area around Natarbora, many people surrendered to the Indonesian army as life in the jungle and mountains became increasingly unbearable. From the 1980s only a small number of guerrillas remained in the mountains to continue the armed struggle, supported by civilians in the Indonesian controlled villages, towns, and resettlement areas. Throughout this period, Natarbora remained a center of "logistics" for FALINTIL—a place where civilians prepared, cooked, and supplied food to the armed guerrillas, supplied them with medicines and shoes, and passed on messages. *Estafeta* (messengers) played a critical role. Many were young people and children who raised fewer suspicions among the Indonesian army than adults. One former *estafeta* described how journeys to the hinterland had to be made barefoot, demonstrating with his body how the messenger had to constantly bend over, reaching behind to smooth over their footprints with a small branch.[3]

Peoples' acute experiences of suffering, hardship, and deprivation during the early years of the occupation have led the mountains and forests to become charged spaces that loom large in local and national imaginaries. Aciksoz has referred to the mountains in Kurdish guerrilla imaginaries in Turkey as "objects of reverence, sites of redemption, silent witnesses of sacrifice, and tombs of heroic martyrs" (Aciksoz 2020, 19). In Timor-Leste, the mountains and forests are similarly evoked as ambivalent spaces of both refuge and death, heroism and suffering. They are spaces that are "sacralised in the poetics of national struggle," seeped in "sedimentary layers of resistance and martyrdom" (Aciksoz 2020, 17). These imaginaries are reinforced through famous poems and songs such as Francisco Borja da Costa's stirringly nationalist *Foho Ramalau* (Mount Ramalau), penned in 1974, which urges Timorese to cast off the shackles of colonialism. The song became the unofficial FRETILIN anthem during the Indonesian occupation and is frequently sung today.

The affective charge of the mountains and forests is further enhanced by their spiritual potency, inhabited as they are by various spirit beings, including nature spirits and ancestral spirits. Andrew McWilliam and Elizabeth Traube (2011, 11) write of how people sought protection from their spirit guardians during the Indonesian occupation, including those that inhabited the mountains and forests and those from their ancestral origin villages. Many FALINTIL guerrillas speak today of how they solicited "help from the 'hidden world'" not only to ensure their own survival but to ensure the success of the resistance (McWilliam and Traube 2011, 11). Indeed, it is a widely held view, even among members of the political elite, that the success of the national liberation struggle was at least in part made possible by "an alliance between the human and more-than-human realms" (McWilliam and Traube 2011, 11).

These imaginaries of the mountains and forests were vividly conjured during my conversations with Natarbora residents, given depth and texture through highly personalized accounts of struggle, survival, and loss. Former guerrillas spoke of how they had survived with the help of both human and more-than-human forces—the local civilians who fed and clothed them, the ancestors who guided them—and by carrying *biru* (protective amulets), which, charged with *lulik*, protected them from bullets (see Winch 2020). Civilians told stories of how they had survived by eating what they could: wild sago palm, sweet potato, tubers, the trunks of banana trees, leaves (often described as bitter), and even their own clothing. They spoke of hunger and illness, of the deaths of loved ones. Themes of disorientation, of being constantly on the move because of the ongoing Indonesian assaults from the air, were frequently evoked. Death was omnipresent in these narratives, as was the anguish of abandoning bodies. As one Natarbora resident put it, "they died—so many that we didn't feel human anymore."[4]

A Visit to the Natarbora Commission

My first visit to the Natarbora commission was in April 2018. Having arranged the visit in advance with the help of a prominent former FALINTIL commander in Manatutu municipality, Sebastiao Soares (code name "Mau Kuri"), a group of members of the commission had been expecting me. Mau Kuri and I arrived at the small, rather decrepit-looking local veteran's office to find a group of middle-aged and younger men in their thirties waiting for us in a covered outdoor area. Most were dressed in simple farmer's clothing. Seated on mismatched plastic chairs in a large semicircle, many were smoking cigarettes. My eye was immediately drawn to a large handmade cloth banner reading "Our presence is important to them" that hung outside the veterans' office. "Them," one of the men told me, referred to the spirits of the dead whose bodies lay in the ossuary, who were cheered by the company of the living. Biscuits, bananas, and sweet coffee were quickly offered by a woman who hovered in the background but was otherwise silent. José Ramos, the head of the Natarbora commission, a charismatic and articulate former member of the youth clandestine (who is married to prominent political leader José Ramos-Horta's niece), made some brief introductions of the other men in the group, referring to many of them by their resistance code names. Neatly dressed in long trousers and a shirt, his manner of speech suggested an education level beyond that of many of the other men.

José invited me to see the ossuary, or *uma mahon* (shade house), for the dead that stood next to the veteran's office. A solid structure made of timber and a tin roof, it was framed with three flags: the Timor-Leste national flag, the FRETILIN flag, and the FALINTIL flag, immediately establishing a link between the historical era of the resistance and the independent state. Inside the *uma mahon*, national flags draped many identical, state-issued wooden coffins that lined sturdy wooden shelves in orderly rows. One small, separate room was set aside for those of "superior rank" and included the remains of key resistance leader José Ramos-Horta's brother, a former high-ranking FALINTIL commander. José explained that the *uma mahon* now contained the remains of two thousand bodies gathered by the commission since 2015. It had recently put a temporary hold on its exhumation efforts: there is simply no space for more coffins. This raises an additional set of concerns for the commission, which claims to have identified further sites containing twelve thousand sets of human remains requiring exhumation.

Many of the coffins were carefully labeled with the person's name (where known), their rank (where applicable), cause of death (where known), and the location where the remains were found. José also showed me the commission's sophisticated computer system, which records the details of each body for easy retrieval and cross-checking. Strikingly, the "rank" noted on several coffins was *populasaun partisipativa* (participating population). I was told that these coffins contained the remains of those who had died while sheltering with the FALINTIL during the period of the *bases de apoio* or those who assisted them from the towns. Among the *populasaun partisipativa* were men, women, and children who had cooked, washed clothes, acted as security, and supplied food and messages to the FALINTIL and had died from hunger, illness, or military operations. They too were now martyrs (even if they were not yet formally recognized by the state).

Another striking feature of the *uma mahon* was the number of coffins labeled *deskoñesidu* (unknown). Who were these unknown bodies, I wondered, and how did they come to be there? Some, according to José, contained the remains of East Timorese from other parts of the country who had fled to Natarbora during the early years of the occupation and subsequently died in the area. Even though these dead are "strangers" (in the sense that they were not born in the area and connected through place-based kinship networks), they could not be left abandoned and neglected in the bush. Others contained the remains of the dead who had no surviving family members to search for them. José spoke of the commissioner's sense of responsibility for gathering these bones, which—as both human beings and former community members—could not be neglected. Among the *deskoñesidu* were seventy coffins said to contain the bodies of people from the nearby municipality of Maubisse who had been exhumed from one site. The commission believed them to be members of a large family group that had attempted to walk from Maubisse to Natarbora in 1975 in search of shelter and food, dying along the way from eating poisonous wild plants. Other *deskoñesidu* were the yet-to-be-identified remains of five hundred bodies discovered in a mass grave in nearby Soibada, which had been discovered by a woman farming her fields.

Close by the *uma mahon* stands what the commission members refer to as their "mini-museum," a simple wooden structure with a thatched roof, which I was also invited to see. Inside, I dutifully signed the visitor's book and began to look around. The walls were covered with photographs of the commission's activities, including photographs of the recent exhumation of the bodies in the Soibada mass grave. Next to the photo display was a second room, small and unassuming, in which three walls were covered with small boxes covered with clear plastic containing what was described as "evidence." Here, personal items gathered from the dead were displayed: small pieces of clothing, twine that was used to tie peoples' wrists when captured, coins, combs, strands of hair, and pieces of broken plates, gold bracelets, *biru*, machetes, and bullets. A fourth wall was lined with a series of pegs containing keys to the individual boxes. In a marked divergence from the "repertoire of bodily practices" (Leahy 2012) encouraged by most museums, commission members explained that families of the dead are permitted to request the keys in order to retrieve and touch these material objects, which are understood to be *lulik* and use them in rituals undertaken at the site. It felt to me that these objects exuded a profound sense of melancholy and loss. Unlike the identical coffins in the ossuary, in which the bones of the deceased were covered, out of sight, these objects evoked something of the character and unique individuality of the dead—the utensils they used, their clothing, and even parts of their bodies (hair)—allowing them to be "imagined as they were in life" (Renshaw 2010, 457).

The Commission's "Vision" and "Mission"

Following the tour, José Ramos was keen to talk more about the commission's activities and what he termed its "vision" and "mission." We sat down again in the large circle of chairs, and he began by recounting the commission's rather unusual founding myth. He explained that local veterans and the people of Natarbora had been consumed with the need to search for

Uma mahon (shade house) for the dead. Photo by author (2019).

the dead since 2001. It was that year that the local area had been struck by a plague of locusts, which had destroyed all the crops, resulting in a devastating hungry season. At that time, a local man had had a dream in which an old man (*katuas*) appeared and asked him why he was looking so sad, to which he had responded that the locusts had eaten all the crops. The *katuas* replied that the locusts were in fact the unsettled spirits of those who died in the war who "did not have a place, a road [i.e., pathway ahead] even though the people are liberated already." Preoccupied with this problem, local veterans had only felt financially able to form the commission in 2015 after they had begun to receive their veterans' pensions.

José presented me with a sheet of A4 paper on which the commission's vision and mission statement was carefully typed. The statement included several actions necessary to the success of the commission's work. The first, which has already been completed, involved requesting, with the assistance of local ritual experts, the land spirits to reopen the "door" to the land that they had closed off during the occupation to prevent the enemy from discovering the FALINTIL. José explained that local FALINTIL guerrillas and ritual experts had held a special ceremony in 1975, which had asked the ancestors and land spirits to "close" this door, providing guerrillas with a protective force field against the Indonesian military. This ritual had the effect of allowing FALINTIL to walk through the *rai lulik* (potent land) without being attacked by the Indonesian military and live protected within it for the next twenty-four years. A request to "open the door" was now needed to ensure that the commission's program of bones collection could proceed without the nature spirits becoming angered.

The second action, which is ongoing, involves the gathering of the remains of *all* those who died isolated and dispersed deaths during the early years of the Indonesian occupation. This is necessary both to dignify the dead and to prepare the way for the state's development projects. The land, commission members stressed, needed to be "swept" of concealed corpses so that the government's forward-looking modernizing agenda of *dezenvolvementu* (development), of which roadbuilding forms a key part, can proceed. The urgency of this action has both moral and practical dimensions. If the government has not met its obligations to repay the dead for the sacrifices, the state will not "go ahead" but will continue to be plagued by instability. Roadbuilding will also be significantly delayed if roadworks are continually halted because of the accidental discovery or unearthing of human remains. This issue is particularly important in Natarbora, where a new road from the yet-to-be completed Suai petroleum supply base to Dili is planned to pass through.

The work of gathering the remains of the dead is arduous, time-consuming, and expensive. There is first a lengthy period of preparation. An expedition is usually initiated when relatives of the dead approach the commission asking for help. If they have some information about the place of death, the commission will corroborate this by seeking out further eyewitnesses. In many cases, the place of death is not known, and the commission will need to enlist the expertise of a *matan do'ok* (spiritual guide) to locate the site where the body lies. Before an expedition begins, relatives of the deceased person will gather together in their *uma lulik* (sacred house) and *hamulak* (undertake ritual prayers) to seek permission from the ancestors to disturb the dead body. They must then find the funding to supply food for the group—rice, chickens, bananas, sweet potato, and cooking oil—and gasoline for transport. Other items are also essential to ensure the expedition is successful: gold and white coins to be offered to the *rai nain* (spirit owners of the land) to request permission to disturb the land; eggs, candles, and *bua malus* (betel nut) for the *matan do'ok* to use in locating the human remains; and *tua mutin* (palm wine) and *tua sabu* (palm brandy) as offerings to the dead. If the correct rituals are not performed, the bodies will not be found. Proposals are often submitted to the Ministry for Veterans Affairs to assist with these necessities.

The traveling group will consist of around twenty people, mostly relatives of the dead but also members of the commission and, where needed, a *matan do'ok*. The group travels by four-wheel-drive vehicles and then, when there are no roads, on foot to remote areas of the landscape where people may camp in tents for up to a month. Members of the police force and military sometimes accompany the group to provide security and assist with the digging and to provide an ambulance for the transportation of human remains. As they move through the landscape the group carries the national Timor-Leste flag, the FRETILIN flag, and the FALINTL flag as a "sign" to the dead that they have come to gather them. Once the group is in the area where the remains are believed to lie, the dead will usually show a sign to the *matan do'ok* to indicate the site where digging should take place.

While the work is exhausting and hot, involving rudimentary tools such as spades and crowbars, the commission members explained that human remains are generally not buried very deeply; in fact, clothing can sometimes protrude from the ground. The spirits of the dead, knowing the commission and their family members are there to help them, also "think of" them, helping them and giving them strength to complete the work. As the dead and the living *hanoin malu* (think of one another), the digging is imbued with a powerful, affective force, a sense of collective moral purpose and mutual care. The remains of the dead are then gently wrapped in *tais* (woven cloth)—another dimension of care—and transported, often via a state ambulance, to the commission's *uma mahon* to await burial in the yet-to-be-completed local Garden of Heroes cemetery. Another ritual is conducted at the *uma mahon* to thank the ancestors for bringing the dead back into the community.

The third action can be completed only after the remains of *all* the dead from the area are gathered. It will involve the ritual "cooling" of the land, which remains "hot" owing to the presence of blood, unhappy spirits, and human remains, to ensure that agriculture will flourish and the community will prosper. And because these human remains come from all parts of Timor-Leste, the commission will be required to invite people from all districts to a *nahe biti bo'ot* (ritual reconciliation), during which everyone confesses their mistakes and apologizes to the spirits. Ritual experts will be invited to walk from the sea to the mountains, cooling the land by sprinkling it with coconut water mixed with pigs' blood.

A particularly interesting feature of the commission members' narration of their vision and mission was that it both reproduced and subtly challenged the state's logics of necro-governmentality. Commission members described their work as "helping" the state, extending its capacity to recover and identify bodies in preparation for their reburial and valorization as martyrs and to pave the way for development projects. Far from contesting the state's necro-governmental project, they want this project to be larger, more expansive. They argue that the bodies in the ossuary belong to the state and that the state is responsible for reburying them in a Garden of Heroes cemetery. They actively persuade families that their dead should be buried together with their *kamarada* (comrades) rather than in family cemeteries. They insist that the state will not become strong (*metin*), it would not "move ahead"; the government would remain unstable, continuing to rise and fall (*tun sai dei't*), unless *all* the dead were gathered and their demands met. In these ways, the commission seems to be bringing the dead within the realm of the state and bringing necro-governmental logics into the lives of Natarbora residents. Symbols of statehood also saturate the commission's work, from the Timor-Leste national flags that drape coffins and are carried into the field to the uniformed police and military that accompany the commission on its expeditions.

Yet it was also clear that the commission members had their own necro-governmental goals and logics that diverged from the state's. Their work is in part a subtle critique of the state's failure to complete its own valorization project and an assertion their own power (a theme to which I return in the following section). Furthermore, the commission members, unlike the state, engage with the dead as agential beings rather than passive substances. The sense of urgency that imbues their work is driven, at least in part, by affective and embodied experiences of restless spirits, impelled by the need to reassert control over dangerous landscapes and a precarious present and future. It seemed almost unbearable for commission members to contemplate the human remains of their former comrades lying abandoned and neglected in the bush, devoid of human attention and care. They spoke of meeting their "promises" to the dead, their former FRETILIN *kamarada* who had not been fortunate enough to survive, describing the gathering and care of the dead as a form of "dignifying" them, an essential form of repayment for their suffering and sacrifices to the nation (see Traube 2007). This work is also critical for intergenerational well-being. Fears were shared that the families of the dead, the *maluk* (close friends) of those who died (those who struggled and suffered alongside them), and the residents of Natarbora will continue to experience bad consequences until all the dead were gathered and they had been given a good resting place. As Mau Kuri put it: "We need to look for the *mate ruin* (the bones of the dead). They will help us *lao ba oin* (go ahead). It's lucky that we lived, they didn't live. If we don't do this the *mate ruin* can have a big impact on our development. We didn't have any help from other countries during our struggle. We have to love our *mate ruin*."[5]

The Resurfacing Dead are Drawn into a Veterans' Politics

The commission's work highlights how the Timor-Leste state continues to draw its legitimacy and power from decentralized resistance networks operating outside formal state channels. A key issue is that the state's ability to construct cemeteries and carry out reburials lags far behind the capacity of the commissions to exhume human remains. The thousands of coffins awaiting reburial in *uma mahon* around the country are visible and material evidence to the state that its obligations to valorize its martyrs have yet to be fulfilled. These coffins now constitute an "archive of remains" (Rudling and Duenas 2021, 129) that is difficult for the state to ignore. Not only do they provide powerful affective material evidence of the state's limits. They are also noisy, demanding, and potentially dangerous spirits who inhabit what Rojas-Perez (2013, 152) refers to as "the temporality of an unfinished past." While they may have been rescued from their abject and neglected state, they remain in an uncertain and liminal realm in the *uma mahon*, not yet properly settled into the world of the ancestors.

This archive of human remains has political utility to the commission. Its material presence reinforces their historical links to the resistance struggle as former members of the clandestine resistance and FALINTIL and their ongoing political relevance and authority in the present. It regenerates the strong affective-relational connections between local guerrillas and the communities that lived alongside them. It is also a powerful assertion to the state that the struggle is not yet over and will not be over until all the nation's dead are exhumed, identified, dignified, and properly reburied. In this sense it offers an implicit critique of the state for its failure to live up to its obligations to valorize and dignify the nation's martyrs (see Kammen 2009; Myrttinen 2013, 2008).

More than this, the commission's archive and its practices are also reinvigorating and reactivating dormant resistance networks. The Natarbora and other commissions organize themselves along the lines of former armed resistance structures (sectors, regions, and zones). They coordinate and cooperate on a nationwide scale (through mobile phones and regular visits to different municipalities), organizing to collect the human remains of members of "their" municipality and bring them "home." Those I have met around Timor-Leste speak of their work with an urgency and passion, as though they have regained something of the motivation and sense of purpose they had through the long years of resistance.

Because the commissions draw on the language of valorization, state leaders are placed in a bind. Political elites cannot deny the importance of their activities. The endless project proposals and requests for vehicles, police escorts for exhumations, ambulances to transport bodies, upgrades to ossuaries, coffins, funds for rituals to appease the spirits, and new cemeteries are very difficult to refuse.[6] Furthermore, it is in no one's interest—not least state officials—to ignore the demands of the dead. Despite being enrolled in the secular rationalities of modern state building and necro-governmentality, these officials—especially those who were once resistance leaders in the mountains and forests—have their own personal understandings and experiences of the spirit realm. Neither are such officials willing to ignore the demands of powerful and potentially unruly living veterans. As the Dili-based officials continue to hand over resources to commissions, their capacity to control the state's necro-governmental project is revealed as limited. This project emerges as precarious, tenuous, and unstable, performed in the face of "internally fragmented, unevenly distributed and unpredictable configurations of political authority" (Hansen and Stepputat 2005, 2).

The Difficulties of Identification and the Anxieties Provoked by the *Deskoñesidu*

There are, however, several ways in which the uncertainties evoked by resurfaced human remains can confound the commission's own necro-governmental goals just as they do the state's. A key issue is that the tens of thousands of bodies gathered by the Natarbora commission and others around the country demand to be individually identified, to be *named*. The perceived imperative to individually identify or name the dead of war or violent conflict is, for Sarah Wagner (2019, 139), a relatively recent phenomenon globally. Yet we now live in what Thomas Laqueur (2015, 366) refers to as "an age of necronominalism; we record and gather the names of the dead in ways, and in places, and in numbers as never before. We demand to know who the dead are. We find unnamed bodies . . . unbearable."

The practice of naming the dead, in Timor-Leste as elsewhere, lies at "the intersection between the intimate and the bureaucratic" (Laqueur 2015, 397). In Natarbora it is important for the state's and the commission's (at times divergent) projects of reordering the violence, chaos, and large-scale bad death of the occupation; it enables the dead to become sorted and reordered, for official records to be created, and for the political and social fabric of the society to be stitched back together (see Wagner 2019). Yet naming the dead is also important for their reintegration into familial networks and their safe settlement into the realm of the ancestors. It allows them to be assigned what Layla Renshaw (2010, 454) refers to as "locally meaningful conceptualizations of identity," contributing to the sense that they are both "known and knowable" and diffusing their dangerous and destabilizing tendencies.

In a context where there is no state or international assistance for identification, members of the Natarbora commission have developed their own practices of identifying the dead that, like those discussed in chapter 2, creatively combine ideas drawn from forensic science with vernacular knowledge and practices. For example, in the many cases where it is not possible to locate the dead through the recollections of eyewitnesses, commissioners are attuned to messages delivered from the dead to living family members through dreams (which often provide clues about their location) and work closely with ritual experts to identify the sites where their human remains lie. Ritual experts in Natarbora use a range of methods of identification, some of which involve the use of chicken eggs. An egg that has been emptied of its contents may be used as a binocular that assists the ritual expert to "see" and locate the place where bodies are buried. In one popular local narrative, a ritual expert is said to have successfully identified the location of human remains from an airplane by using this method. A different egg may be tapped near a potential site of human remains—if it cracks this indicates that bodies lie below. In other cases, a ritual expert throws an egg into the bush, and the place where it lands marks the location of human remains.

Bones, once found, are usually in a dry state and may hold very few visual clues as to their identity. If there are doubts, the expertise of ritual experts is enlisted to determine to which family they belong. These experts use a range of methods. One method, described in chapter 2, is called *koko ran* (testing the blood) and is increasingly referred to as "traditional DNA" (see chapter 2). It involves taking a blood sample from a relative of a missing person and placing it on a small piece of bone. This method is thought to confirm whether the body belongs to that family (see also Robins 2010, 51). Another method, known as a "hair test," involves tying a piece of bone suspected to be from a deceased relative with a piece of hair from a family member. The hair is then set alight. If the fire burns the hair, it is said that the bone belongs to the family. As already discussed, these methods of identification, while grounded in older practices that are imbued with preexisting meaning, are evolving and transforming as they are now applied to the problem of massive bad death and missing bodies. They might be understood as heralding the emergence of new forms of "citizen-led forensics" (Cruz-Santiago 2020) that do not require the presence of scientific experts, are efficient and cost-effective, and draw on forms of knowledge that exceed the scientific-legal boundaries of forensic expertise.

The use of blood and hair in these processes is not coincidental. Like human remains, these substances have a strangely ambiguous status; they can be experienced both as inert things and as extensions of the living themselves, as almost alive. Blood, like human remains, is a transforming, flowing substance. For Janet Carsten (2019, 205), while blood is not "conclusively alive, its uncertain status of animation" imbues it with a capacity to "animate others." It is associated with "life itself" (Carsten 2019, 207). Carsten observes that while the presence or absence of blood is what separates the living from the dead, blood is also "the stuff that connects living persons who are related and that distinguishes different kinds of people from each other" (Carsten 2019, 206). The widespread use of "blood tests" in Timor-Leste signals that blood is the stuff that connects living and dead kin; it is critical to the re-membering of the dead, their enfolding into their kinship networks.

Yet these practices of identification often raise as many questions as they resolve. A key issue is that the "indeterminate materialities" of bones can confound attempts to identify them (see Fontein 2014, 115). The Natarbora commission is well aware of this. During our conversations they made it clear that their methods of identification were not always 100 percent accurate. One concern was that issues can sometimes arise when two different families claim the same set of human remains as their own. These disputes are generally resolved through what commission members describe as the "natural process," in essence deferring to the agency of the spirits. In one case described by the commission, two families claimed the same set of human remains as their deceased relative. After some time, the members of one family became ill, indicating that they had incorrectly claimed the remains and were being punished by the spirits. More of a concern to commission members was their opinion that traditional methods of identification cannot always correctly identify bodies in cases of mass graves where body parts are comingled. This is an urgent concern in the case of the five hundred bodies discovered in the mass grave in Soibada, which have yet to be identified.

These unidentified remains—the *deskoñesidu*—are an acute preoccupation for members of the Natarbora commission and other commissions around the country. The vernacular term used to describe these remains, the Portuguese term *deskoñesidu* (unknown) alludes to their dangerous indeterminacies and their unsettling and destabilizing presence. The thousands of *deskoñesidu* that lie in ossuaries around the country remain in a protracted liminal state, not yet able to take their place within the social order and the community of ancestors. They generate anxieties that provoke members of the commissions around the country to advocate for the state to make DNA technologies available as a supplement to traditional identification methods. Political leaders, too, are preoccupied with the *deskoñesidu*, including those that lie in the ossuaries and those that remain in the landscape. While maintaining that DNA testing is not financially feasible, they are urgently looking for new solutions.

Revealing Complex Subjectivities, Eluding Categorization

The work of categorization is another practice that reveals how resurfacing remains can both reinforce and unsettle the commission's necrogovernmental project. For the commission, not only must bodies be individually identified: they must also be categorized according to their different functions. As one member explained: "Everyone has their place: FALINTIL, clandestine, the population. Now, they are altogether [in the ossuary] but they will be separated. They should be separated, they had different functions."[7]

The commission members argue that this separation should take place at the time of reburial, when those of highest rank will be sent to the national Garden of Heroes cemetery in Metinaro while commanders representing the subregion will be sent to the municipality cemetery in Manatutu. The remainder will be reburied in the *posto* cemetery. Social hierarchy thus maps onto place hierarchy.

The *deskoñesidu* (unknown), Ermera ossuary. Photo by author (2019).

Categorization is a process that works to homogenize the dead *and* differentiate them. As those deemed to be martyrs are drawn into a national community by virtue of their sacrifices to the nation, they are distinguished according to hierarchies of service (namely their rank and their role within the resistance). On one level, producing knowledge about the functions of these bodies contributes to the state's project of constructing sovereign masculine martyr subjects who are set apart from the bodies of the ordinary civilian dead. It also crafts an orderly narrative of the occupation that might contain its destabilizing excesses of grief and encourage the population to move on. But a deeper reading suggests that the commission's practices are expanding the state's narrow, militarized understandings of martyrdom. Just as in the case of the Santa Cruz and Liquiçá church dead, the category of the martyr is being reshaped as it intersects with popular understandings of suffering and sacrifice, a complex politics of veterans' identity, desires for economic security, and the demands of unruly spirits. The scale of the commission's activities brings this dynamic into sharp relief.

At this point it is important to recall that the Natarbora commission, like other commissions, is gathering the remains of both guerrillas and civilians who lived alongside them. Former guerrillas have a profound awareness of the essential role civilians played in cooking and caring for the armed resistance and helping to keep them alive. The close affective relationships formed while living alongside civilians in the *foho* have given them an acute sense of moral responsibility to exhume, care for, and dignify these civilians, who, they argue, are also martyrs. As one interlocuter explained: "People were killed not just by the forces but also by bombs, airplanes. Some were just ordinary people. They died because of the consequences of the war, so we consider them all *herois da patria* [heroes of the nation], even the population. The martyrs are not just those who carried guns."[8]

The bones that now lie in the Natarbora ossuary (and the objects associated with them in the mini-museum) provide a tangible, intimate, and emotional connection to the lives of those who perished. They literally "bring to light" the myriad, entangled relationships that were formed between resistance members and civilians, revealing their complex subjectivities and activating personal *and* political responsibilities among their former *kamarada*. Those who fit within the state's narrow category of martyrdom escape attempts to categorize them as fixed, militarized, subjects, revealing that they are also fathers, mothers, sons, daughters, and friends who demand to be re-enfolded within the networks of their kin. Those who do not fit within this category demand to be re-membered within their kinship networks and also recognized as martyrs deserving of valorization and reburial in a Garden of Heroes cemetery.

Their physical presence is, like the graves of the civilian dead in Liquiçá, a reminder of the suffering and sacrifices of the *povu kiik* (the small people, ordinary people). This is leading to the creation of a new category of martyrdom, at least among the commission members: the *populasaun partisipativa* (participating population). This is a category that draws on the state's logic of sacrifice and yet destabilizes the stark and highly gendered distinction between "veteran" (an armed guerrilla or member of the clandestine) and ordinary civilian. In these ways, the dead and the living are pushing toward an expansion of the category of the martyr and the heroic resistance narrative.

Yet the complex subjectivities revealed by the dead raise another set of problems for the commission. While these subjectivities may resonate with former resistance actors' own lived experiences of the occupation and the multiple, shifting roles they occupied, they are also confronting and potentially destabilizing of their recently acquired veteran subjectivities. Commission members have gained status from their identities as sovereign, masculine veterans, which rely on a clear distinction between those who participated in the resistance and those who did not. This drives them to engage in their own project of ordering and bordering, a continual redrawing of distinctions between martyrs and nonmartyrs, male and female, active and passive, and an assertion of these distinctions as an objective reality. Members of the Natarbora commission carefully explained to me that to be categorized as a martyr, a person must have died due to suffering caused by participation in the resistance. They made it clear that they were not gathering the remains of those killed due to "personal conflicts" (*konfliktu persoal*), or civilians who died from illness or hunger once they had "surrendered" to the Indonesian military and were living in the villages and towns. Those killed during the internal, political conflict between FRETILIN and UDT that took place just prior to the Indonesian occupation are also regarded as falling outside the category of martyr, as are members of FRETILIN killed during internal party purges (see chapter 5). These bodies, if accidentally gathered by the commission, are passed on to their families to care for them.

Despite these assertions, unlike Dili-based state officials who define martyrdom through abstract policies developed in air-conditioned offices far from the communities affected, commission members are continually confronted with, and confounded by, the on-the-ground complexities of the struggle: its multiple forms, the myriad actors involved (men, women, and children), and their diverse and overlapping roles. This leads them to push, for instance, for the recognition of children as martyrs. This is something the state is not prepared to countenance (as it would require acknowledging that children were used in armed conflict, contravening international law). That there are so many bodies of children in the ossuaries now provides *evidence* of the important roles played by young people in supporting the FALINTIL, as messengers, couriers, and spies, evidence that will be difficult for the state to ignore. In these ways, the dead and the living are transforming the narrow boundaries of martyrdom.

New Spaces of Memory, New Practices of Care

Another way in which the resurfacing dead are disrupting the state's necro-governmental logics is by prompting the creation of new spaces of memory around which new practices of care for the dead are coalescing. These spaces not only elude the centralized control of national political elites but also resist an engagement with the dead as abstract and masculine symbols of heroism and state sacrifice. The creation of these spaces emerges from the commission's ethics of care, its desire to dignify the dead and re-member them as part of the community.

One such space is the Natarbora "mini-museum." As previously discussed, the museum displays personal objects associated with the deceased, and families of the dead are permitted to touch these objects, which are imbued with *lulik*, and remove them from the box to use in rituals undertaken at the site. These practices facilitate an intimate exchange with the deceased, bringing the living and the dead into "spatio-temporal co-presence" (Tusinski 2016, 18). The objects in the museum (each of which has its own specific affordances), elicit a "powerful charge of immediacy and direct connection with the dead," not only among surviving relatives but also among those who, like me, had little or no relationship with the dead in life (Renshaw 2010, 461). They enable a personalized identification with the dead, generating empathy, sympathy, and desires to respond.

The objects in the mini-museum tell a different story of the Indonesian occupation than that which is projected by the state's "monumental" narrative. These objects provide "evidence" to the state and the Natarbora population that contributions to the resistance were intensely *local* and relational. They are material traces of the textured, intricate, and everyday dimensions of life during the resistance: of the suffering and grief that it entailed and of the civilian men, women, and children who lived closely alongside and provided critical support to the guerrillas. This evidence disrupts the dominant national narrative of the occupation, which demarcates the broad contours of the struggle and highlights the contributions of key "national" leaders such as Xanana Gusmao and Taur Matan Ruak. Commission members explain that the museum contains the *riku soin* (riches) of the struggle. They express hopes that it will become a site where future generations of Natarbora residents will learn about their local history and where the state will learn and, in turn, recognize the significance of the struggle in Natarbora within the national story.

The *uma mahon* has emerged as another space where families and the Natarbora commission are developing new practices of care for the dead. Local families regularly visit the *uma mahon* to light candles and lay flowers near their coffins, while those from other municipalities visit on special days, for instance, the 3rd of November (the date when people traditionally visit their dead beyond their family cemeteries). On that date in 2019, my second visit to the Natarbora commission, there was a relaxed atmosphere outside the veteran's office as a slow trickle of motorbikes began to arrive. Families, covered with dust and weary after long and bumpy journeys, chatted and drank coffee with the commission members before entering the *uma mahon* to lay flowers on coffins, light candles, and converse with the deceased. These acts re-member and care for the dead as fathers, brothers, and children, making space for expressions of sorrow, loss, and pain; the disruption of familial networks; and intergenerational well-being.

The commission also organizes regular gatherings in the *uma mahon* to show the dead they are not forgotten. Eating with the dead is a key part of these rituals. In Timor-Leste, the ritual of eating with the dead usually takes place within *uma lulik* or homes and is an important expression of kinship (Tusinksi 2016, 24).[9] The performance of this ritual in the *uma mahon* by those not directly connected to the dead through an ancestral origin house signals that new forms of sociality and connectedness are being created. These rituals usually involve the setting of a table in the *uma mahon* with a large pot of freshly cooked rice, plates, forks, and spoons. As the dead are invited to eat, the living also eat. The ritual act of preparing, feeding, and shared consuming of food is an act of solidarity and empathy with the dead, who, like the living, might be hungry or thirsty. By nourishing the dead, and satisfying their hunger, this practice enacts positive reciprocal relations with the dead that will ensure health and prosperity for the living. These ongoing obligations to feed and satisfy the desires of the dead will continue until the dead are in their final resting place—until they are "emplaced" in the landscape and properly separated from the living—at which point they will no longer be a potential source of danger.

Finally, the resurfaced dead are also driving a local push for another significant new space of memory in Natarbora, a new Garden of Heroes cemetery in the *posto* that will enable the dead to remain close to their families and *kamarada*. Members of the Natarbora commission argue that the government's planned municipality-based heroes cemeteries are too far away for families to visit to pray, light candles, lay flowers, and communicate with the

Eating with the dead. Photo by author (2019).

dead. Families of the dead in Natarbora appear to have accepted this proposal rather than pushing for the dead to be buried in family cemeteries. As one man who had recently recovered his daughter's body from the mountains after more than forty years put it to me: those who died during the conflict need to be buried together because "these dead have become a new community." The commission has persuaded the government to fund the construction of this Garden of Heroes and has successfully argued that this cemetery needs to have a "unique" design that follows the contours of the natural terrain rather being organized in a linear grid pattern. While the potent presence of the dead in this cemetery is likely to reinforce the power of veterans within their territorial domain, the dead and the living are also resisting the state's necro-governmental project of spatiotemporal control of the dead and subverting the central planning practices and regulations that define the rigidity, straight lines, and hard borders of the Garden of Heroes cemeteries.

Conclusion

By providing a window into the painstaking and unique expeditionary work of gathering and identifying human remains, this chapter has generated further insights into the agential dimensions and political implications of Timor-Leste's dead. This work exemplifies the complex necropolitics that is activated as the state's necro-governmental logics encounter other sources of power. While the dead are deployed for diverse political purposes, including former resistance actors' own project of structuring social responses to massive bad death, they are also imbued with "unstable, uncertain and ultimately indeterminate materialities" that exceed their political utility (Fontein 2022, 30). This renders the responses of the living provisional, never "fully and finally complete" (Fontein 2022, 32).

These uncertainties are evident across several domains. First, the dead who remain in a protracted liminal state in the *uma mahon* both demand identification and reburial and also complicate those processes. The *deskoñesidu* are an acute problem for the Natarbora commission and other commissions around the country, provoking anxieties and revealing the limited resources and identification capacities of both the state and the commissions. The resurfaced dead, as they enter into ongoing reciprocal relations of care with the living, also reveal their complex subjectivities, escaping attempts to categorize them as fixed militarized, masculine subjects and assign them to a past temporality. We have also seen how the work of recovering human remains is prompting the creation of new spaces of memory that exceed the defined and bounded spaces of the state's planned heroes' cemeteries.

There is, however, one final way in which the dead disrupt diverse necro-governmental projects: that is as restless spirits who continue to inhabit the landscape. Despite the time and resources invested by the Natarbora commission and others around the country in searching for and exhuming the dead, not all bones do resurface. Many elude detection. There are simply too many victims of bad death who lie in dispersed, remote, and inaccessible locations. Some have no surviving family members to care for them. Just as the restless spirits of the Santa Cruz and Liquiçá church massacres trouble the sites where violence was done to their bodies, so too do the spirits of those who died solitary, isolated deaths in the mountains and forests. They are perhaps even more potent because there are so many of them and because dangerous landscapes are more proximate. Rather than coalescing around massacre sites, these dead are more dispersed. As they continue to render landscapes disordered and dangerous, they cause problems for the living, such as motorbike accidents, and block, in a literal sense, the state's ambitious roadbuilding project. These dead, even more so than the *deskoñesidu* (who at least have been rescued from their abject and neglected state), remain dangerous entities that cannot be easily controlled or defined. They remain an acute preoccupation for rural communities whose livelihoods are precarious. These dead also pose a profound challenge for the state, inhabiting and reminding political leaders of an unfinished past, that those who lost their lives have not yet been repaid for their sacrifices, and disrupting forward-looking projects of development.

All of this suggests that the project of gathering, reburying, and dignifying *all* the conflict dead is arguably an impossible, never-ending one. There will always be bodies that elude detection. For those that have resurfaced, questions will linger as to whether identification practices have been accurate, especially in the case of the *deskoñesidu*. Even as the excessive indeterminacies created by missing bodies in the mountains and forests continue to provoke practices of recovery and reburial, this project is unlikely to gather all the dead and fully and finally stabilize their identities. The dead's excessive indeterminacies will continue to destabilize attempts to draw them into a collective frame of remembrance and fashion them into sovereign, masculine, martyr subjects that might contain the material and spectral legacies of the Indonesian occupation.

The next chapter turns to a category of the dead that is especially difficult to place in the state's valorization program and its criteria of martyrdom: those killed by the resistance movement. In contrast to the memory work taking place around the Santa Cruz and Liquiçá massacres, and the gathering of the human remains of the *populasaun partisipativa* discussed in this chapter, responses to what I call the "treacherous dead" are necessarily less publicly visible. Yet they are not absent. Like other East Timorese who died bad deaths, these dead cannot be left neglected and abandoned, devoid of proper burial: they demand care and attention from the living. As they are cared for, mourned, and re-membered as part of the national and local community, possibilities open for those who have hitherto been marginalized and ungrievable to be visible and acknowledged.

5

The Treacherous Dead of the Badlands

Re-membering Those Killed by the Resistance

Angelo, a softly spoken man in his late sixties, is one of a handful of East Timorese who had participated in a public hearing on the theme of "massacres" organized by Timor-Leste's Commission for Reception, Truth, and Reconciliation (CAVR) in 2003. During that hearing, Angelo had recounted how in 1976 he had witnessed the killing of seventeen members of his extended family, who had been shot and cut down with machetes, in a remote location in Lautem. It was for these reasons that I had first sought him out as an interviewee, in 2006, for a research project on transitional justice. During our first conversation, Angelo had told me a little more about the killings, enough for me to piece together their intimate quality and to glean something of the atmosphere of fear, distrust, and opacity of information that marked the early years of the Indonesian occupation. These acts, Angelo told me, had been perpetrated by members of his own extended family who had recently joined the pro-independence party FRETILIN. Those killed were also members of FRETILIN. While I came away from that interview with more questions than answers, Angelo's recollection of these events brought home to me the extent to which discourses of treason, circulating rumors, the availability of weapons, and preexisting familial tensions could intersect in volatile and potentially lethal ways during the early years of the occupation.

As it turned out, Angelo's telling of his story at the CAVR public hearing would have negative consequences for him personally. By naming the dead publicly Angelo had in effect made a promise to help them by searching for

123

and reburying their bodies, a promise that for over a decade he was unable to fulfill. During that time, he suffered a debilitating illness. I only learned this part of the story in 2017, when I visited Los Palos and stayed, as I usually did, in the small guest house run by Angelo and his wife Jacinta. Although I had remained in touch with Angelo since 2006, I had not spoken to him about the events of 1976 again. He had not wished to talk about them, and I did not wish to pry. However, in my 2017 visit, which happened to coincide with the parliamentary elections, Angelo asked me if I would drive him, his wife, and two of his teenage children to the voting station at the local school in the nearby village of Souro. Along the way Angelo explained that we would first visit his family cemetery to lay flowers and light candles.

It was apparent on our arrival that this was no ordinary cemetery but that it contained the graves of the seventeen family members killed in 1976. As we walked around the small, well-maintained site with its colorful, freshly painted fence of red, blue, and white, Angelo pointed out the headstones of his mother and father, his then eight-months-pregnant wife, and several small children. We carefully lit candles to place on each grave. He explained that the remains of the dead had been collected the previous year during a weeklong expedition to the remote bush location of the massacre. While no actual "bones" were found, soil and rocks had been taken from the site identified by a *lia nain* (ritual expert) as the site of the killings. Through the ritual "mentioning" (*temi*) of their names the *lia nain* had called their wandering spirits to the site. The rocks and soil, now infused with the spirits of the dead, were then carefully wrapped in *tais* (woven cloth) and carried back to Souro, the family's ancestral village, where they were placed in coffins, each carefully labelled with the name and age of the deceased. Through a subsequent three-day ritual involving the participation of over two thousand members of the extended family, the spirits of the dead were properly settled into the ancestral realm. After months of painstaking planning and fundraising, USD 200,000 had been raised for the rituals—an amount only possible owing to significant monetary contributions from Angelo's children living in the UK.

Angelo invited me to return to Souro in four months' time to participate in the *kore metan* "taking off the black" ritual, which customarily takes place one year after death (and in this case was taking place a year after the long-delayed reburial ritual). In a sign that the ancestors were pleased, the rain that had threatened to ruin the ceremony had eased by the evening, and car after car arrived after navigating the muddy roads, with relatives bearing cartons of beer and soft drinks. There was a festive, party atmosphere. Rows of plastic chairs had been arranged in concentric circles under tarpaulins, and large tables had been set out in the middle with food, champagne, and a large cake. Dancing and drinking continued late into the night. The next day I asked Angelo how he felt. "Calm," he told me, "because we have given them [the dead] a good place." Over breakfast, his daughter told me that he had recovered from his debilitating illness.

The dead, however, are not entirely at peace. Before I departed for Dili, Angelo gave me a photocopy of a carefully typed and detailed four-page chronology of the events of the 1976 massacre in a paper envelope that, he explained, he had submitted to the government agency responsible for assessing claims for veteran and martyr status. On the final page, Angelo had made the case that his deceased family members gave their lives for the nation and are innocent, not traitors. They should therefore be recognized, through medals and pensions, as martyrs. He urged me to follow up on the progress of this claim when in Dili. Angelo's actions suggest that while the gathering and reburial of the dead has calmed their restless spirits, the absence of official recognition of their sacrifices leaves residues of doubt about the rightfulness of their past actions, activating new demands from the dead and new responsibilities from the living.

Angelo's recently completed cemetery. Photo by author (2017).

The ambiguities and intimate betrayals that marked the early years of the Indonesian occupation continue into the present, coalescing in stories, like Angelo's, of the "ungrievable" dead (Butler 2009). The families of those killed by FRETILIN gain no assistance to search for their bodies, and the dead are excluded (at least in theory) from the state's valorization program that provides recognition and pensions to martyrs. Even more so than the civilian dead who did not participate in formal resistance structures, these dead do not have a place in the heroic resistance narrative. The state's necro-governmental project, sustained as it is by "ordering and bordering" (Auchter 2013, 293), inevitably renders certain kinds of suffering and certain dead bodies invisible. It is in this sense that the FRETILIN dead inhabit a "Badlands." The Badlands is both a geographic and a figurative space. It comprises the dispersed sites where killings of "traitors" took place, a variegated topography that is interspersed with and layered over other spaces: the city, the town, the hinterlands. It also encompasses the outer fringes of the national imaginary: the relational spaces where the dead who are excluded from the state's narrative of unified and heroic struggle press their demands on those close to them for care and official recognition.

The extensive violence and killings committed by those acting in the name of the resistance against those labeled "traitors" and "collaborators" might be understood as a "public secret" (Taussig 1999, 5). Taussig described the public secret as "that which is generally known but cannot be articulated" (Taussig 1999, 5). Or as Fletcher, summarizing Taussig puts it, it is "something that is in fact widely known, yet about which there remains a certain official silence, as all involved work to sustain the fiction that there is in fact a secret to be hidden" (Fletcher 2012, 434; Taussig 1999, 5). The power of the public secret lies in its ability to fashion social subjects who "know what not to know" (Taussig 1999, 49). In Timor-Leste, the public secret of resistance violence is not only integral to the state's project of necro-governmentality but also to the large numbers of ordinary people who, in the aftermath of the intra-Timorese violence of the 1970s, are deeply invested in the (re)imagining of a cohesive community, both nationally and locally. It is a secret deeply enmeshed with other public secrets: the secret that the national resistance struggle was far messier, less unified and cohesive than it is portrayed and that collaboration with the Indonesian regime was pervasive during the occupation, as was intra-Timorese violence and local betrayals. It is also connected to the public secret that the state's political authority in the present is fragile and contingent; the strength of peoples' relational ties to kin, community, ancestors, and resistance comrades means that their loyalties to the state are balanced against other powerful allegiances and responsibilities. The maintenance of each of these secrets is essential to the other and to the myth of a united struggle and a united political community.

This chapter explores how the vernacular memory work of caring for the treacherous dead, while not exposing the public secret or destroying it, is allowing it to be negotiated in ways that bring the dead back into the local (and sometimes national) political community. It is work that emerges from necessity: from relatives' embodied, visceral reminders of the dead's continuing suffering and from their own desires for the economic security promised by a survival pension. It also emerges from local lived experiences of a conflict that was messy and confusing, in which people played multiple roles, and of peoples' strong bonds and memories of the dead as community members and kin. This pushes toward local reinterpretations of the dead's suffering and deaths as consequences of the war (*konsekuensia funu*) that were necessary to the achievement of national independence. These dead have the "right" to be properly buried and grieved: they too suffered and made sacrifices for the nation.

I explore these dynamics through a focus on two categories of the treacherous dead: those who died in FRETILIN-run "national rehabilitation" (RENAL) prisons, accused of being "reactionaries" in the early years of the occupation, and members of the UDT (União Democrática Timorense, Timorese Democratic Union) and Apodeti (Associação Popular Democrática Timorense, the Popular Democratic Association of Timor), political parties whose members were killed by FRETILIN during the internal political conflict just prior to the Indonesian invasion. I show how, even as the public secret of resistance violence is deeply embedded in the official memorial landscape and cannot be openly challenged, the living and the dead are navigating it in ways that allow some of those who have been rendered publicly ungrievable to become grievable, acknowledged. The first part of the chapter sets the scene for this exploration. I begin by discussing scholarly insights into the category of the "traitor," which provide useful conceptual starting points to make sense of what we see across a range of sites and cases in Timor-Leste. This section is followed by a brief overview of the evolving category of the traitor in East Timor and a discussion of its contemporary resonance.

Traitors and the Treacherous Dead

The category of the traitor performs important political work. For Tobias Kelly and Sharika Thiranagama (2012) the traitor plays a critical role in the reproduction of the social and political order, working to delineate the boundary between insiders and outsiders to a political community. Yet such a figure also raises important questions about sovereignty as an ongoing, contested, and vulnerable political project (Kelly and Thiranagama 2012, 3). This is because, while accusations of treason are assertions of political authority that give "the people" a more tangible and definite presence—especially at times when claims to such authority are frail and contested—these assertions simultaneously expose the very fragility of political community and the contingency of political authority. They are a reminder that all states and political movements aspiring toward sovereignty must cultivate sentiments of loyalty and (national) belonging among constituencies who often have coexisting loyalties and allegiances to households, family, clan, tribe, ethnic group, religious leaders, or spiritual communities (Kelly and Thiranagama 2012, 2, 3, 8, 10; see also Schafers 2020, 120–21). In these ways, the category of the traitor helps to lay bare the "contours of the social labor" that goes into the "making and maintenance of sovereignty" (Schafers 2020, 121). In essence it helps reveal the "public secret" that loyalties to the state are contingent and that the state itself is an unstable entity.

The extent to which accusations of treason work to demarcate the boundaries of a political community *and* reveal the fragility of the political community is especially marked when it comes to the dead. Aciksoz argues that the radical devaluation of traitors produces what Agamben referred to as a "biopolitical body" a "bare life that is stripped of social, legal, and religious protection and included in the political order only through its exclusion" (Aciksoz 2020, 8–9, referring to Agamben 1998). Agamben called this biopolitical body the *homo sacer* (sacred man) who "has been abandoned by both divine and profane laws and may therefore be killed by members of the political community, with impunity". Even after death, the body of the *homo sacer* continues to be excluded from the political order (Acikcoz 2020, 9, referring to Agamben 1998). Not only does the traitor's death not count as sacrifice because "he has been stripped of the worth required for such a divine gesture": he is also denied funeral rites and public mourning (Acikcoz 2020, 9).

Yet, scholarly insights and popular stories remind us that the publicly ungrievable dead are not easily dispensed with. They remain a haunting presence as specters who trouble performances of sovereignty (Auchter 2013, 299). A powerful account of this disruption is provided by Sophocles in his ancient Greek play *Antigone* (441 BCE), which has been extensively analyzed. The story tells of how Antigone is initially prevented from securing a respectable burial for her brother Polynices, regarded as an enemy of the city-state by its ruler Creon. Polynices's body must be left abandoned on the battlefield outside the city wall to be eaten by worms, dogs, and vultures (Kwon 2010, 411). Yet Antigone is unable to subject herself to the law of the state and decides to bury her brother, defending her acts by declaring that "death longs for the same rites for all" and that "the rights of the dead are universal and part of the 'great, unwritten, unshakable traditions'" (verse 505, cited by Kwon 2010, 411). Arrested by Creon, she is sent to a cave to await her death and commits suicide, not aware that Creon—warned that his acts have angered the gods—has ordered her release. Things end badly for Creon too, who is horribly punished by the gods; his own wife and son commit suicide, unable to bear what the king has done (Kelly and Thiranagama 2012, 20).

In Timor-Leste, those killed by FRETILIN similarly long for consolation, care, death rites, and recognition. Their relatives, like Antigone, must navigate between the demands of the state and their deeply felt obligations to the dead. As in the world evoked by Sophocles, the devaluation of the dead is experienced by their living relatives as unbearable, and they are compelled to act. In contrast to Antigone's world, and to Agamben's emphasis on the power of the sovereign to produce "bare life" excluded from the political order, the category of the traitor in Timor-Leste is not absolute. Just like the category of the martyr, there is some room for the living and the dead to negotiate its terms.

The Evolving Category of the Traitor in East Timor

The categories of the traitor (*traidor*) and its other, the nationalist (*nasionalista*), became salient in East Timor during the brief interregnum between the end of Portuguese colonial rule in 1974 and the Indonesian invasion in 1975 (Kammen 2003, 79). Amid the destabilizing political uncertainties of this period, when there was an acute need to imagine East Timor as a unified and tangible "people," the identification and violent punishment of purported acts of treason gave an "undeniable tangibility" to the claims of FRETILIN leaders to speak in the name of the nation (see Kelly 2012, 186). It also gave rise to new tensions between peoples' responsibilities to family and intimate relationships and their support for the resistance.

This was the period of the so-called "internal political conflict" or "civil war" that implicated East Timor's two largest political parties, FRETILIN and UDT, and to a lesser extent, a third, Apodeti. At stake were competing political visions of national independence. While the more radical FRETILIN favored immediate national independence, UDT advocated a more gradual transition on the basis that the Timorese were not yet ready for self-governance.[1] Apodeti, by contrast, favored the integration of the territory into Indonesia. These competing visions soon manifested as competing claims to speak on behalf of the East Timorese people, and the ensuing tensions were fostered by agents of the Indonesian state. Those who remember this time tell of how FRETILIN taunted UDT with slogans such as "UDT eat foreigners' shit" while UDT members accused FRETILIN of being "communists."[2]

In May 1975 a fragile, four-month coalition between FRETILIN and UDT broke down when UDT launched a coordinated armed action (variously called a "coup," a "movement," or an "uprising," depending on one's political persuasion)—against "communist elements" within FRETILIN. FRETILIN responded by calling for "a general insurrection against the *traitors* of the homeland and for the genuine liberation of the Maubere people" (Gusmao 2000, 25, my emphasis; see also Kammen 2003, 79). As Kammen observes, "Effigies of UDT leaders were hung from buildings in Dili and graffiti on bullet-pocked buildings read 'Burn the Traitors' and 'Vigilance against Traitors'" (Kammen 2003, 79). As the ensuing violence spiraled into a conflict that spread from Dili throughout the country, the Portuguese administrator rapidly left Dili to seek protection on the island of Atauro (CAVR 2005, chapter 1). FRETILIN, quickly emerging as the victors, issued a unilateral declaration of independence on 28 November and inaugurated Francisco Xavier do Amaral as the first president of the new Democratic Republic of East Timor the following day. This independence was short lived, with the full-scale Indonesian invasion arriving on 7 December 1975.

Although it lasted for less than three weeks, the internal political conflict has indelibly marked many lives. Between fifteen hundred and three thousand people are thought to have died (CAVR 2005, introduction, 9). The majority were members of UDT and Apodeti, killed by FRETILIN, although mass killings of FRETILIN members were also committed by UDT (CAVR 2005, chapter 1). The violence also became entangled with personal and familial divisions, creating opportunities to settle old scores that often had very little to do with political goals (Braithwaite, Charlesworth, and Soares 2012, 14; CAVR 2005, chapter 1).[3] Personal grievances became intertwined with larger understandings of loyalty to the movement for national liberation. That the conflict is popularly referred to as the *funu maun alin* (war of brothers) provides a sense of the depth and intimacy of the betrayals that took place.

The category of the traitor took on new meanings in the mid- to late-1970s as FRETILIN began to arrest and punish those within its own ranks. The "reactionary" also became a new salient category (Kammen 2003, 80). Many so-called reactionaries were associated with FRETILIN leader Francisco Xavier do Amaral, who, at a time of drastic loss of civilian life in the mountains and the decimation of resistance strategies, called for a radical change of resistance strategy. Diverging from the militant position of the FRETILIN central committee that emphasized mass mobilization as a vital component of the revolutionary struggle, Amaral and his supporters argued that civilians should be allowed to surrender and continue to resist from the towns and villages (CAVR 2005, part 3, 77–78). Negotiation with the Indonesians would be a critical part of that strategy. Thousands of supporters of Amaral's strategy (among them FALINTIL commanders) were arrested, languishing in FRETILIN-run "rehabilitation prisons" (RENAL) or executed through the public spectacle of *justisa popular* (popular justice) (CAVR 2005, part 5, 19). Among them was Amaral himself, who in September 1977, was publicly tried by an extrajudicial FRETILIN tribunal for planning to negotiate with the Indonesian military and accused of high treason. In a bitter twelve-page diatribe on behalf of the FRETILIN Central Committee, then FRETILIN prime minister Nicolau Lobato accused Amaral of being "a saboteur, capitulationist, traitor, lackey of imperialism, counter-revolutionary, racist, obscurantist, feudalist and opportunist." Amaral was ousted from FRETILIN and all leadership positions (cited by Walsh 2012, 3).[4]

By the late 1970s, the "collaborator" had emerged as another salient category. In 1979 the territory had been declared "pacified" by the Indonesian armed forces and most civilians were living in villages and towns under heavy Indonesian military surveillance. The occupation pervaded everyday life at the most local of levels. The regime's elaborate system of spies, informants, and civil defense patrols had recruited thousands of East Timorese (Drexler 2013, 75). The surviving FRETILIN leadership had also been forced to recalibrate resistance strategy, developing a clandestine network made up of tiny locally based "cells" that connected FALINTIL with the population and in which participants were only aware of a very small set of the wider network (Kammen 2003, 81; McWilliam 2005, 35). While civilians often worked secretly for the resistance, passing on information about military plans and strategies, the cell structure made it impossible to be certain of others' loyalties (Drexler 2013, 88). In a context where survival depended on some degree of cooperation with the regime, many struggled with the conflicting demands of supporting and feeding families and tacit cooperation with the Indonesian occupation (Drexler 2013). Countless small acts of complicity, betrayal, and collaboration were committed as desires for power, survival strategies, responsibilities to kin, and obligations to the resistance struggle intersected (see Kelly 2012, 182). These intersections were further inflected by unequal and deeply gendered power relations. The young women who were sacrificed by their families and village chiefs to the Indonesian military to be used for sex in exchange for the security of the family and the village and were subsequently labeled traitors provides perhaps the starkest example of this (see Kent 2015).

Questions of loyalty and people's "true allegiances" emerged as preoccupations in both private and public lives, a source of immense anxiety. The fear of being accused, either publicly or privately, of treason or collaboration with the enemy was a constant threat hanging over everyday interactions. For Schafers (2020, 125), reflecting on research in Palestine, part of the power of the implicit and ever-present threat of collaboration lies with the ambiguity as to where, exactly, the boundary between loyalty and disloyalty lies. Peoples' position in relation to that boundary is never entirely certain, and loyalties are closely observed, leading to a continuous recalibration of behaviors, actions, and interactions (see Schafers 2020, 122, 125). During the Indonesian occupation, East Timorese engaged in performances of what McClintock (2019, 593) refers to as "everyday acts of loyalty," developing a heightened awareness of "potential violations of bonds of solidarity" that could involve public acts of treason as well as personal acts between individuals and among families.

By the late 1990s, the word *traidor* had largely disappeared from the political speeches of East Timor's most prominent leader, FALINTIL commander Xanana Gusmao, replaced with a discourse of "national unity." These shifts had begun in the 1980s, when Gusmao announced that he would resign from FRETILIN and that FALINTIL would be politically neutral, paving the way for a more inclusive resistance that would be open to members of Apodeti, UDT, and others who had not been FRETILIN (Niner 2009, 113; Kammen 2003, 81). In 1998 the National Council of the Timorese Resistance (CNRT) was formed, uniting the historical parties in "one broad front" (Leach 2017). In the new discourse of national unity, the breakdown of the FRETILIN-UDT coalition in 1975 was construed as a "fatal, historic mistake" that had "weakened the nationalist movement" (Gusmao 2000, 214, cited in Leach 2017, 122; see also Niner 2009, 112). The divisions of the internal political conflict were increasingly described in terms such as "our problems in the early years in the mountains" (Gusmao 2000, cited in Kammen 2003, 81). However, just as the traitor-nationalist dichotomy waned, new oppositional terms, "pro-independence" and "pro-autonomy" (supporters of East Timor's continued integration into Indonesia) emerged (Kammen 2003).

The Traitor in the Contemporary Era

In the current era of national independence, accusations of treason, reactionary behavior, and collaboration are no longer ubiquitous. Yet they lurk just beneath the surface, retaining an emotive power and erupting publicly at times when political authority appears fragile or under threat, reigniting historic political party tensions. This term is applied in a general sense to those who are said not to have suffered and struggled for the nation's liberation. This includes those accused of having collaborated with the enemy or those who had jobs in the Indonesian administration, who are said to be unjustly benefiting from the fruits of that struggle in the new era of independence. It can also be applied to diaspora East Timorese, whose loyalties to the nation are sometimes deemed questionable. This group have activated what Angie Bexley (2007, 71) describes as a new "politics of authenticity" in which those who remained in East Timor to wage the struggle on the home front are said to have been engaged in a more "pure struggle," and their suffering more authentic, compared with Timorese who had led "the good life" overseas, returning after independence as an educated elite to claim good jobs and high salaries within the UN and the independent government.[5] The question of whether one had truly sacrificed and struggled for the resistance is not only of symbolic importance; it has become a key marker for determining entitlements to jobs, benefits, government contracts, veterans' pensions, and scholarships to study abroad.

Part of the power of the category of the traitor in the contemporary era is that while it is asserted as definitive and distinct, it remains operationally ambiguous and slippery. Accusations of treason can be invoked to cast a shadow over the behavior of political opponents or other emergent political threats. These accusations avoid opening to scrutiny the violence committed by FRETILIN, UDT, and other political parties in the lead-up to, and during, the early years of the occupation. Elite political leaders, both past and present, have little interest in opening space for discussion of the circumstances in which accusations of treason, collaboration, and reactionary behavior were made and brutal forms of punishment meted out. Instead, a pervasive "epistemic murk" (Taussig 1999, 49; Surin 2001, 206) surrounds this public secret, allowing the myth of a unified Timorese nation to persist.

This is not to suggest that intra-Timorese violence is completely absent from the political discourse. It is, in fact, integral—if implicitly—to the state's project of structuring social responses to the massive bad death of the occupation and remaking the political order. This violence serves as a pedagogical lesson to the population of today, a lesson about the dangers of internal division and the importance of national unity. Yet the acute suffering caused by this violence is not spoken of. Instead, diverse, fragmented, and intimate experiences are collectively enfolded into a single narrative trajectory of how the East Timorese people, once divided by colonial masters, international interference, and internal divisions "came together" once more in a unified and cohesive national struggle. In these ways, the state attempts to control the public secret. This reinforces the secret's power and the state's own authority, reminding citizens that for the collective future of the polity they must continue to know what not to know.

The ambiguity of the category of the traitor also avoids opening to scrutiny the public secret of the pervasiveness of East Timorese collaboration with the Indonesian regime, which continues into the postconflict era. The reality that state building relies on those who have relationships with Indonesian companies, members of the Indonesian military, and Indonesian political leaders (IPAC 2014) speaks to the salience of Ernesto Laclau's argument (1996) that "groups struggling for independence necessarily contain elements of the forces they seek to overcome" (cited by Kelly 2012, 170).[6] For Laclau, "the penetration of the oppressor into the everyday life of the oppressed makes complete separation impossible." The tragedy, he suggests, is that national liberation movements are forced to create their new nations on "foundations produced by the very regimes they are opposed to" (cited by Kelly 2012, 170). Knowing not to know this is essential to the myth of a united people and a liberated, self-reliant state.

For East Timorese on the wrong side of history there are complex dynamics to be negotiated. While their skills and knowledge are necessary for state building, and while they may obtain senior positions within the government, inclusion within the political community requires them to allow the state to control the public secret and tell the story of the "coming together" of the East Timorese people. For families who have not yet recovered the bodies of their deceased relatives or for whom a question mark hangs over the deeds of those relatives, these terms are complicated by the continuing demands of restless, unhappy spirits.

Resistance Violence and the Memorial Landscape

Much can be gleaned about the state's (incomplete) attempts to control the public secret of resistance violence from the official memorialization landscape. Memorialization is a key necro-governmental technology; the strategic emplacement of monuments to national heroes in public places visually reinforces the collective national story of heroic resistance, wholeness, and continuity, rendering some stories visible and others invisible. For instance, a statue of recently deceased, errant FRETILIN resistance leader Francisco Xavier do Amaral—a granite bust of Amaral as an elder statesman—now stands in the center of Dili. Amaral is now recognized as East Timor's first president, his body buried in a prominent position at the apex of the National Garden of Heroes cemetery.[7] His rehabilitation serves the official national narrative of the "coming together" of the East Timorese people. By contrast, the former national "rehabilitation" (RENAL) prisons where many former FRETILIN "reactionaries"—including Amaral—perished, are overgrown with weeds and hidden by thick undergrowth. The suffering experienced by these prisoners at the hands of FRETILIN is not deemed worthy of public remembrance.

In 2017 Pedro Mendonca do Regio accompanied me to visit the ruins of one of Timor-Leste's many RENAL prisons, in Remexio, in the hinterlands behind Dili. Pedro's brother Annanais, a former FALINTIL commander, had been incarcerated in this prison and had perished there, while Pedro had been detained in a nearby prison. Coincidently, this prison, known as Nundamar, was also the place where Amaral had been detained and where two of his children are said to have been killed. After traveling for some time on a poorly maintained and pot-holed dirt road, we came to a stop at the top of a hill where the sea could be glimpsed in the distance. Pedro took me to the edge of an escarpment and pointed to where he said the prison lay, several hundred meters below us. It was covered with thick undergrowth. Pedro, now an elderly man, would not accompany me to take a closer look at the prison and, despite

Statue of Francisco Xavier do Amaral, Dili. Photo by author (2020).

The Treacherous Dead of the Badlands

my requests, would not allow me to make the steep descent on my own. In any case, he said, there was not much to see.

The Nundamar prison lies in an area that was a meeting point for the FRETILIN central committee members in the Central North Sector. According to Pedro, there were three other nearby prisons, Kotomori, Erluli, and Erumori. The prison, like many others, had been little more than a series of *rai kuak* (holes in the ground) covered by wooden bars with a large rock placed on top (see also CAVR 2005). Pedro described it as three holes, each around four meters high, three meters wide, and three meters deep. Each housed around ten prisoners. Prisoners were forced to work during the day (husking corn and cutting wood). At night they slept on the ground. They ate whatever they could, often *ai ferina* (sweet potato). Those who were accused of committing "less serious" offences were sometimes allowed to sit outside the prison, under the trees. Many died here from hunger, disease, a lack of water, or from harsh beatings. Others were executed. Pedro demonstrated by hunching his body into the cramped position in which his brother Annanais was forced to crouch night after night in the subterranean darkness, his wrists bound with harsh twine.

The violence that took place here is not completely invisible, serving as a reminder that the state's control over the public secret is far from absolute. At the time of my first visit, a small makeshift cement white cross stood at the top of the escarpment with the words RENAL colorfully emblazoned on it. Pedro explained how in the absence of any state-sponsored memorialization or exhumation efforts the Remexio community has had to find its own way to remember, care for, and console the restless spirits of deceased RENAL prisoners who congregate at the sites of their former imprisonment and deaths, imbuing them with *lulik* (sacred) potency. Soon after the end of the occupation, when travel was no longer a difficult and dangerous proposition involving navigating checkpoints and obtaining *surat jalanan* (certificates to travel), families came from across Timor-Leste to look for the remains of their loved ones at this place. But the remains of the dead had comingled and disintegrated. Dogs and pigs had eaten them. As in other contexts of partial and comingled remains, this gave rise to specific problems for families. Identification of individual bodies would not be possible even with the use of methods such as *koko ran* (testing the blood), preventing the return of the dead to their families for individualized mourning and care. In addition, as Zoe Crossland (2015, 134) writes, "Mixed bones mean mixed needs and priorities, as relatives must sort out for themselves their obligations not only to their deceased but to other families of the missing." In this case, families collectively decided the site could not be disturbed. Instead, with the help of *lia nain*, they called restless spirits to the site of the mass grave, delivered ritual prayers (*hamulak*), and took clumps

Makeshift cross at the former RENAL prison, Remexio. Photo by author (2018).

of soil and rocks from the site, which had been infused with the spirits of the dead. The rocks and soil were then buried in family cemeteries. With the help of the local priest, the small cross was built. Despite its remote location, signs of local care of this place could be seen in the candle wax that remained at the base of the cross.

The sites where mass killings took place during the *funu maun alin* similarly reflect the state's (incomplete) attempts to control the public secret. The sites where UDT and Apodeti prisoners were killed by FRETILIN during the internal political conflict are forlorn and neglected, highlighting how these dead, more so than the RENAL dead (most of whom were FRETILIN), are portrayed as being firmly on the wrong side of history. The graves at Aisirimou, Saboria, and Aituni, in Aileu municipality, which mark the sites where up to one hundred people were executed by FRETILIN in December 1975 as Indonesian forces advanced, lie far from the main roads, scattered in disparate locations marked by a few simple, concrete graves, beneath which there are presumably a mass of bodies.

Mario, the head of the Aileu victims' association, took me to visit these sites, which are around an hour and a half's winding drive from Dili into the

Neglected graves of UDT and Apodeti victims in Aileu. Photo by author (2017).

central mountains, in 2017. He explained that the graves are occasionally visited by relatives of the dead, especially on significant days such as All Souls' Day, when flowers and candles are placed on them. Yet at the time of my visit, there were no signs of care. The graves were overgrown with abundant weeds. There was no signage providing an explanation of them or markers with the names of the dead. There were no fresh flowers to be seen. These sites exuded a feeling of the abject, that which has been "cast off," thrown away (Auchter 2013, 296). They were spaces that reinforced the lack of spatial incorporation of the deceased into the "proper" place of the dead (see Crossland 2002, 122).

Yet, as in the case of the RENAL site, traces of the violence of the past remain, even if they are even less visible. For instance, in front of the graves in Aisirimou stands an intriguing empty concrete marker where there had once been a plaque. According to Mario, the original plaque placed here in the 1980s—presumably by the Indonesian authorities—had claimed the dead as Indonesian "heroes." After national independence, relatives of the dead had removed it. Yet its traces remain, its material presence and concrete solidity marking what Malathi de Alwis, referring to Derrida, calls "the absence of a presence" (de Alwis 2022, 143, referring to Derrida 1974).

Caring for the RENAL dead

While much can be learned from the memorial landscape about the state's (incomplete) attempts to control the public secret of resistance violence, the picture becomes still richer if we consider the emergent vernacular memory work that is taking place around the treacherous dead. For instance, over the course of several conversations with Pedro Mendonca do Regio between 2017 and 2019, I learned a great deal about how the Remexio community's practices of caring for the RENAL dead have evolved over time, becoming increasingly more public and visible. While the building of the small cross and the preliminary rituals had calmed the restless spirits of those who died at the prison, it had also triggered new responsibilities among the living. The dead, as they were re-enfolded into the community, required ongoing care and expressed new demands.

I first met Pedro in 2017 in his small house in Lahane, Dili, where he now lives. As we sat on plastic chairs on his veranda overlooking a modest vegetable garden and drinking sweet black coffee, Pedro spoke with the air of authority that befitted his status as a member of a powerful local family in Remexio who, after his own incarceration as a reactionary, had re-joined the FALINTIL resistance until his arrest and imprisonment by the Indonesian military. Pedro has been recognized by the state for his contributions to the resistance and is now receiving a veterans' pension. During a long, open-ended conversation, he seemed happy to talk about his experiences as a FRETILIN prisoner, telling me that he had recounted the story of his incarceration to the CAVR as part of its truth-telling process and now has close links with the CAVR and its successor institute, the CNC (Centro Nacional Chega!, National Chega! Center), and Dili-based human rights organizations. Pedro now identifies as the victim of a human rights violation and speaks regularly to school groups about his experiences. During these talks he tells the students that the violence committed by FRETILIN against those in its own ranks was *aat liu* (far worse) than the violence committed by the Indonesian military. He sees these speaking engagements as part of a moral duty that will help ensure this violence will not happen again.

During this first conversation, I learned that since 2001 the families of those who died at Nundamar and the three nearby prisons have organized an annual commemoration of the dead at the cross at the top of the escarpment. Following a mass at the cross, those present descend into the *rai kuak* to light candles and place flowers for the dead. By bringing together families from across Remexio as well as from other parts of Timor-Leste whose loved ones died in these prisons, the commemoration has forged a new community united by shared experiences of grief and loss. Its goal, according to Pedro, is to educate the new generation about the "consequences of the war" (*konsekuensia funu*), consequences that were an inevitable part of the path to independence. In these ways, the annual commemoration subtly works against the exclusions and hierarchies of the dead that are inherent to the state's necro-governmental project. While it does not directly expose the public secret of FRETILIN violence, the commemoration enables its leakage into the public sphere in ways that provide space for the creation of new narratives. The dead can be reclaimed from a position of "bare life," their deaths no longer wasted or disposable but sacrifices for the nation.

Ensuring the continuity of this event has required creativity and strategic thinking. First, the community's engagement with successive local priests has been critical, offering the church's powerful endorsement and enabling the portrayal of the commemoration as a ritual of mourning rather than a political act that challenges the moral boundary between those inside and outside the political community. Second, families have chosen to remember the dead on the 12 November, the date that marks the Santa Cruz massacre. While this date bears little relation to the dates of deaths within the prison, it means that state resources for the (increasingly decentralized) Santa Cruz commemorations can be put toward food, water, and transport. As the RENAL dead are remembered alongside the martyred youth of Santa Cruz, these events are implicitly linked and interwoven into the national narrative of heroic resistance. These developments highlight how the memory of Santa Cruz has "traveled" not only internationally but also within Timor-Leste; it has been negotiated, cross-referenced, and borrowed in ways that facilitate the remembrance of other, less politically palatable traumatic "truths" (see Kent 2012).

The commemoration emboldened Pedro and other families of the dead in Remexio to do more. As in other cases where questions surround the rightfulness of the dead's deeds (as in Angelo's case discussed at the beginning of this chapter), the spirits of the dead had hopes for the rehabilitation of their names. Because they had been FRETILIN members, they sought a place in the story of the resistance and recognition as martyrs. Rehabilitation was also important to the living. Conflicting narratives and doubts regarding the dead's past actions have implications for the social status, intergenerational well-being, and financial security of the dead's families. Dispelling such doubts requires the creation of new narratives and their permeation of both local and national imaginaries (Feijó 2020, 279). For these reasons, Pedro and other families became increasingly invested in their own project of (re)structuring social responses to the dead.

Advocacy for the official rehabilitation of the names of the dead and for their recognition as martyrs has been a key element of this project. Pedro described how he and four other relatives of those who died in the Nundamar prison visited then president Xanana Gusmao at his home in Balibar in the late 2000s to request that he amend the veterans' registration process to allow those who died at the hands of the resistance to be considered for martyrs' pensions. The results of their early advocacy are reflected in the passage of a 2012 parliamentary resolution on the "Rehabilitation of East Timorese who died, were imprisoned, or suffered ill-treatment within the scope of the Timorese resistance."[8] The resolution provides for a select number of people (whose names are attached in an annex) to have access to the medals, pensions, and state burial rites through the veterans' valorization scheme. It also recommends that the "Government take the necessary steps to identify other dead Timorese, arrested, or who have suffered ill-treatment within the scope of the Timorese Resistance" to add to those on the list. Pedro's brother Annanais is among those listed. This advocacy provides another example of how the category of the martyr, and its opposite, the traitor, are negotiated "in the field" by the living and the dead. While the state has reasserted its role in ordering and bordering, redefining the distinction between the grievable and ungrievable, these efforts have also opened the door to future negotiation by former RENAL prisoners and families of dead not yet publicly rehabilitated.

The rehabilitation of the Remexio prison has been another preoccupation of families of the RENAL dead. According to Pedro, this was necessary both to educate a new generation of Timorese about the consequences of the war and to "dignify" the dead whose remains still lay below. For this a plaque inscribing the names of the dead and the circumstances in which they died would be needed. The imperative for the dead to be publicly named is a reminder that the circumstances in which they died and the inability to disinter their bodies from the mass grave has ruptured the link between name and body. In a context where the retrieval and individual identification of bones has been impossible, names might become "the traces of bones" (Auchter 2014, 70–71). Names can stand in for, or point to, the bodies of the dead. Like bodies, they can "create a community between the living and the dead," making the dead present again (Laqueur 2015, 387, 390). However, Pedro was fully aware of the sensitivities that would be raised by such a plaque. "What", he rhetorically asked, "would we write on the plaque? 'Heroes of the nation'? 'Victims of political conflict'? They didn't die at Indonesia's hands so can they be considered heroes? Who is going to make this decision?" As Pedro well knew, the discussions that would need to take place about a plaque would be potentially destabilizing of the sharp dichotomy between the traitor and martyr that lay at the heart of the state's necro-governmental project. Furthermore, more than leaking the public secret, a plaque had the potential to inscribe it in the landscape in a very public way.

Between 2017 and my next visit to Timor-Leste in 2019, families had succeeded in building a permanent monument to replace the makeshift cross at the top of the escarpment. While the national government had continued to ignore their requests for funding and support, local government officials had been prepared to acknowledge the historical significance of the former prison. The Aileu municipality government agreed in 2018 to turn the site of the RENAL prison into a historical place and provided funding toward a new cross, a plaque, and a chapel. Local Remexio families contributed funds for the purchasing of cement and marble for the cross and donated wood for the chapel. Relatives of those who died at Nundamar, Kotomori, Erluli, and Erumori contributed USD 2.50 each to have the name of their deceased family member inscribed on the plaque. There is now a plaque listing the names of thirty-seven deceased persons, restoring the link between the name and the body. The naming of the dead also ascribes them a political value. By identifying each dead person with a name, the plaque subverts the state's necro-governmental logics that would "leave them for dead," bringing them back into the political community.[9] Yet there are limits to how far the community is prepared to leak the public secret. The plaque is inscribed with the words, in Portuguese "Na Ponta da Minha Baioneta Escrevei A História da Minha Libertação" (At the point of my bayonet:

the story of my liberation from RENAL), words that carefully circumvent revealing the circumstances in which the dead died.[10]

The monument was inaugurated in late 2018 with a Catholic mass and customary rituals that involved the calling of the spirits of the dead to leave their old place below—the *rai kuak*—and come to their new home at the top of the hill, transitioning from the darkness into the light above. This was both a transference into the light of a Christian God and proper transference of the dead into the realm of the ancestors where they would finally be at peace. The living would now no longer need to make a treacherous descent into the *rai kuak* to lay flowers and light candles to the dead. Pedro explained how, following the ritual families knew the spirits arrived in their new place. Some dreamt that night that the spirits had climbed the mountain and entered the ancestral realm, while others heard drumming coming from the site of the new monument late in the evening and saw light emanating from the area. As Pedro put it, "We knew it was the spirits of the dead. So, we felt content, it was *los* (right)." The unhappy spirits of the dead, it seems, have finally been released from their prison.

It would be tempting to suggest that this is the end of the story, but I want to resist this neat ending by pointing to two factors that contribute to a lingering sense of unfinished business. First, Pedro and other families know that the thirty-seven names listed on the plaque represent only a fraction of the dead who lie below. There are, they believe, over two hundred bodies at Nundamar and the three nearby prisons. Some families were not in a financial position to provide the USD 2.50 needed to inscribe the name of their deceased relative on the plaque—an additional plaque will be needed. The many unnamed dead who have not yet been reconnected to their bodies may trouble attempts to settle this case of massive bad death. Second, the absence of invited national political leaders from the inauguration ritual disappointed many families and has left an aura of ambiguity around the status of the dead who have been named. Have they been rehabilitated or not? The spirits of the dead may well remain unruly.

Caring for the Dead of the *Funu Maun Alin*

Like the RENAL dead, the unburied UDT and Apodeti members killed by FRETILIN remain uneasy and restless. The public memorialization of these deaths—even at a highly localized scale—is perhaps even more publicly sensitive. That many of these deaths were dispersed, solitary deaths, also makes it difficult to forge a new community around specific sites. Yet these dead, too, continue to press their demands on the living. As they do so, they are activating practices from the living that seek to bring them back into the political community and care for them. In these ways, the public secret of FRETILIN violence seeps into the public realm.

One way in which this occurs is as the bodies of those killed in diverse rural locations are "accidentally" unearthed by commissions for the recovery of human remains. While the commission members argue that the responsibility for searching for the remains of UDT and Apodeti members killed during the *funu maun alin* lies with families, not the commissions, this logic breaks down in practice. As previously discussed (chapter 4), not all the identities of the dead exhumed by the commissions are known in advance. Many are *deskoñesidu* (unknown), who cannot be left in the ground lest they cause ongoing problems for local communities, such as crop failures and motorbike accidents, and prevent state road construction projects from proceeding. These bodies demand to be recovered, identified, and cared for. As they resurface, the dead reveal complex subjectivities that trouble the state's categories of martyr and traitor. Some reveal agonizing choices and sacrifices made for family and loved ones that sometimes had to override loyalties to the nation. Others expose how they were "little people" whose deaths were entangled with complex political struggles over which they had little control. They protest their innocence, presenting evidence that they, too, acutely suffered and made sacrifices for the nation. As in the case of the RENAL dead, the familial care and reburial of these accidentally unearthed bodies may not in itself be enough to bring peace to their spirits or to the living. The ambiguities and conflicting narratives that leave residues of doubt about the rightfulness of the dead's deeds require responses not only from the dead's local communities but also from the state, responses that rehabilitate their names. The dead push for a resignification of their deaths; far from being worthless or wasted, they were consequences of the war, an inevitable part of the struggle. In these ways they trouble their exclusion from the state's heroic narrative.

The leakage of the public secret also takes place as the living are impelled to develop improvised rituals of reconciliation to "clean" (*hamoos*) the "mistakes" of the past through public performances of confession. These rituals, which involve cases of FRETILIN, UDT, and Apodeti violence, are being devised in some divided communities where large numbers of bad deaths were experienced during the *funu maun alin* and where the dead can cause disruption to well-being on a large scale. Here the living are continually reminded that these bad deaths disrupt the flow of life, the connections between houses, and relationships between new generations (see Palmer 2021, 123; Babo-Soares 2004). The future will not unfold in the right way. These rituals involve a "complicated alchemy of remembering, forgetting and remembering to forget" that is as intrinsic to the remaking of local social and political worlds as it is to the remaking of a national political community (Theidon 2006b, 98). They appear to be made possible through what Kimberly Theidon (2006b, 48) refers to as a "cultural logic of exteriority." Drawing on long-term fieldwork in Peru, Theidon describes this as a logic that imagines "bad things" as arriving from elsewhere, allowing the "causes of sociopolitical problems to be located outside the boundaries of the community" (Theidon 2006b, 89). In the case of the *funu maun alin*, this logic allows affected communities to imagine themselves as the *ema ki'ik* (little people), the ordinary East Timorese who had little political understanding or control over the course of events and suffered at the hands of the political divisions and top-down decisions of the *ema bo'ot* (the big people, resistance elite who are now Dili-based political leaders). By creating what Theidon (2006a, 388) refers to as "histories of innocence," reconciliation becomes possible between "intimate enemies."

In Ermera, for instance, local veterans organized a ceremony in 2017 to foster reconciliation among local members of the five historic political parties and their descendants. The ritual took place at the river (Mota Mau Oso), regarded as *lulik*. Local accounts tell of how buffalo and pigs were slaughtered by the riverside, their blood mixed into the river water. *Lulik* objects were brought by families of victims and perpetrators, contributing to the ritual's power. Local representatives of the five political parties accepted responsibility for the mistakes of the past, removed their clothes and plunged into the water as a *lia nain* spoke words to bring about a "*matak malirin* (greening coolness)", a flourishing of good health and vitality (Palmer 2021, 123). The rain that came that night was a sign, according to one participant, that the *malirin* (cool) had arrived. "We have been cleaned. It will no longer be hot."[11]

Other communities have turned to the recently established Centro National Chega! (CNC, the successor organization of the CAVR) to support their local reconciliation rituals. The CNC offers a new language of victims' rights and "truth telling" as a vehicle for national reconciliation as well as important logistical support and an imprimatur of officialdom. Yet communities are carefully controlling the truth that is told and repurposing the CNC's "national" reconciliation focus by addressing the complex *local* impacts of the *funu maun alin* and their legacies. Space is made for the representatives of local political parties and families to speak and for perpetrators to make confessions. Tragic stories of how families were torn apart, and of how fathers killed their own sons, have been told publicly in these spaces for the first time, again by imagining the local community as the *ema ki'ik*.[12]

Through these rituals, communities are engaging in their own forms of sociopolitical reordering that weave the violence of the *funu maun alin* into a narrative of the "consequences of the war." These rituals help to "clean" the mistakes of the past and usher in a "greening coolness" that recalibrates relationships among divided families and communities. However, as with the rituals around the RENAL prison in Remexio, there remains a question mark over their completeness and rehabilitative potential. The absence of national political leaders from them, despite repeated invitations, and the failure of such leaders to devise their own rituals of truth telling and reconciliation is, once again, commonly expressed as a disappointment.[13] All of this suggests that the intricate dance of "revelation and concealment" (Surin 2001, 206) of the public secret of FRETILIN violence will continue as the dead and the living question the grounds for entry into the political community.

Conclusion

This chapter has shown how the vernacular memory work that responds to the treacherous dead, while not revealing, exposing, or destroying the public secret of resistance violence, is allowing it to leak into the public sphere in ways that enable a recognition of the dead's suffering and sacrifices and their reincorporation into the local and national community. This occurs as the human remains of those who died in the *funu maun alin* inadvertently resurface through exhumations undertaken by commissions for the recovery of human remains. It also takes place as families and communities are provoked to respond to the localized intergenerational and community misfortunes caused by unhappy spirits, through memorials and reconciliation rituals. As the dead become materially present as bones or as names inscribed on a plaque, or are made audible through community discussions, they testify that their bad deaths were a consequence of the war and that they continue to suffer. Their suffering must be repaid in the form of proper burial, rehabilitation of their names, and recognition of their sacrifices, requiring actions not only by their families and communities but also by the state.

The unmarked and abject graves at Aisirimou are a reminder that there are limits to the extent to which the public secret can be negotiated. Yet even in here, where publicly visible forms of care, consolation, and recognition do not seem possible, the dead are not entirely absent. By leaving these traces of mass graves unmarked, the state leaves these bodies "for dead," reminding the living that they must continue to "know what not to know." Yet this absence, this "carefully crafted invisibility of the public secret" (Auchter 2014, 56), is itself a reminder that certain lives and deaths are privileged above others.

In these ways the unhappy and restless spirits of those killed by FRETILIN continue to unsettle the state's necro-governmental project that designates them publicly ungrievable, using them only to harness them within a collective, linear, state-sanctioned narrative of "coming together." They help define the conditions by which lives are deemed visible and grievable and count as political lives, questioning the preconditions for entrance to the political community and pushing for a more inclusive and democratizing narrative of what constitutes sacrifices for the nation. Not only that—they remind the living of their *continuing* suffering, that the violence of the early years of the occupation is not yet over.

Conclusion

The dead are omnipresent in Timor-Leste. They are symbols and matter, objects of collective memorialization and mourning, subjects embedded in thick social relations, and unruly and unknowable spirits. In all these guises—and especially in their spirit form—they are lively participants in social and political life. Far from simply being metaphors that persist in memories and stories, or passive symbols harnessed for state building, they are agential beings who "insist on active relations with the living" (Langford 2013, 210). Not only do they deplore the Indonesian necropower that dismembered them from their families and communities; they also push back against the violence of the state's necro-governmental logics that would contain or exclude them.

The Unruly Dead began its story in Dili, the heartland of the state's necro-governmental project. By moving beyond the state-sponsored commemorations of the Santa Cruz massacre and attending to the multiple scales and spaces where memory work takes place, I established that the legacies of this case of massive bad death are not, as they appear at first glance, contained and tamed, assigned to a past temporality. While the young people who died during the massacre have become central to the imagining of a new state and held up as instructive figures to the youth of today, the spirits of those whose bodies have not been recovered prevent the narrative of Santa Cruz from being fully co-opted by the state. The dead deem their treatment as "mere symbols" of the nation insufficient, demanding the recovery of their bodies, a recognition of their distinct personhood and suffering, and their inclusion in "any rites held in their name" as "full participants" (Traube 2020, 13).

As the book moved both figuratively and geographically away from the metropole, the demands of restless spirits whose bodies have not been recovered became even more omnipresent, more difficult to ignore. In the towns and the hinterlands, and the variegated topography of the Badlands that is interspersed within them, the living dwell among the dead. Amid uncertain economic conditions and precarious livelihoods, the restless and unhappy spirits of the dead who remain scattered in the landscape impede the rebuilding of interpersonal and kinship relations and disrupt intergenerational well-being and prosperity in profound and material ways. The dead catalyze urgent practices of recovery, reburial, and care.

It also became clear that those who are excluded from the state's category of martyrdom activate a complex necropolitics, setting in train projects that push for their inclusion in this category while destabilizing its narrow, militarized, masculine boundaries. The civilians who died during the Liquiçá church massacre, the dispersed dead civilians who died in the mountains and forests from hunger and disease, and those who were killed by the East Timorese resistance demand not only proper burial and familial care but also the official recognition of their suffering and sacrifices. As they are cared for, mourned, and reintegrated into the national and local community, a tentative space is also opened for those who have been marginalized and ungrievable to be visible and acknowledged.

The Limits of Re-membering: The Missing Body

A key thread running through the chapters is that spirits of those who died bad deaths in Timor-Leste demand not so much to be remembered but *re*-membered, "gathered in" (Renshaw 2010) from their abject and neglected state in the literal and figurative forests and mountains to be re-enfolded within their networks of kin and community. I have shown that this re-membering, while profoundly important for the remaking of social and political order, also has a fragile, restless, and contingent quality.

The re-membering of Timor-Leste's dead is, to be sure, settling many restless spirits. It is allowing some of the dead to transition from dangerous and unpredictable spirits into benevolent ancestors, making some dangerous landscapes less dangerous. In cases where bodies cannot be found or where they are comingled in mass graves in ways that prevent their individualized recovery and identification, creative practices of calling the spirits of the dead to the sites where violence was done to their bodies and coaxing them to infuse soil and rocks are taking place. These substances then become the "bodies" of the dead. Far from transforming the dead into passive, mute, inert substances, as the dead tangibly receive the material care given to their body, they are able to care for the living, entering into continuing, reciprocal relations with them (see Grenfell 2020, 147; see also Langford 2009; 2013). Similar practices are taking place across other Southeast Asian societies marked by legacies of massive bad death. Caroline Bennett (2018, 184–85) for example has traced how, in Cambodia, the dead from the Khmer Rouge era are being "brought in" from "'the forest'—the wild and untamed post-conflict environment of insecurity and fear," to be reintegrated into the social lives of the living. This is allowing these ghosts to metamorphose from "frightened and frightening entities of haunting into benevolent allies in the reconstruction of post–Khmer Rouge Cambodia" (Bennett 2018, 184–85).

I am cautious about suggesting a linear and reparative trajectory to the re-membering of Timor-Leste's dead. The massive scale of bad death during the Indonesian occupation seems to exceed the capacities of the living to contain it. Furthermore, the "excessive indeterminacies" that imbue Timor-Leste's dead, in their entangled spectral and material presence, profoundly unsettle the living. The dead seem to demand urgent attempts to recover their bodies and stabilize their meanings and identities, while also rendering such attempts contingent, never "fully and finally complete" (Fontein 2014; 2022, 32). Even in cases where bodies can be recovered or where substitute rituals can be undertaken to transform them from unruly beings into protective ancestors, the outcome of such rituals is not certain.[1] Furthermore, as discussed in the case of Angelo and the RENAL victims of resistance violence (chapter 5), the dead, while welcoming rituals to settle their spirits, may ask for more, activating a new set of obligations among the living, setting in train what Langford (2016, 37) refers to as the "bottomless quality to reciprocity with the dead."

The fragility and contingency of re-membering is further complicated by those spirits who cannot be "gathered in" from the mountains and forests. In cases where the location of remains is not known, families do not always have the resources to conduct the expensive rituals required to call their restless spirits and safely settle them. Their spiritual leaders will not always permit such rituals. And some restless spirits have no living family members to call them. The gathering in of the dead is also uneven: shaped by unequal relations of power. Just as some bodies and some spaces are being reclaimed, others are neglected, relegated to the margins of local and national imaginaries. Yet this does not dispel their power. There remain lingering uncertainties and anxieties about disordered landscapes, where bodies of the dead lie just under the surface. The spirits attached to such bodies remain in a protracted liminal realm. They inhabit areas such as the salt lake in Liquiçá, the hinterlands around Natarbora, and the diverse sites in the landscape where people were killed in the *funu maun alin* (war of brothers). These spaces remain charged and potentially dangerous, causing motorbike accidents and making land "hot," difficult to cultivate.

Missing bodies are also a problem for the state. Their excessive indeterminacies exceed containment within the secular necro-governmental logics that are key to the forward-looking project of state building. The scattered bodies of those who died dispersed deaths in the mountains and forests interrupt, in a material sense, the construction of new roads through rural landscapes that are integral to imaginings of modern development. The dead may also resurface during the construction of luxury hotels as occurred during the 2010 construction of the "Pelican Paradise Resort" in Tacitolu, on the outskirts of Dili, when nine blindfolded bodies were accidentally unearthed.[2] These unpredictably resurfacing bodies provide material *evidence* that the violence of the Indonesian occupation is not firmly in the past but remains a potent presence in the present. These dead continue to make their unhappiness and their disruptive presence felt. They cannot, as Auchter (2023, 120) puts it, be "bought off, threatened, or silenced," and as such interrupt "the disciplinary shape of stories told about them" (Langford 2013, 211).

While the myriad ways in which missing bodies interrupt or escape the state's necro-governmental logics has been a theme throughout this book, let me briefly revisit and expand on two cases touched on in earlier chapters that illustrate how "the missing" can block, in quite direct ways, a national political agenda that aims to consolidate a collective memory of the Indonesian occupation and orient the living to the future. The first example concerns the state's attempts to memorialize key resistance figure Nicolau Lobato. As discussed (chapter 1), a monument of Lobato looms large in the urban landscape of Dili, standing just outside the airport at the intersection to the road into town, a commanding, material embodiment of the state's heroic narrative. Yet this monument is mirrored by another powerful, yet incomplete, monument on the other side of Dili: Lobato's empty tomb, which lies at the apex of the Metinaro Garden of Heroes cemetery, indexing the failure of the state to locate and recover his remains more than forty years since his death.

While Lobato was allegedly killed by Indonesian forces in 1978 in the mountains outside Dili, his unrecovered body has an active and unsettling absent presence that generates continual speculation and circulating rumors. A widely held narrative is that the Indonesian military is concealing information about its location and that his head, severed from his body, was taken to Indonesia as a war trophy. From time to time, human remains that are claimed to be Lobato's "resurface," yet far from creating clarity this generates new questions and uncertainties. For example, in 2003 when remains without a skull were found in the backyard of then prime minister Mari Alkatiri in Dili, speculation

Nicolau Lobato's empty tomb in the Garden of Heroes, Metinaro. Photo by author (2023).

arose as to whether they were Lobato's. Bone fragments sent by the United Nations to the Northern Territory Police in Darwin, Australia, for forensic DNA testing were, however, returned without a clear result. Later, the International Forensic Team conducted further tests on the samples that, again, were inconclusive.[3]

The material presence of Lobato's empty tomb, the circulating rumors that surround the whereabouts of his (shockingly dismembered) body, and Lobato's unhappy and restless spirit generate profound uncertainties that interrupt state building and the crafting of new bilateral relations with Indonesia. Timor-Leste's political leaders are caught in a bind as the desire to maintain the bilateral relationship must be continually weighed against the imperative to dignify Lobato by burying his remains in the Garden of Heroes. This prompts intermittent, yet tentative, diplomatic requests for Indonesia to reveal the whereabouts of those remains. That Lobato—perhaps the nation's most significant martyr—has not yet been made "whole," that his body is not yet properly buried and honored, blocks the reconstitution of the political order (see Rojas-Perez 2017, 45). More than this: Lobato's unhappy and restless spirit is widely regarded as a *contributing* factor to ongoing political instability and lack of economic progress in the new nation-state.

The second example of how missing bodies can block the state's necrogovernmental project is the 2018 Kore Metan Nasional (national end of mourning). As discussed in chapter 1, this initiative was aimed at providing a collective, national ritual of symbolic recognition for all those who died during the occupation that would curtail locally led practices of searching for and recovering the dead and encourage the living to focus on the future. Yet it was roundly rejected by citizens on the basis that it was not yet "time" for a *kore metan*—there were still missing bodies that demanded individualized care and proper burial.

In the wake of the ill-devised Kore Metan Nasional, the state has recently embarked on an elaborate new nationwide program to manage the destabilizing presence of missing bodies. The Ministry for Veterans Affairs has developed a questionnaire that seeks to come up with a definitive number of those who died during the conflict as well as details on where and how they died. As with the Kore Metan Nasional, an aim seems to be to end expensive and time-consuming local practices of gathering human remains. State officials are also concerned about the ever-expanding number of claims for martyrs' pensions and the growing number of funding proposals from local commissions for the recovery of human remains for food, transport, coffins, ambulances, new cemeteries, rituals, and upgrades to ossuaries.[4] The questionnaire is being taken to each family's *uma lulik* (sacred house), where families are enlisting the expertise of ritual leaders to fill it in, who, in turn, are communicating with the ancestral realm to determine the "accurate" information. Once the dead have been counted, families will be asked to call the spirits of the missing dead to infuse a small rock from their ancestral land. These rocks will collectively form the plinths of new monuments to be built in each *posto* (subdistrict), providing a centralized place to care for and remember those whose bodies remain missing.

Compared with the Kore Metan Nasional, this initiative has a more "bottom-up" flavor and involves the spirits of the dead as active agents. It is a creative response that, in a context of constrained resources and political imperatives, might allow the living and the dead to engage in a new form of relational and collective truth telling, a counting and accounting for those who lost their lives through communication with the spirit realm. Yet, just as with the Kore Metan Nasional, the aim of "resolving" the legacies of massive bad death once and for all, and drawing the dead into centralized, state-sanctioned places of memory, seems destined to failure. There are already signs that this initiative is generating new uncertainties and activating a new set of debates.[5] The dead are likely to remain unruly.

Transforming necro-governmentality

Timor-Leste's dead are not only disrupting or escaping the state's necro-governmental logics. They are also *transforming* those logics by activating new spaces of memory, new communities, and new social and political practices. By decentering the state and paying attention to the memory work of a multiplicity of actors—veterans' groups, survivors' groups, NGOs, families of the dead—I have been able to bring these transformative capacities into view.

A key thread running through the chapters is that while the state's necro-governmental project is introducing new militarized, martyr subjectivities and discourses and new spaces for the containment and remembering of the dead, it is not displacing a familial ethics of care. Instead, it is providing the basis on which new relationships between the living and the dead are being forged. Furthermore, this project seems to be intensifying the demands of the dead and changing the nature of their demands by introducing new prospects for the official recognition of their unacknowledged suffering and sacrifices. As we have seen, ongoing citizen-led practices of searching for the dead are leading an increasing number of dead bodies to resurface and to a growing number of claims for martyr status. In these ways, the state's logics and technologies of necro-governmentality are *enlivening* the dead, providing new opportunities for them to make their demands felt. These demands are integrally entangled with the rapid change and unpredictable dynamics of state building and the new anxieties, expectations, and forms of precarity it is producing (even if they are not simply symptoms of the concerns of the living).

As the dead resurface, they are difficult to ignore. While their potent spectral presence may have dissipated, they gain an affective and visible *material* presence that raises new uncertainties and new questions about what is to be done about their identification, reburial, and recognition. They become drawn into a complex necropolitical terrain where other actors (for instance veterans' groups) seek to harness their power for their own political projects and where the dead remain their own unruly source of power. The civilian dead, those who died in massacres, FRETILIN prisons, and those who died painful, lonely, and dispersed deaths in the mountains and forests where they were left uncared for, testify to the suffering and sacrifices of the *povu kiik* during the Indonesian occupation. As the dead and the living push for recognition of that suffering and those sacrifices, they work toward the enlargement of the category of the martyr. Even those who are reburied in the Gardens of Heroes do not become a passive and compliant community of fixed martyr subjects but leak out of the orderly spaces designed to contain them, demanding ongoing reciprocal relations with their kin.

The interplay between diverse necro-governmental logics and forms of power is also creating new spaces of memory. These include the spaces created by the ritual lighting of candles in Dili neighborhoods in the evening after the formal Santa Cruz commemoration; the annual gathering around the Angel memorial in Liquiçá to remember those who died in the Liquiçá church massacre; the mini-museum in Natarbora where families come to touch the objects associated with the dead; and the Natarbora ossuary, where people from all districts visit their dead on the 3rd of November. The memorial in Remexio, where families from around Timor-Leste visit to re-member and care for those who died in the FRETILIN "rehabilitation" prison is another new space of memory. These spaces are not the monumental spaces of national commemoration, nor are they the dangerous, unpredictable spaces of landscapes inhabited by restless spirits. They go beyond the intimate space of kinship relations. They are spaces where new communities of the living and the dead, united by shared experiences of violated socialities, are being formed and where reciprocal forms of care can take place.

These new spaces of memory are not simply spaces of care and repair. They are also spaces where the silences and exclusions of the state's necro-governmental project can be navigated and at times subtly challenged. They are spaces that keep alive the need to address *continuing* losses and absences, maintaining a demand for absent bodies to be made present (see Walker, 2015, 111).

They are spaces where the civilian dead remind the living of the state's unfulfilled obligations to the *povu kiik* (small people) who lost their lives during the long struggle for independence, activating practices of monument construction and advocacy for plaques and pensions that are expanding the official category of the martyr. They are also spaces that work against the imposition of national memorial narratives and official sites of collective remembrance, spaces where the multiple stories and everyday dimensions of resistance, struggle, and suffering become present. These spaces reveal the intimate and the political to be entangled and co-constituting, shaped by the relational interactions of the living and the dead.

Rethinking Postconflict Peace Building

How does this study of vernacular memory work invite different ways of thinking about the remaking of social and political order after mass violence? Two points stand out. First, this book destabilizes liberal narratives of peace building and transitional justice that promise the containment of massive bad death through prosecutions, truth telling, exhumations, reburials, and memorialization so that the living can move on, a state built. The evolving vernacular memory work taking place in Timor-Leste is a reminder of the limits of narratives of "resolution" and "closure" when it comes to massive bad death and missing bodies. This work seems to embody a demand for "a more ethical relation to the past," rejecting the idea of the past as something "dead," as something that automatically "distances" from the present (Bevernage 2012, 348), and reminding the state that the violence of the Indonesian occupation is not over and done with, contained and controlled. This demand challenges scholars to develop more open-ended narratives of peace building that do not assume a linear trajectory or make a stark delineation between life and death, acknowledging the continuing presence of the past in the present.

Second, and crucially, the book insists that more attention needs to be paid to the power of the dead to act on the living. Timor-Leste's dead have shown that they are not simply substances to be harnessed in the service of political ends, or problematic symbolic legacies of traumatic events of the past that must be managed through counting, management, exhumation, reburial, and recognition. Just as the living work with the dead, enrolling them in diverse projects of sociopolitical reordering, the dead, in their emotive materiality and their affective presence, work on the living. They provoke uncertainties that are not always easily resolvable and always threaten to overwhelm any "political utility" they may have (Fontein 2014, 134). As they catalyze diverse responses, they raise new questions about suffering, sacrifice, and reward as well as whose lives (and deaths) matter in the national imaginary. Put another way, Timor-Leste's dead push for new understandings of "the political" that encompass a community of the living and the dead.

These insights are not simply theoretical but push for new forms of research and engagement on postconflict interventions. There is growing interest in the political import of local memory work in conflict-affected societies: in how practices of memorialization and commemoration can be both an agent and an obstacle to social change (for example, see Brown 2013; Gutman and Wustenberg 2023). Scholarly work on "necropolitical activism" (Leshem 2015) or "corpse politics" (Verdery 1999, 108)—on how funerals and other staged practices around dead bodies can challenge the national and global politics that lead to the erasure and abandonment of certain categories of the dead—is also burgeoning (see, for example, Stumer 2018). These studies, while insightful, have tended to focus on the agency of the living and their conscious and deliberate actions, neglecting the dead. There needs to be more attention to the dead as unpredictable agents in memory work and necropolitical activism, agents who may drive these processes in unexpected directions. This in turn opens up new avenues for thinking about social and political change. As the idea of the "individual [living human] knower as an autonomous centre of coherent thought and action" (Brigg 2016, 2) is disrupted, it is possible for a renewed orientation to the many interconnected elements and actors that can "support destructive relations to shift or new patterns of political order to emerge" (Brown 2020, 428).

The book also calls for a rethinking of postconflict interventions concerned with the search, exhumation, and identification of human remains. Over the past two decades there has been a notable rise in mass grave exhumations as part of international human rights investigations in the aftermath of mass violence, connected to the global expansion in human rights discourse and practice and significant advances in DNA technology (Ferrandiz and Robben 2015, 6–9). It is now a widespread assumption that families have a "right to know" what has happened to their loved ones and that recovering human remains will also benefit the society as a whole by addressing traumatic legacies of mass violence (Moon 2014, 52; Rojas-Perez 2015, 192).[6] Some scholars have heralded a "forensic turn" that is characterized by "the arrival of forensic pathologists and anthropologists on the scene of mass violence and genocide as the decisive agents of practice in the search for bodies" and in the assembling of the "truth" about the circumstances of their deaths (Anstett and Dreyfus 2015, 4; see also

Dziuban 2017). Facilitating this "turn" is the movement of forensic professionals, along with their expertise, their equipment, and their ideas around the globe (Anstett and Dreyfus 2015, 4).

The book pushes scholars and practitioners to think critically about the possibilities and limits of the forensic turn. It serves as a reminder, first, that this shift is far from global. As we have seen, international forensic investigations have not been prioritized in Timor-Leste, just as they have not been prioritized in many other countries in the Global South, underscoring the degree to which such investigations are entangled in histories of inequality and colonialism, in which some bodies have always been treated differently from others. As Rosenblatt (2015, 29) bluntly puts it, there are enormous disparities between "the effort and expense spent on the identification of relatively light-skinned bodies in countries considered part of (or on the doorstep of) the West, compared with the effort and expense put into identifying dark-skinned bodies in non-Western countries."[7]

Second, the book raises questions about the extent to which internationally supported searches for missing bodies necessarily contribute to the healing of individuals and the peace of postconflict societies (see Anstett and Dreyfus 2015, 6). In Timor-Leste, the exhumations conducted by the SCIU and framed within a narrow prosecutorial paradigm *complicated* processes of healing and peace building. At the time of the closure of the SCIU in 2003, 250 sets of human remains relating to the unit's investigations of 1999 crimes were handed over to the Timor-Leste government. They are currently being stored in shipping containers on the grounds of the Dili district hospital, slowly decomposing due to frequent electricity breakdowns. In a context where the Timor-Leste government has neither the funding nor the inclination to complete the forensic analysis required for their identity to be established in accordance with accepted international standards, these leaky transforming substances and unsettled and dangerous spirits remain a troubling potent legacy of international justice in Timor-Leste.[8]

Even investigations underpinned by a paradigm of forensic humanitarianism oriented toward families' needs have raised as many issues as they have solved. As the case of the Santa Cruz exhumations led by the International Forensic Team (chapter 2) showed, some families were not prepared to trust forensic DNA technologies if the findings contradicted their own relational and embodied knowledge of the dead acquired through dreams. As they grew frustrated with the slow pace and lack of results of the IFT's work, they hired an excavator and began to conduct their own digging. It seems likely that any future organized searches for the dead will, far from creating resolution, only bring to the fore diverse and sometimes competing forms of "expertise" as relatives of the dead, spiritual leaders, veterans' groups, and politicians each bring with them their own sensibilities, loyalties, interests, knowledge, and interpretations (see Fontein 2022, 29).

For these reasons, it is vital that scholars and practitioners pay more attention to the "complex terrain" opened up by the interplay of scientific and vernacular knowledge, political interests and struggles, and the emotive materiality of human remains themselves (see Dziuban 2017). There is also a need to go beyond calls for more resources for exhumations, the counting of the dead, and memorials to remember them, to consider how the dead might be included, not simply as objects, but as subjects of these interventions.[9]

Localized practices of exhuming and identifying the dead also need more attention. As we have seen, in a context of limited support from the state and international actors, East Timorese have evinced an extraordinary capacity to respond to the profound disruptions and unsettling legacies of massive bad death through their own evolving ritual practices. Practices that involve communication with the spirit realm, the interpretation of dreams and embodied experiences, and "testing the blood" (*koko ran*) are critical to the remaking of social and political worlds even as they challenge scientific "truths" and their narratives of objectivity and reliability. These practices are bringing the dead in from the mountains and forests even when the bodies themselves cannot be found. They are also allowing for the establishment and binding of individuated and relational identity with specific human remains and other substances. Diverse practices of citizen-led forensics are taking place in other parts of the world (see Cruz-Santiago 2020 on Mexico; Reineke 2022 on the U.S.-Mexico border; Fontein 2014, 2022 on Zimbabwe; Ngo 2021 on Vietnam; Rudling and Duenas 2021 on Colombia). There is much that can be learned from these practices about alternative understandings of truth, justice, and peace, which could help avoid an overprivileging of exhumation and identification models based on international forensic expert assistance. Even in societies where there are strong calls for such assistance, the massive scale of bad death and the limited resources that are often available in such contexts will mean that only a small percentage of deaths will conceivably be investigated through forensic means (see Cruz-Santiago 2020, 365).

Final Reflections: The Agential Dead in Timor-Leste and Beyond

As I draw this book to a close, I would like to briefly revisit my reasons for bringing the dead to the center of this study of vernacular memory work and ascribing them agency. Could I not have written this book by focusing on the living? Hasn't a focus on the agency of the dead detracted from a full consideration of the agency of the living and their political, social, and economic struggles? No. To take the agential dimensions of the dead seriously *is* to take seriously the experiences and knowledge of a people who have been systematically marginalized.[10] Had I occluded the dead from this story, I would not have done justice to the profoundly unsettling and dismembering experiences of the Indonesian occupation and their material, affective, and spectral reverberations into the present. I would like to think that by expanding the scope and subjects of memory work, and moving beyond traditional Western constructs of agency, subjectivity, and materiality, it has been possible to gain a deeper insight into what is at stake for a community of the living and the dead. This book is an attempt to center the dead in debates on memorialization, recognition, reward, social repair, and state formation: to take them seriously, not simply as objects or as stand-ins for the trauma and sacrifices of the living but as members of the political community as well. I would also like to think it has fostered a richer understanding of the diverse actors and interests involved in necropolitics.

Finally, my aim in writing this book is not to hold up Timor-Leste as a case of radical otherness that reinscribes difference between the Global North and the Global South. I hope that this book might also raise new questions and prompt new ways of thinking about the legacies of settler colonialism in the Global North. Writing of the U.S., Jean Langford (2013, 211) invites us to consider "the spirits of those who died in national sacrifice or national terror in order to initiate and sustain U.S. democracy and capitalism: African slaves; soldiers and civilians in numerous wars; countless early residents of this continent, dead from smallpox, shrinking lands, heartbreak, alcohol, bullets." She suggests that all these dead "belong to a U.S. nation-state of mind; all these uneasy ghosts are part of a repressed story of national freedom."

In Australia, where I live, the unknown numbers of First Nations people who died during the "Frontier Wars" of shootings, poisonings, introduced disease, and starvation might likewise be understood as part of our repressed story of nationhood.[11] While the presence of restless spirits may feel less immediate here than in Timor-Leste, and there is even less space for them to make their demands felt in our secular, modernist imaginings of statehood, these spirits have not been dispelled. They continue to haunt the state, disrupting attempts to define, once and for all, which deaths are valued by the nation (ANZAC deaths, not Frontier War deaths). These dead also possess a powerful *material* presence that pushes for actions to redress the violence that was a consequence of their original theft, challenging systematic injustices at the heart of colonialism (see Fforde et al. 2022; Kent et al. forthcoming).[12] Acknowledging these dead as part of our social and political worlds might enable us to engage more fully with the *continuing* violence of settler colonization and develop more complex narratives of our own state formation.

Across Timor-Leste, human remains and unhappy restless spirits are being brought in from the forests, mountains, and mass graves. The work of searching, exhumation, reburial, and commemoration is allowing the dead to be remembered as part of their families and communities and to engage in reciprocal forms of care. It is also generating a complex necropolitics as the dead push back against state-building logics that would contain or exclude them. In their potent spectrality and their emotive materiality, the dead are prompting urgent actions from the living that are making a tentative space for those whose lives have been marginalized, invisible, or ignored to be visible, grievable, acknowledged. They are also pushing for a more ethical relationship to the past, rejecting the idea that the massive bad death of the Indonesian occupation is over, distant from the present.

This book highlights the need to take seriously the profoundly disruptive legacies of massive bad death and the urgent responses they provoke from the living. These legacies are experienced in Timor-Leste as the demands of unhappy and restless spirits for proper burial, recognition, and care. Studies of postconflict recovery and rebuilding have not taken the dead seriously. Their agential dimensions and their political implications have been underexplored. Timor-Leste's dead have revealed themselves to be not simply evidence of past harm, symbols to be deployed in political projects, or substances that must be managed and contained; they are members of the political community, participants in the ongoing remaking of social and political worlds.

Glossary

ai laran	forests
adat	custom
Apodeti	Associação Popular Democrática Timorense, Popular Democratic Association of Timor
bases de apoio	resistance support bases
biru	protective amulet
bua malus	betel nut
CAVR	Comissão de Acolhimento, Verdade e Reconciliação de Timor Leste, Commission for Reception, Truth, and Reconciliation
CNC	Centro Nacional Chega!, National Chega! Center, the successor institute to the CAVR
CNRT	Conselho Nacional de Resistência Timorense, National Council of Timorese Resistance
CNV	National Veterans Council
deskoñesidu	unknown [dead bodies]
estafeta	messenger during the East Timorese resistance
FALINTIL	Forças Armadas da Libertação Nacional de Timor-Leste, Armed Forces for the National Liberation of East Timor
foho	mountains
F-FDTL	Falintil-Forcas de Defesa de Timor-Leste, Timor-Leste Armed Forces
FRETILIN	Frente Revolucionária de Timor-Leste Independente, Revolutionary Front for an Independent East Timor
funu maun alin	war of brothers (internal political conflict)

IFT	International Forensic Team
kamarada	comrade
koko ran	testing the blood ("traditional DNA")
kore metan	taking off the black (a ritual that customarily takes place a year after death to signify the end of the mourning period)
Kore Metan Nasional	National End to Mourning (government initiative)
lia nain	ritual expert, "custodian of the words"
lulik	sacred, taboo, hidden
maluk	close friend
matan do'ok	ritual expert, literally, "one who can see far"
mate ruin	bones of the dead
mate restu	survivor, literally, "leftovers from the dead"
populasaun patisipativa	participating population
posto	administrative post, subdistrict
povu ki'ik	small people, ordinary people
rai nain	spirit owners of land
Rate La'ek	Without Graves (widows' group in Liquiçá)
RENAL	National Rehabilitation Prison
RENETIL	Resistência Nacional dos Estudantes de Timor-Leste, National Resistance of East Timorese Students
SCIU	Serious Crimes Investigations Unit
suco, suku	village
tais	traditional East Timorese woven cloth
traidor	traitor
UDT	União Democrática Timorense, Timorese Democratic Union
ukun rasik an	self-government
uma lulik	spirit house, sacred house
uma mahon	shade house, protective house (for the dead)
UNTAET	United Nations Transitional Administration in East Timor

Notes

Introduction

1. See Robert Cribb (2001) for a discussion of how the number two hundred thousand was arrived at, and John Roosa (2007) for a discussion of the difficulties of determining a precise number of deaths.

2. Interview in Natarbora, November 2017.

3. My fieldwork was funded by an Australian Research Council Discovery Early Career Researcher Award (DE150100857). The ethical aspects of the project were approved by the Australian National University Human Ethics Research Committee. In most cases, interviewees elected to be identified by name. In a small number of cases, I have disguised people's identities by using a pseudonym.

Chapter 1. From Necropower to Necro-governmentality

1. See Government Press Release, "Extraordinary Meeting of the Council of Ministers on August 25th, 2015," Dili, 25 August 2015. http://timor-leste.gov.tl/?p=13122&lang=en&lang=en.

2. See Government Press Release, "Celebration of Desluto Nacional," Dili, 4 September 2015. http://timor-leste.gov.tl/?p=13180&lang=tp.

3. Kelly Silva (2017) has made a similar argument about the government's instrumentalization of *tara bandu* ritual practices to engage people in the market economy.

4. These terms have been understood differently by different authors. For a discussion, see Huttunen (forthcoming), 33.

5. The justification given for such support was a concern that East Timor would become a communist state used as a base for incursions by unfriendly powers into Indonesia and could inspire secessionist sentiments across the Indonesian archipelago.

6. Hannah Loney's monograph provides a vivid account of the impact of this period in women's lives. In it, Luisa Gonzaga recounts her experiences of walking from Tutuala to Mount Matebian during this period, explaining, "People just collapsed and died as they were walking." The others had to step over the corpses, "even if it was your

mother or father, your husband or your children—it didn't matter, you just had to keep going because the enemy was coming" (Loney 2018, 54).

7. The CAVR (2005, chapter 7.3) estimates that between 84,200 and 183,000 people died in the famine, which lasted from 1977 to 1979.

8. There are resonances with the early Catholic missions during Portuguese times. These missions, even as they coerced East Timorese to abandon their beliefs in *lulik*, burned sacred houses, and erected crosses on *lulik* land, did not, in the end, succeed. Rather, as Judith Bovensiepen argues, the planting of Catholic signs, including crosses, was regarded not as replacing *lulik* but, rather, as evidence of the strength of the spiritually potent landscape (Bovensiepen 2009, 329).

9. The idea of sacrifice resonates with both nationalist and Catholic understandings of this concept, while also gaining its purchase by connecting with widespread "normative beliefs around reciprocity" that foreground the state's obligations to care for those who struggled, suffered, and gave their lives for the nation (Roll 2020, 312). As Elizabeth Traube (2011, 135) suggests, according to the ideology of animist rituals, "those who suffer to bring something forth must be repaid for their 'fatigue' (*kolen*)."

10. The resistance is commonly understood to be divided into three "fronts": the armed front, the clandestine front, and the diplomatic front.

11. Constitution of the Democratic Republic of Timor-Leste (English translation), section 11.

12. National Parliament Decree Law 3/2006, Statute of the National Liberation Combatants, as amended by Law 9/2009 of 29 July 2009, article 4.

13. Ibid.

14. The original legislation lists five privileged organisations: FRETILIN, FALINTIL, CRRN, CNRM, and CNRT, constructing a cluster of "true" or "core" resistance organizations. This marginalized armed FALINTIL splinter groups, such as Sagrada Familia; clandestine groups, such as National Resistance of Timorese Students (RENETIL); and informal networks. In 2009 the parliament amended the law to allow for membership in other organizations recognized by the leadership of these five groups (Roll 2014, 104).

15. See Government Decree Law 16/2008, Pensions for Combatants and Martyrs of National Liberation. This law has been amended five times, see Decree Laws 25/2008, 35/2009, 25/2010, 42/2011, and 6/2012. A single lump sum payment has also been introduced for indirect heirs of martyrs. See Government Decree Law no. 30/2012, Single Lump Sum for National Liberation Combatants and Families of Martyrs.

16. See https://hdr.undp.org/sites/default/files/Country-Profiles/MPI/TLS.pdf. The multidimensional poverty index measures each person's overlapping deprivations across ten indicators in three equally weighted dimensions: health, education, and standard of living.

17. See Democratic Republic of Timor-Leste, program of the 9th Constitutional Government, July 2023.

18. Interview with adviser to the secretary of state for veterans' affairs, July 2023.

19. Ibid. According to this adviser, there was USD 2.4 million set aside for cemetery construction in the 2020 state budget. At the time of writing, seven Garden of Heroes cemeteries contain human remains. See also the program of the 9th Constitutional Government, July 2023.

20. These have also consumed a significant amount of resources. For instance, as of November 2019, the Laga cemetery, which is driven by the advocacy of key resistance leader Cornelio Gama, aka L7, and members of Sagrada Familia, a prominent resistance group, had been funded USD 200,000. Interview with adviser to secretary of state for veterans' affairs, Dili, November 2019.

21. Government Decree Law 30/2017, Special Cemeteries of National Liberation Combatants Gardens of Heroes of the Fatherland.

22. Conversation with José Ramos, Natarbora, July 2017.

Chapter 2. The Martyred Youth of the Metropole

1. Other 1999 killings involving churches include the Suai church massacre and the attacks on the Canossian convent and the residence of Bishop Belo in Dili (Leach 2017, 108; Rei 2007; Loney 2018, 134).

2. Some of the key clandestine youth groups were the Organização Juventude Catolica Estudantes de Timor-Leste (OJECTIL, the Catholic Youth and Students Organisation of Timor-Leste), which later became the Organização Juventude Estudantes de Timor-Leste (OJETIL, Organisation for Youth and Students of Timor-Leste), the Indonesia-based Resistência Nacional dos Estudantes de Timor-Leste (RENETIL, National Resistance of East Timorese Students), and the Frente Iha Timor Unidos Nafatin (FITUN, Always United Front of Timor). The literal meaning of Fitun in Tetun is "star."

3. Interview with Liurai Tasi, Dili, November 2019. Liurai Tasi is a code name meaning "lord of the sea."

4. Ibid.

5. See also interview with Max Stahl in Andrew Sully and Max Stahl's documentary, "Anatomy of a Massacre," 2010.

6. Ibid.

7. He was assisted by Dutch activist Saskia Kouwenberg, who hid the film cartridges in her underwear.

8. Resolutions were also passed by the US Congress, the European Parliament, and Canada, condemning Indonesia. The Netherlands and Denmark suspended aid (Jardine 1995, 17; Braithwaite, Charlesworth, and Soares 2012, 82–83). Slowly, Western democracies such as Australia and the United States began to suspend training and defense technologies to the Indonesian military (Braithwaite, Charlesworth, and Soares 2012, 40, 73). Activists also began to gain more support from the United Nations, which led to the passage of a resolution by the UN Commission on Human Rights critical of Indonesian practices in East Timor in 1993 (Jardine 2000, 58).

9. Santa Cruz also increased the visibility of youth contributions to the nationalist struggle and catalyzed further youth recruitment (Bexley 2009, 76; Bexley and Tchailoro 2013, 409).

10. East Timor Alert Network, East Timor Update no. 17, November 20–29, 1992, "East Timor Massacre Remembered Worldwide"; no. 18, October 5–November 30, 1992, "Orchestrated Commemorations in Dili," "Armed Troops Patrol Dili Streets." Held by the National Library of Australia.

11. East Timor Alert Network, East Timor Update, no. 18, October 5–November 30, 1992, "Dili tightly monitored"; no. 18, October 5–November 30, 1992, "The Hearts and Minds War," "Mourning in Timor." Held by the National Library of Australia.

12. East Timor Alert Network, no. 41–42, November 3, 1995–January 31, 1996, "Timor Capital Quiet during Massacre Anniversary," "East Timor Marks Massacre." Held by the National Library of Australia.

13. Interview with Liurai Tasi, Dili, November 2019.

14. Ibid.

15. "Halibur Sira Ne'be moris no Halakaan sira ne'be laiha ona,"

16. "Aktifis Timor Leste pro merdeka an belaku merdeka tetap Merdeka."

17. The event also became an occasion for the representatives of East Timor's five main political parties to display their commitment to reconciliation; this was significant, as they had, by this point, reached consensus to support a referendum on East Timor's self-determination. On the large cross inside the cemetery grounds, the organisers had written "Reconciliacaio Nacional," and the representatives of the political parties collectively laid a wreath on the large cross. Interview with Liurai Tasi, Dili, November 2019.

18. Ibid.

19. See McCosker (2004) for a discussion of the ambiguous and affective power of these—or similar—photographs of East Timorese suffering that circulated internationally during the 1990s.

20. Indeed, at the time of the twentieth anniversary of Santa Cruz, the secretary of state for veterans' affairs explained that the organizers of the original 1991 demonstration "could only count their involvement as one day of service" for the resistance. Many contested this, arguing that preparations for the protest had taken several years (International Crisis Group 2011, 8).

21. From 1989 Gregorio was involved in the establishment of a new organization called CRNJT (Commission of National Resistance for Youth Timor-Leste) that was linked to OJETIL (the main organization of youth activists in Timor-Leste). It was envisaged that CRNJT would be in the front line during demonstrations in order to protect OJETIL from being discovered by Indonesian authorities.

22. Interview with Gregorio Saldanha, Dili, November 2019.

23. Ibid.

24. Other estimates of the missing, such as that of the CAVR, are higher, although less up to date than the 12 November committee figures.

25. Interview with Soren Blau, Melbourne, December 2019.

26. Ibid.

27. Ibid.

28. Ibid.

29. Ibid.
30. Interview with Gregorio Saldanha, Dili, November 2019.
31. Interview Soren Blau, Melbourne, December 2019.
32. Interview with Gregorio Saldanha, Dili, November 2019.
33. Interview with Liurai Tasi, Dili, November 2019.
34. For example, from their shared experiences of grief and loss, families of victims and the *mate restu* have created a community that supports one another through financial assistance to those in need and by attending events such as weddings and funerals.

Chapter 3. Civilian Sacrifices in the Town

1. Other demands often include a designated national day to remember the 6th of April and a commission to search for the bodies of the missing.
2. This was an attempt that backfired. The Liquiçá church massacre has instead become known for revealing the degree of coordination between the military and the police (who had been entrusted by the UN with providing security during the referendum) and the militia (Robinson 2003, 192).
3. Multiple witnesses suggest that military officers in plain clothes participated in the attack (CAVR 2005, 255).
4. This includes the leader of the Aitarak, Eurico Guterres, who later became the only person convicted and imprisoned in Indonesia for crimes against humanity in East Timor. Indicted by the Indonesian ad hoc tribunal in 2002 that was set up to try human rights cases relating to East Timor in 1999, he was sentenced to ten years in jail after being found guilty of involvement in the killings that took place in the Carrascalão house. He was then acquitted and released by the Indonesian Supreme Court in 2008 (Hughes, C. 2015).
5. By contrast, the Indonesian provincial police report said that only five people had died in the attack and its aftermath (CAVR 2005, part 7.2, 251).
6. For example, Mari Alkatiri once disparagingly referred to them as *sarjana supermee* (supermee graduates—named after a popular brand of Indonesian instant noodle) (Kent 2012, 128).
7. Some of the most prominent NGOs are Yayasan Hak (Rights Foundation), Fokupers (Forum for Women's Communication), AcBIT (Association Chega! Ba Ita, Association "Chega!" for Us), and AJAR (Asia Justice and Rights).
8. During the church services, the martyrdom of the dead was imbued with a transcendent, religious dimension, their suffering and sacrifices described in the priests' sermons as paralleling those made by Christ. Now safely dispatched to heaven, the dead had transcended their suffering and now watched over the living while their spirits and their principles remained alive. They served as a symbolic message to the Liquiçá population of today, especially the youth, to respect the sacrifices and the principles of the martyrs of the past by leading their lives as disciplined, Christian citizens committed to work for the rebuilding of their country and their local community.
9. Interview with organizer of the Liquiçá church commemorations, Liquiçá, April 2018.

10. Interview with former member of the youth clandestine in Liquiçá, April 2018.

11. At the time of writing, local residents had begun to discuss plans for a new monument—much larger than the angel memorial, to be placed at a prominent site in the center of the town. The angel, some argue, is not visible enough (tucked away as it is near the church), and the area has become too small to accommodate the growing number people who attend the commemorations. How this new monument will further shift the ground on which relations between the living and the dead, and the subjectivities of the dead, are forged remains to be seen.

Chapter 4. The "Participating Population" of the Hinterlands

1. See Government Media Release: National Council of Combatants of National Liberation to be Formally Established, Dili, April 17, 2015. http://timor-leste.gov.tl/?p=11693&lang=en.

2. Interview with adviser to the state secretary for veterans' affairs, Dili, November 2019.

3. Interview in Natarbora, April 2018.

4. Interview in Natarbora, April 2018.

5. Interview with Mau Kuri, April 2018.

6. For instance, the Natarbora commission successfully approached the government's Ministry for Veterans' Affairs and political leaders for personal donations for upgrades to the ossuary. Thanks to prominent political leader José Ramos Horta, the commission was able to upgrade an originally simple wooden structure to a sturdy iron construction with a tin roof.

7. Interview in Natarbora, April 2018.

8. Ibid.

9. For Tusinski (2016, 24), acts of "preparing, giving and consuming food" play an important role in mediating connections between the living and the dead. On significant days, spirits are invited into the house and are "offered gifts of *bua malus* (betel nut), cigarettes, water, fermented palm wine (tua), and palm-leaf-wrapped coconut rice balls (katupa)." The leftover food is then eaten by their living counterparts (Tusinski 2016, 24). In these ways, the acts of eating and feeding are "mutually entangled" in a "dialectic exchange of consumable substance: the fed feed and the feeders are fed" (Tusinski 2016, 25).

Chapter 5. The Treacherous Dead of the Badlands

1. Two other smaller parties also formed, *Klibur Oan Timor Aswain* (KOTA, Association of Timorese Warrior Sons) and *Trabalhista* (Labor) party (CAVR 2005, 9).

2. Interview with former UDT secretary general, Domingos de Oliveira, Dili, July 2016.

3. According to the Commission for Reception and Reconciliation, the violence was most intense in Liquiçá, Ermera, Ainaro, Manufahi, and Manatuto, though it was not confined to these districts (CAVR 2005, chapter 1).

4. He was also found guilty of "superstition, megalomania, and polygamy" (Walsh 2012, 3).

5. These debates echo those in Cambodia, where it is said that dual citizens "arrived during the good times; they would leave during the bad times." Furthermore, these returning refugees who had lived in luxury while others suffered are said not to "know what Khmer Angkor are, what really poor people, people in difficulty are" (Poethig 2004, 77).

6. Many members of Xanana Gusmao's first and second cabinet, for instance, were drawn from those who supported integration with Indonesia, "a strategy that helped sponsor a boom in investment and construction activities by Indonesian firms" (IPAC 2014).

7. It is adjacent to an empty tomb that awaits Xanana Gusmao and another empty tomb that awaits the yet-to-be-located remains of Nicolau Lobato.

8. See National Parliamentary Resolution 10/2012, on the Rehabilitation of East Timorese Who Died, Were Imprisoned, or Suffered Ill-Treatment within the Scope of the Timorese Resistance. Pedro explained that he complained to Gusmao during his meeting that the questionnaire used to register claimants for martyrs' pensions asked "Where did the person die?" and "How?" yet did not include an option for "Death due to FRETILIN." According to Pedro, following this meeting Gusmao wrote a memo advising the registration team to allow for the option of death due to "political conflict." However, as of 2018, no families of those killed by FRETILIN who had registered as claimants had had their loved ones officially verified as martyrs (interview with adviser to secretary of state for veterans' affairs).

9. I am grateful to Damian Grenfell for this observation and phrasing.

10. These words are an adaption of a verse in a poem by famous Timorese poet Francisco Borja da Costa.

11. Interview with Victor Soares, Dili, April 2018.

12. Interview with Hugo Fernandes, CNC director, online, July 2022.

13. Ibid.

Conclusion

1. Langford (2013, 213) makes a similar observation of Cambodian spirits, writing that the distinction between dangerous spirit and benevolent ancestor is not always clear cut, as "the dead's status as one or the other is often indeterminate, unstable, and subject to metamorphosis."

2. While there was initial speculation that some of the dead may be Santa Cruz victims, their clothing suggested they were likely to be people taken for execution from Dili prisons. See East Timor Law and Justice Bulletin, "Remains of Nine Found in Timor Graves," https://www.easttimorlawandjusticebulletin.com/2010/03/remains-of-nine-found-in-timor-graves.html.

3. See Barker, Anne. 2018. "East Timor's Latest Attempt to Find the Body of its First Prime Minister Nicolau dos Reis Lobato." ABC News, 21 February 2018. https://www.abc.net.au/news/2018-02-21/new-push-to-find-ex-east-timor-pm-dos-reis-lobartos-body/9468250.

4. Interview with adviser to secretary of state for veterans' affairs, July 2023.

5. Several issues have already emerged. Some people have refused to fill out the questionnaire as it is not clear whether those who died during the *funu maun alin* will be counted. Some families have expressed concerns that they don't know the cause of each dead family member's death. In some cases, there are no heads of houses, or *lia nain*, with the authority to "correctly" count the dead or call their spirits. Families have expressed concerns about providing misinformation or miscounting the dead, which might lead to punishment from the ancestors. Interviews in Dili, Natarbora, and Iliomar, July 2023.

6. These developments are reflected in the emergence of a new human right, the "right to truth" (Moon 2014, 52).

7. A comparison of exhumations in the former Yugoslavia and Rwanda is a case in point. "Only two major forensic exhumations of mass graves were conducted in Rwanda, compared with upward of sixteen thousand bodies exhumed from hundreds of graves in Bosnia, with more exhumations and ongoing identification work still underway" (Rosenblatt 2015, 29).

8. Interviews with ICRC staff, Dili, Timor-Leste, and forensic specialist at the Dili district hospital, July 2018.

9. Rosenblatt (2015, 32) makes a similar point, arguing that while the new language of humanitarian forensic work expresses a great deal about the duties of forensic teams to living victims of violence, it still has little to say about its responsibilities to the dead.

10. See Chao (2022, 213) for a similar point about taking seriously the possibility of plants as agents.

11. The extent of frontier violence is unknown yet is beginning to be mapped. See, for example, the University of Newcastle's Colonial Frontier Massacres map, https://c21ch.newcastle.edu.au/colonialmassacres/introduction.php.

12. The First Nations–led movement for the repatriation of "Old People" (ancestral remains) who were stolen from their communities and lands and taken to museums and universities, and the evolving practices to settle their spirits, is evidence of this.

Works Cited

Acikcoz, Salih Can. 2020. *Sacrificial Limbs: Masculinity, Disability, and Political Violence in Turkey*. Oakland: University of California Press.

Agamben, Giorgio. 1998. *Homo Sacer: Sovereign Power and Bare Life*. Stanford, CA: Stanford University Press.

Agard-Jones, Vanessa. 2013. "Bodies in the System." *Small Axe* 17 (3 (42)): 182–92.

Agliomby, John. 1999. "Mass Graves Found in Timor: Legacy of Indonesian Troops and Militia Uncovered." *The Guardian*, 21 December 1999.

Allerton, Catherine. 2009. "Introduction: Spiritual Landscapes of Southeast Asia." *Anthropological Forum* 19 (3): 235–51.

Anstett, Élisabeth, and Jean-Marc Dreyfus. 2015. "Introduction: Why Exhume? Why Identify?" In *Human Remains and Identification: Mass Violence, Genocide, and the "Forensic Turn,"* edited by Élisabeth Anstett and Jean-Marc Dreyfus, 1–13. Manchester: Manchester University Press.

Arthur, Catherine E. 2019. *Political Symbols and National Identity in Timor-Leste*. London: Palgrave Macmillan.

Auchter, Jessica. 2013. "Border Monuments: Memory, Counter-Memory, and (B)ordering Practices along the US-Mexico Border." *Review of International Studies* 39 (2): 291–311.

Auchter, Jessica. 2014. *The Politics of Haunting and Memory in International Relations*. Abingdon, UK: Routledge.

Auchter, Jessica. 2016. "Paying Attention to Dead Bodies: The Future of Security Studies." *Journal of Global Security Studies* 1 (1): 36–50.

Auchter, Jessica. 2020. "Burial, Reburial and the Securing of Memory." *Interdisciplinary Political Studies* 6 (1): 113–37.

Auchter, Jessica. 2023. "Ghosts." In *The Routledge Handbook of Memory Activism*, edited by Yifat Gutman and Jenny Wüstenberg, 117–21. London: Routledge.

Babo-Soares, Dionisio. 2004. "Nahe Biti: The Philosophy and Process of Grassroots Reconciliation (and Justice) in East Timor." *Asia Pacific Journal of Anthropology* 5 (1): 15–33.

Barad, Karen. 1996. "Meeting the Universe Halfway: Realism and Social Constructivism without Contradiction." In *Feminism, Science, and the Philosophy of Science*, edited by Lynn Hankinson Nelson and Jack Nelson, 161–94. Synthese Library. Dordrecht: Springer Netherlands.

Barad, Karen. 2007. *Meeting the University Half-Way: Quantum Physics and the Entanglement of Matter and Meaning*. Durham, NC: Duke University Press.

Barad, Karen. 2013. "Posthumanist Performativity: Toward an Understanding of How Matter Comes to Matter." *Women, Science, and Technology: A Reader in Feminist Science Studies* 28 (3): 473–94.

Barnes, Susana. 2011. "Origins, Precedence and Social Order in the Domain of Ina Ama Beli Darlari." In *Land and Life in Timor-Leste: Ethnographic Essays*, edited by Andrew McWilliam and Elizabeth G. Traube, 23–46. Canberra: ANU Press.

Barthes, Roland. 1980. *Camera Lucida: Reflections on Photography*. Translated by Richard Howard. New York: Hill and Wang.

Bear, Laura. 2007. "Ruins and Ghosts: The Domestic Uncanny and the Materialization of Anglo-Indian Genealogies in Kharagpur." In *Ghosts of Memory*, edited by Janet Carsten, 36–57. Oxford: Blackwell.

Bennett, Jane. 2010. *Vibrant Matter: A Political Ecology of Things*. Durham, NC: Duke University Press.

Bennett, Caroline. 2018. "Living with the Dead in the Killing Fields of Cambodia." *Journal of Southeast Asian Studies* 49 (2): 184–203.

Bevernage, Berber. 2012. "'Unpopular Past': The Argentine Madres de Plaza de Mayo and Their Rebellion against History." In *Popularizing National Pasts: 1800 to the Present*. Edited by Berger, Stefan, Chris Lorenz, and Billie Melman. Taylor and Francs.

Bexley, Angie. 2007. "The Geracao Foun, Talitakum and Indonesia: Media and Memory Politics in Timor-Leste." *Review of Indonesian and Malaysian Affairs* 4 (1): 71–90.

Bexley, Angie. 2009. "Youth at the Crossroads: The Politics of Identity and Belonging in Timor-Leste." PhD diss., Australian National University.

Bexley, Angie, and Nuno Tchailoro. 2013. "Consuming Youth: Timorese in the Resistance Against Indonesian Occupation." *Asia Pacific Journal of Anthropology* 14 (5): 405–22.

Bignall, Simone, Steve Hemming, and Daryle Rigney. 2016. "Three Ecosophies for the Anthropocene: Environmental Governance, Continental Posthumanism and Indigenous Expressivism." *Deleuze Studies* 10 (4): 455–78.

Blau, Soren. 2020. "Working for the Living and the Dead: Challenges Associated with Personal Identification from Skeletal Remains in Timor-Leste." In *The Dead as Ancestors, Martyrs, and Heroes in Timor-Leste*, edited by Lia Kent and Rui Graça Feijó, 197–216. Amsterdam: Amsterdam University Press.

Blau, Soren, and Luis Fondebrider. 2011. "Dying for Independence: Proactive Investigations into the 12 November 1991 Santa Cruz Massacre, Timor Leste." *The International Journal of Human Rights* 15 (8): 1249–74.

Blau, Soren, and Naomi Kinsella. 2013. "Searching for Conflict Related Missing Persons in Timor-Leste: Technical, Political and Cultural Considerations." *Stability: International Journal of Security and Development* 2 (1): 1–14.

Bovensiepen, Judith. 2009. "Spiritual Landscapes of Life and Death in the Central Highlands of Timor-Leste." *Anthropological Forum* 19 (3): 323–38.

Bovensiepen, Judith. 2014. "Lulik: Taboo, Animism, or Transgressive Sacred? An Exploration of Identity, Morality, and Power in Timor-Leste." *Oceania* 84 (2): 121–37.

Bovensiepen, Judith. 2015. *The Land of Gold: Post-Conflict Recovery and Cultural Revival in Independent Timor-Leste*. Ithaca, NY: Southeast Asia Program Publications, Cornell University.

Bovensiepen, Judith. 2018. "Death and Separation in Postconflict Timor-Leste." In *A Companion to the Anthropology of Death*, edited by Antonius C. G. M. Robben, 59–70. Oxford: John Wiley & Sons.

Bovensiepen, Judith M. 2021. "Can Oil Speak? On the Production of Ontological Difference and Ambivalence in Extractive Encounters." *Anthropological Quarterly* 94 (1): 33–63.

Braidotti, Rosi. 2013. "Posthuman Humanities." *European Educational Research Journal* 12 (1): 1–19.

Braithwaite, John, Hilary Charlesworth, and Adérito Soares. 2012. *Networked Governance of Freedom and Tyranny: Peace in Timor-Leste*. Canberra: ANU Press.

Brigg, Morgan. 2016. "Engaging Indigenous Knowledges: From Sovereign to Relational Knowers." *Australian Journal of Indigenous Education* 45: 152–58.

Brigg, Morgan. 2018. "Beyond the Thrall of the State: Governance as a Relational-Affective Effect in Solomon Islands." *Cooperation and Conflict* 54 (2): 154–72.

Brown, Anne. 2009. "Security, Development and the Nation-Building Agenda—East Timor." *Conflict, Security and Development* 9 (2): 141–64.

Brown, Anne. 2015. "State Formation and Political Community in Timor-Leste—the Centrality of the Local." *RCCS Annual Review* 7: 113–31.

Brown, Anne. 2020. "The Spatial Turn, Reification and Relational Epistemologies in 'Knowing about' Security and Peace." *Cooperation and Conflict* 55 (4): 421–41.

Brown, Anne, and Alex Freitas Gusmao. 2009. "Peacebuilding and Political Hybridity in East Timor." *Peace Review: A Journal of Social Justice* 21 (1): 61–69.

Brown, Kris. 2013. "'High Resolution' Indicators in Peacebuilding: The Utility of Political Memory." *Journal of Intervention and Statebuilding* 7 (4): 492–513.

Budiardjo, Carmel, and Siem Soei Liong. 1984. *The War Against East Timor*. London: Zed Books.

Butler, Judith. 2009. *Frames of War: When Is Life Grievable?* London: Verso.

Byrne, Denis, and Birgit Ween. 2015. "Bridging Cultural and Natural Heritage." In *Global Heritage: A Reader*, edited by Lynn Meskell, 94–111. Chichester, UK: John Wiley & Sons.

Carsten, Janet. 2007. "Introduction: Ghosts of Memory." In *Ghosts of Memory*, edited by Janet Carsten, 1–35. Oxford: Blackwell.

Carsten, Janet. 2019. *Blood Work: Life and Laboratories in Penang*. Durham, NC: Duke University Press.

CAVR, 2005. *Chega! Report of the Commission for Reception, Truth and Reconciliation*. Dili, Timor-Leste.

Chao, Sophie. 2022. *In the Shadow of the Palms: More-Than-Human Becomings in West Papua*. Durham, NC: Duke University Press.

Chapman, Audrey R., and Patrick Ball. 2001. "The Truth of Truth Commissions: Comparative Lessons from Haiti, South Africa, and Guatemala." *Human Rights Quarterly* 23 (1): 1–43.

Chidester, David. 2000. "Mapping the Sacred in the Mother City: Religion and Urban Space in Cape Town, South Africa." *Journal for the Study of Religion* 13 (1–2): 5–41.

Colombo, Pamela, and Estela Schindel. 2014. "Introduction: The Multi-Layered Memories of Space." In *Space and the Memories of Violence: Landscapes of Erasure, Disappearance and Exception*, edited by Estela Schindel and Pamela Colombo, 1–17. Palgrave Macmillan Memory Studies. London: Palgrave Macmillan.

Cribb, Robert. 2001. "How Many Deaths? Problems in the Statistics of Massacre in Indonesia (1965–1966) and East Timor (1975–1980)." In *Violence in Indonesia*, edited by Ingrid Wessel and Georgia Wimhöfer, 82–99. Hamburg: Abera.

Crockford, Fiona. 2007. "Contested Belonging: East Timorese Youth in the Diaspora." PhD diss., Australian National University.

Crossland, Zoë. 2002. "Violent Spaces: Conflict over the Reappearance of Argentina's Disappeared." In *Matériel Culture: The Archaeology of Twentieth-Century Conflict*, edited by Colleen M. Beck, Willian Gray Johnson, and John Schofield, 115–31. London: Routledge.

Crossland, Zoë. 2009. "Of Clues and Signs: The Dead Body and Its Evidential Traces." *American Anthropologist* 111 (1): 69–80.

Crossland, Zoë. 2013. "Evidential Regimes of Forensic Archaeology." *Annual Review of Anthropology* 42: 121–37.

Crossland, Zoë. 2015. "Epilogue." In *Necropolitics: Mass Graves and Exhumations in the Age of Human Rights*, edited by Francisco Ferrándiz and Antonius C. G. M. Robben, 240–52. Philadelphia: University of Pennsylvania Press.

Crossland, Zoë, and Alexander Bauer. 2017. "Im/materialities: Things and Signs." *Semiotic Review* 4.

Cruz-Santiago, Arely. 2020. "Lists, Maps, and Bones: The Untold Journeys of Citizen-Led Forensics in Mexico." *Victims and Offenders* 15 (3): 350–69.

Das, Veena, Arthur Kleinman, Margaret Lock, Mamphela Ramphele, and Pamela Reynolds, eds. 2001. *Remaking a World: Violence, Social Suffering, and Recovery*. Berkeley: University of California Press.

David, Lea. 2017. "Against Standardization of Memory." *Human Rights Quarterly* 39: 296–318.

de Alwis, Malathi. 2022. "Visual Inscriptions upon Landscapes of Loss: Memorializing Thileepan in Sri Lanka." In *Seeing South Asia: Visuals Beyond Borders*, edited by Dev Nath Pathak, Biswajit Das, and Ratan Kumar Roy, 127–47. Milton, UK: Taylor and Francis.

De Cesari, Ciara. 2010. "Creative Heritage: Palestinian NGOs and Defiant Arts of Government." *American Anthropologist* 112 (4): 625–37.

Democratic Republic of Timor-Leste. 2010. "Timor-Leste Strategic Development Plan 2011–2030." http://timor-leste.gov.tl/wp-content/uploads/2011/07/Timor-Leste-Strategic-Plan-2011-20301.pdf.

Democratic Republic of Timor-Leste. 2023. "Program of the 9th Constitutional Government, July 2023". https://www.laohamutuk.org/misc/gov9/230713ProgramaIXGovernoEn.pdf.

Derrida, Jacques. 1974. *Of Grammatology*. Translated by Gayatri Chakravort Spivak. Baltimore: John Hopkins University Press.

de Vries, Hugo, and Nikkie Wiegink. 2011. "Breaking Up and Going Home? Contesting Two Assumptions in the Demobilization and Reintegration of Former Combatants." *International Peacekeeping* 18 (1): 38–51.

Douglas, Mary. 1966. *Purity and Danger: An Analysis of Concepts of Pollution and Taboo*. London: Routledge and K. Paul.

Drexler, Elizabeth. 2013. "Fatal Knowledges: The Social and Political Legacies of Collaboration and Betrayal in Timor-Leste." *International Journal of Transitional Justice* 7 (1): 74–94.

Drozdzewski, Danielle, Sarah De Nardi, and Emma Waterton. 2016. "The Significance of Memory in the Present." In *Memory, Place and Identity: Commemoration and Remembrance of War and Conflict*, edited by Danielle Drozdzewski, Sarah De Nardi, and Emma Waterton, 1–16. London: Routledge.

Drozdzewski, Daniella, Emma Waterton, and Shanti Sumartojo. 2019. "Cultural Memory and Identity in the Context of War: Experiential, Place-Based and Political Concerns." *International Review of the Red Cross* 101: 251–72.

Durand, Frederic. 2004. *Catholicisme et protestantisme dans l'île de Timor 1556–2003*. Toulouse: IRASEC.

Dziuban, Zuzanna. 2017. *Mapping the "Forensic Turn": Engagements with Materialities of Mass Death in Holocaust Studies and Beyond*. Vienna: New Academic Press.

East Timor Law and Justice Bulletin. 2010. "Remains of Nine Found in Timor Graves." https://www.easttimorlawandjusticebulletin.com/2010/03/remains-of-nine-found-in-timor-graves.html.

Edkins, Jenny. 2003. *Trauma and the Memory of Politics*. Cambridge: Cambridge University Press.

Everth, Thomas, and Laura Gurney. 2022. "Emergent Realities: Diffracting Barad within a Quantum-Realist Ontology of Matter and Politics." *European Journal for Philosophy and Science* 12 (3): 1–20.

Feijó, Rui Graça. 2020. "On the Politics of Memory: Cult of Martyrs, Contested Memories and Social Status." In *The Dead as Ancestors, Martyrs, and Heroes in Timor-Leste*, edited by Lia Kent and Rui Graça Feijó, 263–82. Amsterdam: Amsterdam University Press.

Ferguson, James, and Akhil Gupta. 2002. "Spatializing States: Towards an Ethnography of Neoliberal Governmentality." *American Ethnologist* 29 (4): 981–1002.

Fernandes, Clinton. 2015. "Accomplice to Mass Atrocities: The International Community and Indonesia's Invasion of East Timor." *Politics and Governance* 3 (4): 1–11.

Ferrandiz, Francisco, and Antonius C. G. M. Robben. 2015. "Introduction: The Ethnography of Exhumations." In *Necropolitics: Mass Graves and Exhumations in the Age of Human Rights*, edited by Francisco Ferrandiz and Antonius C. G. M. Robben, 1–38. Manchester: University of Manchester Press.

Fforde, Cressida, Edward Halealoha Ayau, Jilda Andrews, Laurajane Smith, and Paul Turnbull. 2022. "Emotion and the Return of Ancestors: Repatriation as Affective Practice." In *The Oxford Handbook of Museum Archaeology*, edited by Alice Stevenson, 65–85. Oxford: Oxford University Press.

Fletcher, Robert. 2012. "The Art of Forgetting: Imperialist Amnesia and Public Secrecy." *Third World Quarterly* 33 (3): 423–39.

Fontein, Joost. 2010. "Between Tortured Bodies and Resurfacing Bones: The Politics of the Dead in Zimbabwe." *Journal of Material Culture* 15 (4): 423–48.

Fontein, Joost. 2011. "Graves, Ruins, and Belonging: Towards an Anthropology of Proximity." *Journal of the Royal Anthropological Institute* 17 (4): 706–27.

Fontein, Joost. 2014. "Remaking the Dead, Uncertainty and the Torque of Human Materials in Northern Zimbabwe." In *Governing the Dead: Sovereignty and the Politics of Dead Bodies*, edited by Finn Stepputat, 114–40. Manchester: Manchester University Press.

Fontein, Joost. 2022. *The Politics of the Dead in Zimbabwe, 2000–2020: Bones, Rumours and Spirits*. Melton, Woodbridge, Suffolk: James Currey.

Fontein, Joost, and John Harries. 2009. *Report of the "Bones Collective" Workshop, 4–5, December 2008, What Lies Beneath: Exploring the Affective Presence and Emotive Materiality of Human Bones*.

Fontein, Joost, and John Harries. 2013. "The Vitality and Efficacy of Human Substances." *Critical African Studies* 5 (3): 115–26.

Fox, Nick J., and Pam Alldred. 2019. "The Materiality of Memory: Affects, Remembering and Food Decisions." *Cultural Sociology* 13 (1): 20–36.

Freeman, Lindsey A., Benjamin Nienass, and Rachel Daniell. 2016. "Memory | Materiality | Sensuality." *Memory Studies* 9 (1): 3–12.

Graham, Mary. 1999. "Some Thoughts about the Philosophical Underpinnings of Aboriginal Worldviews." *Worldviews: Environment, Culture, Religion* 3: 105–18.

Grenfell, Damian. 2008. "Reconciliation: Violence and Nation Formation in Timor-Leste." In *Rethinking Insecurity, War and Violence: Beyond Savage Globalization?*, edited by Damian Grenfell and Paul James, 193–205. London: Routledge.

Grenfell, Damian. 2012. "Remembering the Dead from the Customary to the Modern in Timor-Leste." *Local-Global: Identity, Security, Community* 11 (2012): 86–108.

Grenfell, Damian. 2015. "Of Time and History: The Dead of War, Memory and the National Imaginary." *Communication, Politics and Culture* 48 (3): 16–28.

Grenfell, Damian. 2020. "Unfulfilled Peace: Death and the Limits of Liberalism in Timor-Leste." In *The Dead as Ancestors, Martyrs, and Heroes in Timor-Leste*, edited by Lia Kent and Rui Graça Feijó, 137–58. Amsterdam: Amsterdam University Press.

Guillou, Anne Yvonne. 2020. "Comments" responding to Carol Kidron's "The 'Perfect Failure' of Communal Genocide Commemoration in Cambodia: Productive Friction or 'Bone Business.'" *Current Anthropology* 61 (3): 326–27.

Gusmao, Xanana. 2000. *To Resist Is to Win! The Autobiography of Xanana Gusmao with Selected Letters and Speeches.* Edited by Sara Niner. Richmond, VA: Aurora Books with David Lovell Publishing.

Gutman, Yifat, and Jenny Wustenberg. 2023. "Introduction: The Activist Turn in Memory Studies." In *The Routledge Handbook of Memory Activism,* edited by Yifat Gutman and Jenny Wustenberg, 1–2. London: Routledge.

Hansen, Thomas Blom, and Finn Stepputat. 2005. "Introduction." In *Sovereign Bodies: Citizens, Migrants, and States in the Postcolonial World,* edited by Thomas Blom Hansen and Finn Stepputat, 1–36. Princeton, NJ: Princeton University Press.

Haraway, Donna. 2015. "Anthropocene, Capitalocene, Plantationocene, Chthulucene: Making Kin." *Environmental Humanities* 6 (1): 159–65.

Hearman, Vannessa. 2022a. "Displacement, Urban Transformations and Resistance in Indonesian-Occupied Dili, East Timor." In *Spatial Histories of Occupation: Colonialism, Conquest and Foreign Control in Asia,* edited by David Baillargeon and Jeremy E. Taylor, 25–50. London: Bloomsbury Academic.

Hearman, Vannessa. 2022b. "Challenges in the Pursuit of Justice for East Timor's Great Famine (1977–1979)." *Third World Quarterly* forthcoming: 1–18.

Hertz, Robert. 1960 [1907]. "A Contribution to the Study of Collective Representations of Death." In *Death and the Right Hand.* Translated by Rodney and Claudia Needham. Aberdeen, UK: University Press Aberdeen.

Hinton, Alexander Laban. 2018. *The Justice Façade: Trials of Transition in Cambodia.* Oxford: Oxford University Press.

Hirsch, Marianne. 2019. "Introduction: Practicing Feminism, Practicing Memory." In *Women Mobilizing Memory,* edited by Ayşe Gül Altýnay, María José Contreras, Marianne Hirsch, Jean Howard, Banu Karaca, and Alisa Solomon, 1–23. New York: Columbia University Press.

Hirsch, Marianne, and Leo Spitzer. 2017. "Small Acts of Repair: The Unclaimed Legacy of the Romanian Holocaust." In *Memory Unbound: Tracing the Dynamics of Memory Studies,* edited by Lucy Bond, Stef Craps, and Pieter Vermeulen, 83–108. New York: Berghahn Books.

Hodge, Joel. 2013. "The Catholic Church in Timor-Leste and the Indonesian Occupation: A Spirituality of Suffering and Resistance." *South East Asia Research* 2 (1): 151–70.

Hughes, Caroline. 2015. "Poor People's Politics in East Timor." *Third World Quarterly* 36 (5): 908–28.

Hughes, Rachel. 2015. "Ordinary Theatre and Extraordinary Law at the Khmer Rouge Tribunal." *Environment and Planning D* 33 (4): 714–31.

Hughes, Rachel. 2023. "In Place of Justice." *Dialogues in Human Geography* 13 (1): 159–61.

Hunter, B. H., and J. Carmody. 2015. "Estimating the Aboriginal Population in Early Colonial Australia: The Role of Chickenpox Reconsidered." *Australian Economic History Review* 55 (2): 112–38.

Huttunen, Laura. 2016. "Liminality and Missing Persons." *Conflict and Society* 2 (1): 201–18.

Huttunen, Laura. 2020. "Conceptualising Disappearances: From Bosnia-Herzegovina to the Present-Day Migration Order." In *Social Disappearance: Explorations between Latin America and Eastern Europe*, edited by Estela Schindel and Gabriel Gatti, 109–21. Dossiers, Forum Transregionale Studien 1.

Huttunen, Laura. Forthcoming. *Violent Absences, Haunting Presences: Human Disappearances, Political Landscapes and Cultural Practices*. Manchester: Manchester University Press.

Ingold, Tim. 2005. "Epilogue: Towards a Politics of Dwelling." *Conservation and Society* 3 (2): 501–8.

International Crisis Group. 2011. "Timor-Leste's Veterans: An Unfinished Struggle?" *Asia Briefing 129*, Dili/Jakarta/Brussels, 18 November.

IPAC (Institute for Policy Analysis of Conflict). 2014. "Timor-Leste after Xanana Gusmao." *IPAC Report No. 12* (16 July). Jakarta: IPAC.

Jackson, Zakiyyah I. 2013. "Animal: New Directions in the Theorization of Race and Posthumanism." *Feminist Studies* 39 (3): 669–85.

Jamar, Astrid. 2022. "Accounting for Which Violent Past? Transitional Justice, Epistemic Violence, and Colonial Durabilities in Burundi." *Critical African Studies* 14 (1): 73–95.

Jardine, Matthew. 1995. *East Timor: Genocide in Paradise*. Tuscon, AZ: Odonian.

Jardine, Matthew. 2000. "East Timor, the United Nations, and the International Community: Force Feeding Human Rights into the Institutionalised Jaws of Failure." *Pacifica Review: Peace, Security and Global Change* 12 (1): 47–62.

Jeffrey, Alex. 2013. *The Improvised State: Sovereignty, Performance and Agency in Dayton Bosnia*. Malden, MA: Wiley-Blackwell.

Jeffrey, Alex. 2019. *The Edge of Law: Legal Geographies of a War Crimes Court*. Cambridge: Cambridge University Press.

Johnson, Andrew Alan. 2020. *Mekong Dreaming: Life and Death along a Changing River*. Durham, NC: Duke University Press.

Johnson, Peter. 2008. "The Modern Cemetery: A Design for Life." *Social and Cultural Geography* 9 (7): 777–90.

Jones, Briony. 2021. "The Performance and Persistence of Transitional Justice and Its Ways of Knowing Atrocity." *Cooperation and Conflict* 56 (2): 163–80.

Kammen, Douglas. 2003. "Master-Slave, Traitor-Nationalist, Opportunist-Oppressed: Political Metaphors in East Timor." *Indonesia* 76: 69–85.

Kammen, Douglas. 2009. "Fragments of Utopia: Popular Yearnings in East Timor." *Journal of Southeast Asian Studies* 40 (2): 96–136.

Kammen, Douglas. 2015. *Three Centuries of Conflict in East Timor*. New Brunswick, NJ: Rutgers University Press.

Kelly, Tobias. 2012. "In a Treacherous State: The Fear of Collaboration among West Bank Palestinians." In *Traitors: Suspicion, Intimacy, and the Ethics of State-Building*, edited by Tobias Kelly and Sharika Thiranagama, 169–87. Philadelphia: University of Pennsylvania Press.

Kelly, Tobias, and Sharika Thiranagama. 2012. "Introduction." In *Traitors: Suspicion, Intimacy, and the Ethics of State-Building*, edited by Tobias Kelly and Sharika Thiranagama, 1–23. Philadelphia: University of Pennsylvania Press.

Kennedy, Rosanne, Jonathon Zapasnik, Hannah McCann, and Miranda Bruce. 2013. "All Those Little Machines: Assemblage as Transformative Theory." *Australian Humanities Review* 55 (108): 45–66.

Kent, Lia. 2011. "Local Memory Practices in East Timor: Disrupting Transitional Justice Assumptions." *International Journal of Transitional Justice* 5 (3): 434–55.

Kent, Lia. 2012. *The Dynamics of Transitional Justice: International Models and Local Realities in East Timor*. London: Routledge.

Kent, Lia. 2015. "Remembering the Past, Shaping the Future: Memory Frictions and Nation-Making in Timor-Leste." In *SSGM Discussion Paper* (No. 1).

Kent, Lia. 2016a. "After the Truth Commission: Gender and Citizenship in Timor-Leste." *Human Rights Review* 17 (1): 51–70.

Kent, Lia. 2016b. "Transitional Justice and Peacebuilding." In *An Introduction to Transitional Justice*, edited by Olivera Simić, 201–22. London: Routledge.

Kent, Lia. 2019. "Transitional Justice and the Spaces of Memory Activism in Timor-Leste and Aceh," *Global Change, Peace and Security* 31 (2): 181–99.

Kent, Lia. 2020. "Gathering the Dead, Imagining the State? Examining the Work of Commissions for the Recovery of Human Remains in Timor-Leste." In *The Dead as Ancestors, Martyrs, and Heroes in Timor-Leste*, edited by Lia Kent and Rui Graça Feijó, 283–304. Amsterdam: Amsterdam University Press.

Kent, Lia, and Rui Graça Feijó. 2020. "Introduction: Martyrs, Ancestors and Heroes: The Multiple Lives of Dead Bodies in Independent Timor-Leste." In *The Dead as Ancestors, Martyrs, and Heroes in Timor-Leste*, edited by Lia Kent and Rui Graça Feijó, 15–43. Amsterdam: Amsterdam University Press.

Kent, Lia. 2023. "Travelling and Multiscaler Memory: Remembering East Timor's Santa Cruz Massacre from the Transnational to the Intimate." *Memory Studies* (online first).

Kent, Lia, Steve Hemming, Daryle Rigney, and Cressida Fforde. Forthcoming. "The Dead as Agents of Truth Telling." *Journal of Sociology*.

Kent, Lia, and Naomi Kinsella. 2015. "A Luta Kontinua (The Struggle Continues)—The Marginalization of East Timorese Women within the Veterans' Valorization Scheme," *International Feminist Journal of Politics* 17 (3): 473–94.

Khalili, Laleh. 2007a. *Heroes and Martyrs of Palestine: The Politics of National Commemoration*. Cambridge: Cambridge University Press.

Khalili, Laleh. 2007b. "Heroic and Tragic Pasts: Mnemonic Narratives in the Palestinian Refugee Camps." *Critical Sociology* 33 (4): 731–59.

Kidron, Carol. 2012. "Alterity and the Particular Limits of Universalism." *Current Anthropology* 56 (3) 733–54.

Kidron, Carol. 2020. "The 'Perfect Failure' of Communal Genocide Commemoration in Cambodia: Productive Friction or 'Bone Business'?" *Current Anthropology* 61 (3): 304–34.

Kirmayer, Lawrence J., Robert Lemelson, and Mark Barad (eds). 2007. *Understanding Trauma: Integrating Biological, Clinical, and Cultural Perspectives*. Cambridge: Cambridge University Press.

Klep, Katrien. 2012. "Tracing Collective Memory: Chilean Truth Commissions and Memorial Sites." *Memory Studies* 53 (3): 59–269.

Krmpotich, Carol, Joost Fontein, and John Harries. 2010. "The Substance of Bones: The Emotive Materiality and Affective Presence of Human Remains." *Journal of Material Culture* 15 (4): 371–84.

Kwon, Heonik. 2006. *After the Massacre: Commemoration and Consolation in Ha My and My Lai*. Berkeley: University of California Press.

Kwon, Heonik. 2008. *Ghosts of War in Vietnam*. Cambridge: Cambridge University Press.

Kwon, Heonik. 2010. The Ghosts of War and the Ethics of Memory. In *Ordinary Ethics: Anthropology, Language, and Action*, edited by Michael Lambek, 400–413. New York: Fordham University Press.

Kwon, Heonik. 2012. "Rethinking Traumas of War." *South East Asia Research* 20 (2): 227–37.

Kwon, Heonik. 2017. "Revolution in the Afterlife." *Religions* 8 (8): 1–9.

Langford, Jean. 2009. "Gifts Intercepted: Biopolitics and Spirit Debt." *Cultural Anthropology* 24 (4): 681–711.

Langford, Jean. 2013. *Consoling Ghosts: Stories of Medicine and Mourning from Southeast Asians in Exile*. Minneapolis: University of Minnesota Press.

Langford, Jean. 2016. "The Immeasurable Debt to the Dead: Insights from Khmu Spirit Economies." In *Global Modernities and the (Re-)Emergence of Ghosts: Voices from Around the World*, edited by Tijo Salverda, Andrea Hollington, Sinah KloB, Nina Schneider, and Oliver Tappe, 35–38. Germany: Global South Studies Center, University of Cologne.

Laqueur, Thomas W. 2015. *The Work of the Dead: A Cultural History of Mortal Remains*. Princeton, NJ: Princeton University Press.

Leach, Michael. 2008. "Difficult Memories: The Independence Struggle as Cultural Heritage in East Timor." In *Places of Pain and Shame: Dealing with "Difficult Heritage,"* edited by William Logan and Keir Reeves, 158–76. London: Routledge.

Leach, Michael. 2017. *Nation-Building and National Identity in Timor-Leste*. London: Routledge.

Leach, Michael. 2020. "Remembering the Martyrs of National Liberation in Timor-Leste." In *The Dead as Ancestors, Martyrs, and Heroes in Timor-Leste*, edited by Lia Kent and Rui Graça Feijó, 67–90. Amsterdam: Amsterdam University Press.

Leahy, Helen Rees. 2012. *Museum Bodies: The Politics and Practices of Visiting and Viewing*. London: Routledge.

Legg, Stephen. 2005b. "Contesting and Surviving Memory: Space, Nation, and Nostalgia in Les Lieux de Mémoire." *Environment and Planning D: Society and Space* 23 (4): 481–504.

Leshem, Noam. 2015. "'Over Our Dead Bodies': Placing Necropolitical Activism." *Political Geography* 45: 34–44.

Li, Tanya Murray. 2007. *The Will to Improve: Governmentality, Development, and the Practice of Politics*. Durham, NC: Duke University Press.

Lincoln, Martha, and Bruce Lincoln. 2015. "Toward a Critical Hauntology: Bare Afterlife and the Ghosts of Ba Chúc." *Comparative Studies in Society and History* 57 (1): 191–220.

Loney, Hannah. 2018. *In Women's Words: Violence and Everyday Life during the Indonesian Occupation of East Timor, 1975–1999*. Brighton: Sussex Academic Press.

Lorimer, Hayden. 2005. "Cultural Geography: The Busyness of Being 'More Than Representational.'" *Progress in Human Geography* 29: 83–94.

MacDonald, Sharon. 2013. *Memorylands: Heritage and Identity in Europe Today*. London: Routledge.

MacGinty, Roger. 2013. "The Local Turn in Peace Building: A Critical Agenda for Peace." *Third World Quarterly* 34 (5): 763–83.

MacGinty, Roger. 2017. "A Material Turn in International Relations: The 4×4, Intervention and Resistance." *Review of International Studies* 43 (5): 855–74.

Maddrell, Avril, and James D. Sidaway. 2010. "Introduction: Bringing a Spatial Lens to Death, Dying, Mourning and Remembrance." In *Deathscapes: Spaces for Death, Dying, Mourning and Remembrance*, edited by Avril Maddrell, 1–18. London: Routledge.

Maier, Charles. 1988. *The Unmasterable Past: History, Holocaust, and German National Identity*. Cambridge, MA: Harvard University Press.

Major, Laura. 2015. "Unearthing, Untangling and Re-articulating Genocide Corpses in Rwanda." *Critical African Studies* 7 (2): 164–81.

Mbembe, Achille. 2003. "Necropolitics." Translated by Libby Meintjes. *Public Culture* 15 (1): 11–40.

McClintock, Louisa, M. 2019. "With Us or Against Us? Nazi Collaboration and the Dialectics of Loyalty and Betrayal in Postwar Poland, 1944–1946." *Theory and Society* 48: 589–610.

McCosker, Anthony. 2004. "East Timor and the Politics of Bodily Pain: A Problematic Complicity." *Continuum: Journal of Media and Cultural Studies* 18 (1): 63–79.

McWilliam, Andrew. 2005. "Houses of Resistance in East Timor: Structuring Sociality in the New Nation." *Anthropological Forum* 15 (1): 27–44.

McWilliam, Andrew. 2008. "Fataluku Healing and Cultural Resilience in East Timor." *Ethnos* 73 (2): 217–40.

McWilliam, Andrew. 2011. "Exchange and Resilience in Timor-Leste." *Journal of the Royal Anthropological Institute* 17: 745–63.

McWilliam, Andrew. 2019. "Stone Archives and Fortified Histories in Timor-Leste." *The Asia Pacific Journal of Anthropology* 39 (1): 247–60.

McWilliam, Andrew, and Elizabeth Traube. 2011. "Introduction." In *Land and Life in Timor-Leste: Ethnographic Essays*, edited by Andrew McWilliam and Elizabeth Traube, 1–24. Canberra: ANU E-Press.

Metsola, Lali Matti. 2006. "'Reintegration' of Ex-combatants and Former Fighters: A Lens into State Formation and Citizenship in Namibia." *Third World Quarterly* 27 (6): 1119–35.

Mitchell, Timothy. 1991. "The Limits of the State: Beyond Statist Approaches and Their Critics." *American Political Science Review* 85 (1): 77–96.

Moon, Claire. 2014. "Human Rights, Human Remains: Forensic Humanitarianism and the Human Rights of the Dead." *International Social Science Journal* 65 (215–16): 49–63.

Moon, Claire. 2020. "Extraordinary Deathwork: New Developments and the Social Significance of Forensic Humanitarian Action." In *Forensic Science and Humanitarian Action: Interacting with the Dead and the Living*, edited by Roberto C. Parra, Sara C. Zapico, and Douglas H. Ubelaker, 37–48. Chichester: John Wiley and Sons.

Muzaini, Hamzah. 2015. "On the Matter of Forgetting and 'Memory Returns.'" *Transactions of the Institute of British Geographers* 40 (1): 102–12.

Myerhoff, Barbara. 1982. "Life History among the Elderly: Performance, Visibility and Remembering." In *A Crack in the Mirror: Reflexive Perspectives in Anthropology*, edited by Jay Ruby, 99–117. Philadelphia: University of Pennsylvania Press.

Myrttinen, Henri. 2013a. "Phantom Menaces: The Politics of Rumour, Securitisation and Masculine Identities in the Shadows of the Ninjas." *Asia Pacific Journal of Anthropology* 14 (5): 471–85.

Myrttinen, Henri. 2013b. "Resistance, Symbolism and the Language of Stateness in Timor-Leste." *Oceania* 83 (3): 208–20.

Myrttinen, Henri. 2014. "Claiming the Dead, Defining the Nation: Contested Narratives of the Independence Struggle in Post-Conflict Timor-Leste." In *Governing the Dead: Sovereignty and the Politics of Dead Bodies*, edited by Finn Stepputat, 95–113. Manchester: Manchester University Press.

Nagy, Rosemary. 2008. "Transitional Justice as Global Project: Critical Reflections." *Third World Quarterly* 29 (2): 275–89.

Navaro-Yashin, Yael. 2009. "Affective Spaces, Melancholic Objects: Ruination and the Production of Anthropological Knowledge." *Journal of the Royal Anthropological Institute* 15 (1): 1–18.

Ngo, Tam. 2021. "Bones of Contention: Situating the Dead of the 1979 Sino-Vietnamese Border War." *American Ethnologist* 48 (2): 192–205.

Nicholson, Dan. 2001. "The Lorikeet Warriors: East Timorese New Generation Nationalist Resistance, 1989–99." Unpublished honors thesis, University of Melbourne.

Niner, Sara. 2009. *Xanana: Leader of the Struggle for Independent Timor-Leste*. Melbourne: Australian Scholarly Publishing.

Nixon, Rob. 2011. *Slow Violence and the Environmentalism of the Poor*. Cambridge, MA: Harvard University Press.

Obradovic-Wochnik, Jelena. 2020. "Hidden Politics of Power and Governmentality in Transitional Justice and Peacebuilding: The Problem of 'Bringing the Local Back In,'" *Journal of International Relations Development* 23: 117–38.

Ong, Aihwa. 2006. *Neoliberalism as Exception: Mutations in Citizenship and Sovereignty*. Durham, NC: Duke University Press.

Painter, Joe. 2002. "Governmentality and Regional Economic Strategies." In *Habitus: A Sense of Place*, edited by Jean Hillier and Emma Rooksby, 115–39. Aldershott, UK: Ashgate.

Palmer, Lisa. 2015. *Water Politics and Spiritual Ecology: Custom, Environmental Governance and Development*. London: Routledge.

Palmer, Lisa. 2021. *Island Encounters: Timor-Leste from the Outside In*. Canberra, ANU Press.

Palmer, Lisa, and Andrew McWilliam. 2018. "Ambivalent 'Indigeneities' in an Independent Timor-Leste: Between the Customary and National Governance of Resources." *Asia Pacific Viewpoint* 59 (3): 265–75.

Palmer, Lisa, and Andrew McWilliam. 2019. "Spirit Ecologies and Customary Governance in Post-Conflict Timor-Leste." *Bijdragen Tot de Taal-, Land- En Volkenkunde* 175 (4): 474–505.

Perera, Sasanka. 2001. "Spirit Possessions and Avenging Ghosts." In *Remaking a World: Violence, Social Suffering and Recovery*, edited by Veena Das, Arthur Kleinman, Margaret Lock, Mamphela Ramphele, and Pamela Reynolds, 157–200. Berkeley: University of California Press.

Pinto, Constancio, and Matthew Jardine. 1997. *East Timor's Unfinished Struggle: Inside the Timorese Resistance*. Boston: South End Press.

Poethig, Kathryn. 2004. "Sitting Between Two Chairs: Cambodia's Dual Citizenship Debate." In *Expressions of Cambodia: The Politics of Tradition, Identity and Change*, edited by Leakthina Chau-Pech Ollier and Tim Winter, 73–85. London: Routledge.

Rei, Naldo. 2007. *Resistance: A Childhood Fighting for East Timor*. Queensland: University of Queensland Press.

Reineke, Robin. C. 2022. "Forensic Citizenship among Families of Missing Migrants along the U.S-Mexico Border." *Citizenship Studies* 26 (1): 21–37.

Renshaw, Layla. 2010. "The Scientific and Affective Identification of Republican Civilian Victims from the Spanish Civil War." *Journal of Material Culture* 15 (4): 449–63.

Rigney, Ann. 2020. "Mediations of Outrage: How Violence against Protesters Is Remembered." *Social Research* 87 (3): 707–33.

Robben, Antonius C. G. M. 2015. "Exhumations, Territoriality, and Necropolitics in Chile and Argentina." In *Necropolitics: Mass Graves and Exhumations in the Age of Human Rights*, edited by Francisco Ferrandiz and Antonius C. G. M. Robben, 53–75. Philadelphia: University of Pennsylvania Press.

Robins, Simon. 2010. "An Assessment of the Needs of Families of the Missing in Timor-Leste." *Report for the Postwar Reconstruction and Development Unit*. York, UK: University of York.

Robins, Simon. 2013. *Families of the Missing: A Test for Contemporary Approaches to Transitional Justice*. London, Routledge.

Robinson, Geoffrey. 2003. "East Timor 1999: Crimes Against Humanity." *A Report Commissioned by the United Nations Office of the High Commissioner for Human Rights* (OHCHR). Dili: Hak Association and ELSAM.

Robinson, Geoffrey. 2009. *"If You Leave Us Here, We Will Die": How Genocide Was Stopped in East Timor*. Princeton, NJ: Princeton University Press.

Rojas-Perez, Isaias. 2013. "Inhabiting Unfinished Pasts: Law, Transitional Justice and Mourning in Postwar Peru." *Humanity* (Spring 2013): 149–70.

Rojas-Perez, Isais. 2015. "Death in Transition: The Truth Commission and the Politics of Reburial in Postconflict Peru." In *Necropolitics: Mass Graves and Exhumations in the Age of Human Rights*, edited by Francisco Ferrandiz and Antonius C. G. M. Robben, 185–212. Philadelphia: University of Pennsylvania Press.

Rojas-Perez, Isaias. 2017. *Mourning Remains: State Atrocity, Exhumations, and Governing the Disappeared in Peru's Postwar Andes*. Stanford, CA: Stanford University Press.

Roll, Kate. 2014. "Inventing the Veteran, Imagining the State: Post-Conflict Reintegration and State Consolidation in Timor-Leste, 1999–2012." PhD diss., University of Oxford.

Roll, Kate. 2018a. "Street Level Bureaucrats and Post-Conflict Policy-Making: Corruption, Correctives, and the Rise of Veterans' Pensions in Timor-Leste." *Civil Wars* 20 (2): 262–85.

Roll, Kate. 2018b. "Reconsidering Reintegration: Veterans Benefits as State-Building." In *The Promise of Prosperity: Visions of the Future in Timor-Leste*, edited by Judith Bovensiepen, 139–53. Canberra: ANU Press.

Roll, Kate. 2020. "Selling Names: The 'Material Dimension' of State Recognition of Martyrs in Timor-Leste." In *The Dead as Ancestors, Martyrs, and Heroes in Timor-Leste*, edited by Lia Kent and Rui Graça Feijó, 305–26. Amsterdam: Amsterdam University Press.

Roosa, John. 2007. "How Does a Truth Commission Find Out What the Truth Is? The Case of East Timor-Leste's CAVR." *Pacific Affairs* 80 (4): 569–80.

Rosenblatt, Adam. 2015. *Digging for the Disappeared: Forensic Science after Atrocity*. Stanford, CA: Stanford University Press.

Rosiek, Jerry Lee, Jimmy Snider, and Scott L. Pratt. 2019. "The New Materialisms and Indigenous Theories of Non-Human Agency: Making the Case for Respectful Anti-Colonial Engagement." *Qualitative Inquiry* 26 (3–4): 331–46.

Rothschild, Amy. 2016. "Democratization of Perpetration." *Conflict and Society* 1 (1): 92–108.

Rothchild, Amy. 2017. "Victims versus Veterans: Agency, Resistance and Legacies of Timor-Leste's Truth Commission." *International Journal of Transitional Justice* 11 (3): 443–62.

Rothschild, Amy. 2020. "Remembering the Dead in Post-Independence Timor-Leste: Victims or Martyrs?" In *The Dead as Ancestors, Martyrs, and Heroes in Timor-Leste*, edited by Lia Kent and Rui Graça Feijó, 219–42. Amsterdam: Amsterdam University Press.

Rudling, Adriana, and Lorena Vega Duenas. 2021. "Liquid Graves and Meaning Activism in the Colombian Armed Conflict: The 'Bottom-up' Recovery and Memorialisation of Victims of Forced Disappearance." *Journal of the British Academy* 9 (s3): 121–37.

Sakti, Victoria Kumala. 2013. "Thinking Too Much: Tracing Local Patterns of Emotional Distress After Mass Violence in Timor-Leste." *Asia Pacific Journal of Anthropology* 14 (5): 438–54.

Sakti, Victoria Kumala. 2020. "The Politics of Loss and Restoration: Massive Bad Death in the Oecussi Highlands." In *The Dead as Ancestors, Martyrs, and Heroes in Timor-Leste*, edited by Lia Kent and Rui Graça Feijó, 159–78. Amsterdam: Amsterdam University Press.

Sather-Wagstaff, Joy. 2017. "Making Polysense of the World: Affect, Memory and Heritage." In *Heritage, Affect and Emotion: Politics, Practices and Infrastructures*, edited by Divya P. Tolia-Kelly, Emma Waterton, and Steve Watson, 12–29. Abingdon, UK: Routledge.

Schafers, Marlene. 2020. "Walking a Fine Line: Loyalty, Betrayal, and the Moral and Gendered Bargains of Resistance." *Comparative Studies of South Asia, Africa and the Middle East* 40 (1): 119–32.

Schramm, Katharina. 2011. "Introduction: Landscapes of Violence: Memory and Sacred Space." *History and Memory* 23 (1): 5–22.

Shaw, Rosalind. 2007. "Memory Frictions: Localizing the Truth and Reconciliation Commission in Sierra Leone." *International Journal of Transitional Justice* 1 (2): 183–207.

Shepherd, Christopher. 2019. *Haunted Houses and Ghostly Encounters: Ethnography and Animism in East Timor*. Copenhagen: Nordic Institute for Asia Studies (NIAS) Press.

Siapno, Jacqueline. 2012. "Dance and Martial Arts in Timor Leste: The Performance of Resilience in a Post-Conflict Environment." *Journal of Intercultural Studies* 33 (4): 425–42.

Silva, Kelly. 2017. "Managing Resources, Persons and Rituals: Economic Pedagogy as Government Tactics." In *Transformations in Independent Timor-Leste: Dynamics of Social and Cultural Cohabitations*, edited by Susana de Matos Viegas and Rui Graça Feijó, 193–209. London: Routledge.

Squire, Vicki. 2014. "Desert 'Trash': Posthumanism, Border Struggles, and Humanitarian Politics." *Political Geography* 39 (March 2014): 11–21.

Stepputat, Finn. 2014. "Governing the Dead? Theoretical Approaches." In *Governing the Dead: Sovereignty and the Politics of Dead Bodies*, edited by Finn Stepputat, 11–32. Manchester: Manchester University Press.

Stoller, Paul. 1994. "Ethnographies as Texts/Ethnographers as Griots." *American Ethnologist* 21 (2): 353–66.

Stumer, Jenny. 2018. "The Dead Are Coming: Border Politics and Necropower in Europe." *Cultural Politics* 14 (1): 20–39.

Sully, Andrew, and Max Stahl, dirs. 2010. *Anatomy of a Massacre*. Documentary, Cordell Jigsaw Productions Pty Ltd.

Surin, Kenneth. 2001. "The Sovereign Individual and Michael Taussig's Politics of Defacement." *Neplanta: Views from South* 2 (1): 205–20.

Taussig, Michael T. 1999. *Defacement: Public Secrecy and the Labor of the Negative.* Stanford, CA: Stanford University Press.

Taylor, John G. 1999. *East Timor: The Price of Freedom.* New York: Zed Books.

Theidon, Kimberly. 2006a. *Intimate Enemies: Violence and Reconciliation in Peru.* Philadelphia: University of Pennsylvania Press.

Theidon, Kimberly. 2006b. "The Mask and the Mirror: Facing Up to the Past in Postwar Peru." *Anthropologica* 48 (1): 87–100.

Thu, Pyone Myat, and Debra S. Judge. 2017. "Household Agricultural Activity and Child Growth: Evidence from Rural Timor-Leste." *Geographical Research* 55 (2): 146–47.

Till, Karen. 2008. "Artistic and Activist Memory-work: Approaching Place-based Practice." *Memory Studies* 1 (1): 99–113.

Till, Karen. 2012. "Wounded Cities: Memory-Work and a Place-Based Ethics of Care." *Political Geography* 31 (1): 3–14.

Till, Karen, and Anna-Kaisa Kuusisto-Arponen. 2015. "Towards Responsible Geographies of Memory: Complexities of Place and the Ethics of Remembering." *Erdkunde* 69 (4): 291–306.

Tomsky, Terri. 2011. "From Sarajevo to 9/11: Travelling Memory and the Trauma Economy." *Parallax* 17 (4): 49–60.

Traube, Elizabeth. 2007. "Unpaid Wages: Local Narratives and the Imagination of the Nation." *Asia Pacific Journal of Anthropology* 8 (1): 9–25.

Traube, Elizabeth. 2011. "Planting the Flag." In *Land and Life in Timor-Leste: Ethnographic Essays*, edited by Andrew McWilliam and Elizabeth G. Traube, 117–40. Canberra: ANU Press.

Traube, Elizabeth. 2020. "Preface: The Dead, the State and the People of Timor-Leste." In *The Dead as Ancestors, Martyrs, and Heroes in Timor-Leste*, edited by Lia Kent and Rui Graça Feijó, 9–14. Amsterdam: Amsterdam University Press.

Trindade, Jose "Josh." 2011. "Lulik: The Core of Timorese Values." Paper presented at 3rd Timor-Leste Studies Association (TLSA) Conference, Dili, 30 June.

Trindade, Josh. 2015. "Relational Dimensions within Timor-Leste Customary Society." Conference paper presented at the 5th Timor-Leste Studies Association Conference, Timor-Leste: The Local, the Regional and the Global, Liceu Campus, University of Timor-Leste, Dili, Timor-Leste, 9–10 July.

Tsing. Anna. 2015. *The Mushroom at the End of the World: On the Possibility of Life in Capitalist Ruins.* Princeton, NJ: Princeton University Press.

Turner, Victor. 1967. *The Forest of Symbols: Aspects of Ndembu Ritual.* Ithaca, NY: Cornell University Press.

Tusinski, Gabriel. 2016. "Fates Worse Than Death: Destruction and Social Attachment in Timor-Leste." *Social Analysis* 60 (2): 13–30.

van Henten, Jan Willem, and Ihab Saloul. 2020. "Introduction." In *Martyrdom: Canonisation, Contestation and Afterlives*, edited by Ihab Saloul and Jan Willem van Henten, 11–31. Amsterdam: Amsterdam University Press.

Vásquez, Noemí Pérez. 2022. *Women's Access to Transitional Justice in Timor-Leste.* Oxford: Hart.

Verdery, Katherine. 1999. *The Political Lives of Dead Bodies: Reburial and Postsocialist Change.* New York: Columbia University Press.

Viegas, Susana de Matos. 2020. "Ancestors and Martyrs in Timor-Leste." In *The Dead as Ancestors, Martyrs, and Heroes in Timor-Leste*, edited by Lia Kent and Rui Graça Feijó, 47–66. Amsterdam: Amsterdam University Press.

Viegas, Susana de Mato, and Rui Graça Feijó. 2017. "Territorialities of the Fallen Heroes." In *Transformations in Independent Timor-Leste: Dynamics of Social and Cultural Cohabitations*, edited by Susana de Mato Viegas and Rui Graça Feijó, 94–110. London: Routledge.

Volkan, Vamik D. 2001. "Transgenerational Transmissions and Chosen Traumas: An Aspect of Large-Group Identity." *Group Analysis* 34 (1): 79–97.

Wagner, Sarah. 2019. "Conclusion." *Forensic Anthropology* 2 (2): 139–42.

Walker, Rebecca. 2015. "Absent Bodies and Present Memories: Marking Out the Everyday and the Future in Eastern Sri Lanka." *Identities: Global Studies in Culture and Power* 22 (1): 109–23.

Walsh, Pat. 2012. "Winter of East Timor's Patriarchs." Edited version of a talk given at the Friends of Aileu, METAC dinner held at the Hume Global Learning Center in Melbourne, 4 May. https://patwalsh.net/wp-content/uploads/PW_Winter-of-East-Timor-patriarchs.pdf.

Warren, Kay B. 1993. "Interpreting *la violensia* in Guatemala: Shapes of Mayan Silence and Resistance." In *The Violence Within: Cultural and Political Opposition in Divided Nations*, edited by Kay B. Warren, 25–56. Boulder, CO: Westview.

Webster, David. 2013. "Languages of Human Rights in Timor-Leste." *Asia Pacific Perspectives* 11 (1): 5–21.

Weissert, Markus. 2015. "Memories of Violence, Dreams of Development: Memorialisation Initiatives in the Peruvian Andes." PhD diss., Free University of Berlin.

Wigglesworth, Ann. 2013. "The Growth of Civil Society in Timor-Leste: Three Moments of Activism." *Journal of Contemporary Asia* 43 (1): 51–74.

Willerslev, Rane. 2007. *Soul Hunters: Hunting, Animism, and Personhood among the Siberian Yukaghirs.* Berkeley: University of California Press.

Winch, Bronwyn. 2020. "*Sempre La'o ho ita*: Ancestral Omnipresence and the Protection of the Living in Timor-Leste." In *The Dead as Ancestors, Martyrs, and Heroes in Timor-Leste*, edited by Lia Kent and Rui Graça Feijó, 115–36. Amsterdam: Amsterdam University Press.

Winchell, Mareike. 2023. "Critical Ontologies: Rethinking Relations to Other-Than-Humans from the Bolivian Andes." *Journal of the Royal Anthropological Institute* 29 (3): 611–30.

Zucker, Eve. 2013. *Forests of Struggle: Moralities of Remembrance in Upland Cambodia.* Honolulu: University of Hawai'i Press.

Index

abject, 94, 139, 149
affect, 7–11, 17, 45, 54, 84, 92–94, 155
Agamben, Giorgio, 25, 128
agency, 4–5, 15–16, 30–31, 44, 78, 113–14, 120, 157, 160–61
Alkatiri, Mari, 151–52
All Souls' Day, 3–4
Amaral, Francisco Xavier do, 130–31, 134–35
Amnesty International, 78
Antigone (Sophocles), 128–29
Apodeti (Associação Popular Democrática Timorense), 127, 129, 144
Araújo, Rui Maria de, 21
Argentine Forensic Anthropology Team (EAAF), 63–64
Arthur, Catherine, 28
Asosiasaun Hak, 58
Auchter, Jessica, 42
Australia, 24, 160–61

bad death: disruption of, 6, 8, 12, 144–45, 161; narratives of closure, 156; scale of, 5–6, 10–11, 83; social responses to, 57–58; and unruliness, 8, 143, 148, 171n1. *See also* death; *lulik* landscape; necropower
Balide Comarca, 60

Barthes, Roland, 54
Bennett, Caroline, 150
Bennett, Jane, 17
Bexley, Angie, 133
Blau, Soren, 64
blood tests, 113–14, 136, 159. *See also* traditional DNA
BMP (Besi Merah Putih), 76–77, 86
Borja da Costa, Francisco, 59, 103
Bovensiepen, Judith, 9

Cambodia, 11, 150, 171n1, 171n5
care, 75–76, 88–92, 118–20, 139–40
Carrascalão, Manuel, 77
Catholicism, 3, 21, 28–29, 46–47, 51, 73, 84, 93, 143, 166n8–166n9
CAVR (Commission for Reception, Truth, and Reconciliation), 25, 40–42, 53, 123–24, 140. *See also* CNC (Centro Nacional Chega!)
Chao, Sophie, 15
citizen-led forensics, 113
citizenship, 12–13, 35, 81. *See also* national identity
clandestine resistance/front, 25–27, 35, 51, 60, 131
clothing, 47–49, 65, 103, 105–6, 145
CNC (Centro Nacional Chega!), 43–44, 140, 145–46. *See also* CAVR

191

CNC (*continued*)
(Commission for Reception, Truth, and Reconciliation)
CNRT (National Council of the Timorese Resistance), 132, 166n14
CNV (National Veterans Council), 101
commemoration, 12, 70, 79–82, 140–41, 148. *See also* prosecutions
cooling the land, 9–10, 93, 109, 145. *See also lulik* landscape
CRNJT (Commission of National Resistance for Youth Timor-Leste), 168n21
Crossland, Zoe, 136

David, Lea, 80
dead bodies: abandonment of, 24–25, 29, 102; accidental discovery of, 144, 151; comingling of, 136, 149; as evidence, 42, 53, 63, 86, 117–18; hiding of, 26–27, 77; identification of, 64–69, 111–14, 159; inability to find, 149–54; materiality of, 11–13, 83–84, 110; recovery of, 13, 18–19, 22, 33, 37, 62–63, 66, 90, 96, 98, 108, 120. *See also deskoñesidu*; mortuary rituals
the dead: and affect, 7–11, 17, 84, 155; agency of, 4–5, 13, 15–16, 20, 30–31, 44, 92, 157, 160–61; counting of, 41–42, 153, 166n7, 172n5; dignity of, 107; eating food with, 119–20, 170n9; felt presence of, 8, 61–62, 65–67, 72, 74, 148, 155; individuality of, 106, 112, 120–21, 142; as part of community, 70–71, 83, 108–9, 120, 139–40, 155–56; and transitional justice, 41; unruliness of, 8, 10, 12–13, 66–71, 92–94, 100–101, 116, 143, 148, 154–55, 171n1. *See also deskoñesidu*; spirits
death: euphemisms for, 27; hierarchies of, 13, 18, 35–38, 49, 60, 68, 72, 79, 84, 95, 104–5, 114–15, 117, 146–47, 166n14; and isolation, 31, 97, 143–44; symbolism of, 21–22, 46, 74, 148. *See also* bad death; martyrdom; mortuary rituals; necro-governmentality; necropolitics
deathscapes, 76, 92–93
dehumanization, 42
desacralization, 29
deskoñesidu, 105–6, 111–14, 121–22, 144. *See also* dead bodies; the dead
Dili, 21, 26, 33, 37, 44, 46, 49, 58, 70, 85, 130
DNA testing, 64–65, 114, 153, 157. *See also* traditional DNA
dreams, 6–8, 52, 64–70, 91, 112, 158–59

East Timor. *See* Timor-Leste
ethics of care, 88–92, 98, 154
exhumation, 42, 63, 66, 83, 88–89, 158–59

FALINTIL (Forças Armandas da Libertação Nacional de Timor-Leste), 4, 27, 38, 51, 76–77, 84, 89, 99, 101–2, 104, 108, 118, 132, 166n14
famine, 25, 42, 166n7
F-FDTL (Falintil-Forcas de Defesa de Timor-Leste), 37
film, 53, 56
FITUN (Frente Iha Timor Unidos Nafatin), 167n2
Foho Ramalau (Costa), 103
Fondebrider, Luis, 64
Fontein, Joost, 11
forensic humanitarianism, 63–64, 158, 172n9. *See also* necro-governmentality
FRETILIN (Frente Revolucionária de Timor-Leste Independente), 12, 19–20, 24, 33, 52, 102, 104, 108, 123, 126–27, 129–30, 132, 134–35, 137, 140, 155, 166n14, 171n8
funu maun alin, 130–31, 143, 146, 172n5

Garden of Heroes cemeteries, 19, 22–23, 31, 37–39, 61, 67, 74–75, 83, 87, 91, 96, 151–52
Gonzaga, Luisa, 165n6

Grenfell, Damian, 10, 41
Gusmao, Xanana, 118, 132, 141, 171n6
Guterres, Eurico, 169n4

heroism, 22–23, 79, 98
Hughes, Caroline, 84–85
Hughes, Rachel, 43
human rights, 33, 41, 56–57, 62–63, 78
Human Rights Watch, 78
Huttunen, Laura, 26, 165n4

imagined community, 27–28, 30, 70. *See also* state formation
Indonesian occupation: ambiguities during, 126–27; collaboration under, 134; defenses of, 55; hero narratives during, 22–23, 79; international perceptions of, 53–55, 62–63, 167n8; legacies of, 5–9, 12; strategies of necropower, 23, 76, 131; violence by resistance forces, 139–40. *See also* Timor-Leste
International Forensic Team (IFT), 50, 63–66

Jakarta, 51, 78
Jeffrey, Alex, 43

Kammen, Douglas, 42–43
Kelly, Tobias, 127
Khalili, Laleh, 32
Khmer Rouge, 11, 150
Kore Metan Nasional, 21–23, 44, 153
kore metan ritual, 14, 21–23, 44, 124, 153. *See also* mortuary rituals
Kuri, Mau, 110
Kwon, Heonik, 5, 82

Laclau, Ernesto, 134
Langford, Jean, 15, 29
Laqueur, Thomas, 112
Liquiçá church massacre, 19, 50–51, 73–79, 92–93, 169n2
Liurai Tasi, 52, 56, 69–70

Lobato, Nicolau, 33–34, 131, 151–54
locusts, 6, 107
Loney, Hannah, 165n6
Los Palos, 37
lulik (sacred,/taboo/hidden), 8–9, 28, 92–93, 103, 106, 118, 136, 145, 166n8
lulik landscape, 8–9, 92–93. *See also* bad death; cooling the land

martyrdom: criteria of, 35–36, 82–84, 86–87, 95, 148–49, 166n14; and hierarchy of remembrance, 49, 54, 60–61, 104–5; and national identity, 32–33, 58–59, 79, 116, 169n8; as necropower, 27–29, 56, 98; recognition of, 18, 35–37, 90–92, 140–42. *See also* death; pensions; valorization; victimhood
masculinity, 33, 35, 98
mass graves, 43, 62, 105–6, 114, 149–50, 157, 172n7
mate restu (survivors), 60, 68, 71–72, 169n34
Maubara salt lake, 83, 86, 94
McWilliam, Andrew, 103
memory work, 49; as assemblage, 16–17; funding sources, 79–80, 82, 108, 124; and instability, 49–50; local practices of, 14, 70, 157, 159; and retelling stories, 59–62; scope of, 160–61; and social engagement, 91; spaces of, 87–94, 118–20, 155–56; and the state, 13, 154; and temporality, 71. *See also* public memory; re-membering
Mitchell, Timothy, 44
monuments, 13–14, 33, 57, 94, 134, 142–43, 151, 155, 170n11
mortuary rituals, 7–8, 10, 13–14, 28–29, 38, 89–90, 124. *See also* dead bodies; death; *kore metan* ritual
Mount Matebian, 102

naming, 69, 112, 123–24, 142
Natarbora, 3–4, 6, 58, 97, 101–2, 104–10
Natarbora commission, 104–10
National Council of the Timorese Resistance (CNRT), 132
National Heroes Day, 21, 33
national identity, 35–36, 55, 71, 81, 128, 160–61, 166n9. *See also* citizenship; patriotism
National Resistance Museum, 33
necro-governmentality, 18–19, 22–23, 29–31, 43–45, 71, 80, 121, 126–27. *See also* death; forensic humanitarianism
necropolitical activism, 157
necropolitics, 148–49. *See also* death
necropower, 18–19, 23–26, 51–52, 57. *See also* bad death
new materialisms, 15–16
Nundamar prison, 136–38, 141–42. *See also* RENAL ("rehabilitation") prisons

Oekussi, 37
OJECTIL (Organização Juventude Catolica Estudantes de Timor-Leste), 167n2
OJETIL (Organização Juventude Estudantes de Timor-Leste), 167n2, 168n21
"One Minute's Silence" (da Costa), 59
ossuary, 67, 83–84, 104–5, 114, 153, 170n6

patriotism, 35–36. *See also* national identity
pensions, 35–37, 61, 89, 100–101, 107, 125, 171n8. *See also* martyrdom
photographic evidence, 53, 56
popular justice, 131
postconflict peace building, 156–59
prosecutions, 33, 40–43, 62–64, 73, 79–82. *See also* commemoration; transitional justice; war crimes
protest, suppression of, 26, 50–51
public memory, 56–57. *See also* memory work

public secret, 20, 126–27, 133–37, 144, 146

Ramos, José, 104
Ramos-Horta, José, 74, 104
Rangel, Sebastiáo Gomes, 51
Rate Laek, 85, 88
Regio, Pedro Mendonca do, 135
Rei, Naldo, 51–52
re-membering, 57, 70, 119, 149–54. *See also* memory work
Remexio, 155
RENAL ("rehabilitation") prisons, 127, 131, 135, 142–43, 145, 150, 155. *See also* Nundamar prison
RENETIL (Resistência Nacional dos Estudantes de Timor-Leste), 78, 166n14, 167n2
Renshaw, Layla, 112
repatriation, 172n12
Rights Association, 58
Rigney, Ann, 54
roadbuilding, 107–8, 121
Rojas-Perez, Isaias, 18, 30–31
Roll, Kate, 36, 61, 99
Roosa, John, 41
Ruak, Taur Matan, 118–19
Rwanda, 43

Saffin, Janelle, 64
Saldanha, Gregorio, 60–61, 67–68
Santa Cruz massacre, 18, 46–53, 64, 68–69, 71, 78–79, 167n9, 168n20; legacy of, 54–55
Santos, Rafael dos, 77
SCIU (Serious Crimes Investigations Unit), 40, 42–43, 63, 86, 158
slogans, 47–49, 52, 104
slow violence, 24
spirits: agency of, 113–14; costs of rituals, 150; possession by, 89–91; protection by, 103; as unknowable, 95. *See also* the dead

spirit world, 9–10, 14–15, 56, 65, 97–98, 159
Stahl, Max, 53–54, 59, 64
state formation, 5–7, 13, 18–19, 27–28, 30, 32, 49–50, 56–59, 99–100. *See also* imagined community
Subianto, Prabowo, 33
Suharto, 55–56

Taussig, Michael, 29
Tetum, 14. *See also* Timor-Leste
Theidon, Kimberly, 145
Thiranagama, Sharika, 127
Timor-Leste: diaspora of, 133; hegemonic narratives of, 18–19, 22–23, 32–33, 38, 49, 56–59, 82, 99–100, 118–19; imagined community of, 27–28, 57–58, 81, 129, 132; independence referendum, 12, 21, 76–77; international perceptions of, 53–55, 62–63, 78, 83, 165n5; and necro-governmentality, 23–24, 29–31; politics of, 16–17, 62, 99, 123–24, 145, 168n17; and poverty, 36, 88. *See also* Indonesian occupation; Tetum
torture, 56, 60
traditional DNA, 67, 113–14. *See also* blood tests; DNA testing
traitors, 127–32, 134, 142. *See also* treason
transitional justice, 39–40, 43–44, 79–80, 85–86. *See also* prosecutions
Traube, Elizabeth, 103
trauma, 14, 49, 85
treason, 123–24, 126–27. *See also* traitors

truth by numbers, 41
12 November Committee, 47, 59–62, 71–72

UDT (União Democrática Timorense), 19, 127, 129–30, 144
United Kingdom, 24
United Nations (UN), 12, 21, 36, 39–40, 43, 52, 79–80, 86
United Nations Transitional Administration in East Timor (UNTAET), 23, 39–40, 79–80
United States, 24
unruliness (of the dead), 8, 10, 13, 66–71, 92–94, 100–101, 116, 143, 148, 154–55, 171n1
usable past, 79

valorization, 35–36, 99–100, 109, 111. *See also* martyrdom
victimhood, 40, 82–85, 145. *See also* martyrdom
Victorian Institute of Forensic Medicine (VIFM), 63–64, 66
Vietnam, 5

war crimes, 33, 42–43, 80. *See also* prosecutions
war of brothers, 130–31
Webster, David, 55
Western epistemology, 5, 16, 31, 78, 160
women, 35, 91, 102, 117–18, 131, 165n6

Yugoslavia, 43

Critical Human Rights

Researching Perpetrators of Genocide
  Edited by KJELL ANDERSON and ERIN JESSEE

Memory's Turn: Reckoning with Dictatorship in Brazil
  REBECCA J. ATENCIO

The Khmer Rouge Tribunal: Power, Politics, and Resistance in Transitional Justice
  JULIE BERNATH

Prisoner of Pinochet: My Year in a Chilean Concentration Camp
  SERGIO BITAR; translated by ERIN GOODMAN; foreword and notes by PETER WINN

Legislating Gender and Sexuality in Africa: Human Rights, Society, and the State
  Edited by LYDIA BOYD and EMILY BURRILL

Bread, Justice, and Liberty: Grassroots Activism and Human Rights in Pinochet's Chile
  ALISON J. BRUEY

Archiving the Unspeakable: Silence, Memory, and the Photographic Record in Cambodia
  MICHELLE CASWELL

Court of Remorse: Inside the International Criminal Tribunal for Rwanda
  THIERRY CRUVELLIER; translated by CHARI VOSS

How Difficult It Is to Be God: Shining Path's Politics of War in Peru, 1980–1999
  CARLOS IVÁN DEGREGORI; edited and with an introduction by STEVE J. STERN

After Genocide: Memory and Reconciliation in Rwanda
  NICOLE FOX

Trauma, Taboo, and Truth-Telling: Listening to Silences in Postdictatorship Argentina
NANCY J. GATES-MADSEN

From War to Genocide: Criminal Politics in Rwanda, 1990–1994
ANDRÉ GUICHAOUA; translated by DON E. WEBSTER

Innocence and Victimhood: Gender, Nation, and Women's Activism in Postwar Bosnia-Herzegovina
ELISSA HELMS

Inside Rwanda's "Gacaca" Courts: Seeking Justice after Genocide
BERT INGELAERE

Practical Audacity: Black Women and International Human Rights
STANLIE M. JAMES

Amending the Past: Europe's Holocaust Commissions and the Right to History
ALEXANDER KARN

The Unruly Dead: Spirits, Memory, and State Formation in Timor-Leste
LIA KENT

Civil Obedience: Complicity and Complacency in Chile since Pinochet
MICHAEL J. LAZZARA

Torture and Impunity
ALFRED W. MCCOY

Systemic Silencing: Activism, Memory, and Sexual Violence in Indonesia
KATHARINE E. MCGREGOR

Elusive Justice: Women, Land Rights, and Colombia's Transition to Peace
DONNY MEERTENS

Conflicted Memory: Military Cultural Interventions and the Human Rights Era in Peru
CYNTHIA E. MILTON

Historical Justice and Memory
Edited by KLAUS NEUMANN and JANNA THOMPSON

The Wars inside Chile's Barracks: Remembering Military Service under Pinochet
LEITH PASSMORE

Buried Histories: The Anti-Communist Massacres of 1965–1966 in Indonesia
JOHN ROOSA

The Human Rights Paradox: Universality and Its Discontents
Edited by STEVE J. STERN and SCOTT STRAUS

Human Rights and Transnational Solidarity in Cold War Latin America
Edited by JESSICA STITES MOR

South-South Solidarity and the Latin American Left
JESSICA STITES MOR

Remaking Rwanda: State Building and Human Rights after Mass Violence
Edited by SCOTT STRAUS and LARS WALDORF

Beyond Displacement: Campesinos, Refugees, and Collective Action in the Salvadoran Civil War
MOLLY TODD

Long Journey to Justice: El Salvador, the United States, and Struggles against Empire
MOLLY TODD

The Social Origins of Human Rights: Protesting Political Violence in Colombia's Oil Capital, 1919–2010
LUIS VAN ISSCHOT

The Soviet Union and the Gutting of the UN Genocide Convention
ANTON WEISS-WENDT

The Politics of Necessity: Community Organizing and Democracy in South Africa
ELKE ZUERN